Biblical Leadership Series

"Follow the Leader"
Dr. J. L. Williams

Follow the Leader

Copyright © 2010 by **Dr. J.L. Williams**

Published by:

Integrity Publishers Inc.
P.O. Box 789,
Wake Forest, NC 27588
U.S.A.
info@integritypublishers.org

ISBN 13: **978-0-9828630-7-7**

Printed in United States

TABLE OF CONTENTS

ACKNOWLEDGMENTS

Every leader knows well that authentic leadership is a *team effort.* No worthy leader **leads alone.** The role of leadership is to activate as many people as possible in the pursuit of the vision or goal. Any goal or vision that can be achieved by one person by himself or herself is not very worthy or challenging. Worthy visions and worthwhile goals are so BIG that they require many people working together to achieve them. Therefore, leadership worthy of the title is a *corporate* activity – not an *individual* one.

Certainly the writing of this book has been a *team effort.* Even though the primary reading and writing has been from my own life and experiences – the transcription of those notes and events has been made possible by my staff. So I want to give due credit where credit is due!

First, I want to express my deep appreciation to the early members of the "New Directions" musical teams who were my initial training ground in the basics of discipleship and mentoring. It was through the dynamic of those hundreds of relationships with high school and college students that I learned the *priority of people* in God's plan for leadership development. The relationships that Patt and I developed with those first teenagers confirmed to us that God builds leaders through *individuals* – not through *institutions.* God showed us through those wonderful relationships that His *plan* has always been *people* – not *programs.* Over 45 years later we continue to rejoice in the "abiding fruit" (Jn. 15:16) that has come from those early days of ministry and mentoring. Today, scores of those young people that we "learned on" are leaders in their own right. Many have gained a significance and influence that far exceeds our own – which is "pay day" for every parent or leader!

Secondly, I thank God for the hundreds of National pastors around the world who have sat through leadership seminars I have taught in their various countries. It was their persistence in asking me for my "teaching notes" that gradually provoked me into writing this book. So, it has been my desire to enhance their lives and leadership for the Kingdom of God that has motivated me to carve out the time in my schedule to expand my notes into manuscript form. I joyfully invest the principles of this book in their ministries!

Thirdly, I want to thank my wife, Patt, for the untold hours she has allowed me to "work late" and "get up early" to sit at my computer writing! As is the case with almost every author's wife, she has been a "writer's widow" during the many long days and late nights of isolation and separation while I have completed this book. Just like in parenting, she has sacrificed far more than I have!

Finally, I want to thank my staff who graciously "covered for me" while I hibernated in my study between trips writing and rewriting this manuscript. Several of my Executive Secretaries and assistants have read...re-read...typed...proofed and re-proofed this book scores of times. So as you read this book, say a prayer of thanksgiving to God for my support team who went far above and beyond the call of duty to get this book into your hands.

My final prayer is that you will read this book *carefully and prayerfully* – and then *lead for God's glory!* As you study these practical principles, I pray that you will be freshly motivated to play *"follow the leader"* the rest of your life – walking closely and carefully in the steps of the Lord Jesus! He is the greatest leader of history – and is worthy of following in every area of your life and leadership!

For His Kingdom & Glory,
J.L.

Dr. J.L. Williams
JL, Patt, & Friends
Founder: New Directions International
Board Member: Impact of Hope International
Professor-at-Large: Carolina Evangelical Divinity School
P.O. Box 4066
Glen Raven, NC 27216
Mobile: 336.684.3131
Home: 336.226.2178
http://www.jlwilliams.org

INTRODUCTION

Whether you're talking about a church or a business, a hospital or a university,
a nation or an athletic team, nothing rises above its leadership – nothing.
So whenever and wherever there is a successful enterprise, whether it's
a prosperous business, a winning team, a growing church,
you will find a competent leader who has made it so.
It didn't just happen. He made it happen.[1]
(Paul Powell, Getting The Lead Out of Leadership)

Growing up almost every child played the popular game known as *"Follow the Leader."* It was a favorite childhood game where one child was the leader and the other children followed. In the process, all of the *followers* had to imitate the *leader*, and do everything he or she did – whether hopping on one foot...rolling over...standing on your head...jumping a log...walking a wall...climbing a tree...or flying like an airplane. The challenge for the leader was to keep all of his playmates interested in what he was doing – so that they would continue to follow his leadership and stay close behind him. If his leadership was too dull and boring, the other children would lose interest and stop following. If his leadership was too daring and dangerous, many would also not follow. In either case, a new leader would emerge for the others to follow.

A successful childhood leader had to find a good balance between *challenge and comfort...risk and reality...suspense and safety...adventure and ability... spontaneity and predictability.* As we were growing up, some of us were more naturally inclined toward leading. Others of us preferred following. Most all of us as children did some of both. However, all of us started out in life as *followers* - children who followed the leadership of our parents. As young children, our first following instincts were directed exclusively toward them. We wanted to always be at our parent's side, or follow close behind them – gripping their hand, or holding to their leg for security! As we grew, we ventured further and further from our parent's side. The more we individuated, the more we gradually divided our following between our parents and our older brothers or sisters. When we became teenagers, we preferred to follow our friends. But over the years as we grew and matured, some of us found that we preferred the challenge of leading – while others of us liked the security of following others.

However, the game of *"Follow the Leader"* does not end with childhood. It is a lifelong activity. Most all of us are followers by nature. If we had a bad leadership experience as a child, we will be insecure and timid about accepting a leadership position as adults. If we had a bad experience following someone as a child or teenager, we will have a problem trusting leaders and other authority figures in our adult life.

To be a good leader or a good follower – and life is a balance of both – we need to understand both *leadership* and *followership*. Neither can be understood apart from the other. Leadership is meaningless without followers; and following necessitates leaders. In this study we are going to primarily focus on *leadership*. We will study the subject of *following* secondarily within the context of leadership. Let's continue the game of *"Follow the Leader"* as we go through this study...

WORLD LEADERSHIP CRISIS

Simply put, our world today is facing a great *crisis of leadership!* Whether on a local, regional, national or international scale, people are literally *dying for a lack of good leadership!* Whether in America, Asia, Africa, Australia, or Antarctica, the problem is always the same – *leadership!* Even though our world faces many economic, educational, environmental, and ethnic problems – the real problem is one of *leadership.* These many socio-economic-political problems are just the *fruit of the problem.* The real *root of the problem* is one of *leadership* – either *poor leadership... prideful leadership...passive leadership...*or *perverted leadership.* A good example of this is a statement by an African diplomat. In the midst of a refugee crisis and famine brought on by tribal warfare, he lamented: *"Africa is starving for leadership more than she is starving for food!"*

It is this kind of leadership crisis that will ultimately create the political-economic-ethnic vacuum that will open the way for the final *antichrist* of history. This false political-spiritual leader will deceive the masses of the world. The Bible warns that the **"...*spirit of antichrist*...is coming and even *now* is already in the world"** (I Jn. 2:18-22; 4:3; II Jn. 7). The primary way we can identify the **"spirit of antichrist"** is that it is opposed to the ultimate authority of the *Incarnate Christ* – the Lord Jesus! This is the spirit that rejects the historic Christ as *God Incarnate* (Mtt. 24:5, 11, 24; II Thess. 2:5-12; Rev. 13:14; 20:7). At almost every level of leadership in the world today, there is a growing hostility toward the *Lordship of Christ*. World leaders may pay Jesus Christ lip service as a great moral example – but they will never surrender their temporal authority to His ultimate authority. They will not submit their thrones to His throne! Whether on a personal or political level, the *spirit of antichrist* will tolerate no rival to its total supremacy. Their name must eclipse all other names – including that **"...Name that is above every name...the Name of Jesus"** (Phil. 2:9-10). Their power must have no limits, and their glory must outshine all. This is the tyranny of the *reign of ego* in every heart! It is the *enthronement of self* that is the very essence of sin. It is also the source of untold political intrigue...abuse of power...continuous warfare...ethnic cleansing...and environmental plunder the world over! It annually results in the disruption of nations...the displacement of people...the starvation of masses...the disease of multitudes...and murder of untold millions of people. This *reign of self* reduces people to slaves...refugees...victims. It ultimately leads to personal...emotional...mental...spiritual...relational...economic... and environmental death! Truly, submitting to the wrong leadership – whether personally or politically – has devastating consequences!

Richard Phillips, in his excellent book, *The Heart of an Executive*, said this about the tragedy of false leaders:

> *It is painful to observe... men and women placed in the executive's chair – a seat of possibility, meaning and importance – only to squander it all over tawdry ambition and shortsighted gain. How hard it is to see the servant's place taken by a charlatan... The counterfeit leader is reprehensible in the extreme, just as burdensome to the heart of God as he is to the backs of men.*[2]

Jesus expressed this universal need for leadership when He said that mankind are like **"...*sheep without a shepherd*"** (Matthew 9:36). Jesus was stating this truth, because He clearly understood that people are basically *followers* rather than *leaders*. Simply put, this social truth means that *if people do not have a good shepherd to follow, they are very vulnerable to the deceits and deceptions of a false leader.* Without a "Good Shepherd" to follow, people will be led astray by *hirelings...false prophets...charlatans... deceivers...counterfeits...demigods...mega-lomaniacs.* In the absence of true and trustworthy leadership, people will follow:

> Religious false prophets
> Political false prophets
> Educational false prophets
> Economic false prophets
> Social false prophets

Like the story of the "Pied Piper," the primary instrument of leadership may be *music* – which is easily seen through the youth culture, so influenced by music and musicians. Or the instrument of leadership may be *sports...entertainment...education...science...politics...economics...*or *religion.* Almost any ability or position can provide a person the platform of leadership.

CHURCH LEADERSHIP CRISIS

Just as there is a leadership vacuum in the other realms of society, *many churches are also experiencing a leadership crisis.* Regardless of whether the institution is sacred or secular, when there are major problems there is almost always a *crisis at the top.* That means that many denominations, mission agencies, para-church organizations, and national churches are facing leadership crisis at the highest levels. From the pope...to cardinals...to bishops...to elders...to deacons...to local pastors, many segments of the people of God are languishing for a lack of godly visionary leadership. The church does not need:

> Better plans - but better leaders!
> Not better methods - but better leaders!
> Not better programs - but better leaders!
> Not better organization - but better leaders!
> Not better facilities - but better leaders!
> Not better financing - but better leaders!

However, in the midst of this *ecclesiastical leadership crisis*, the church does not need *worldly leaders.* The church's greatest need is for authentic *Biblical leaders!* She does not need more charismatic *"men of the flesh."* The body of Christ needs leaders who are truly *"men of the Spirit."* The church of Jesus Christ needs leaders who are more concerned with building a spiritual *organism* than a worldly *organization.* That means that she needs *righteous leaders* rather than *religious leaders* – ones who are more interested in *inner character* than *outward conduct.* The church needs godly leaders who are more concerned with *integrity* than *intellectualism...*who seek higher *degrees of the Spirit* rather than more *degrees from schools...* who desire *anointing* more than *academics...purity* rather than *power... faith* rather than *fame...posterity* rather than *prosperity...favor with God* rather than *favor with man!*

Both the *world* and the *church* are suffering for a lack of the "right stuff" at the top – or the *right kind of leadership!*

If it is indeed true that both the world and church are facing a *leadership crisis,* we must ask some crucial questions to crystallize our thinking:

- What is a leader?
- Where do leaders come from?
- What are some of the marks of a true leader?
- What is the difference between a worldly leader and a worthy leader?

DEFINING LEADERSHIP

There are many good books in both the secular and spiritual realm that deal with the subject of leadership (See Bibliography and Suggested Reading List). There are many different definitions of leadership to choose from. I am obviously more interested in the subject of leadership from a spiritual and Biblical perspective. Even though I have learned a lot about leadership from reading prominent secular authors, *all authentic leadership originates from God* – whether or not the leader acknowledges it. *All truth is God's truth.* All valid leadership principles come from the Hand of a gracious God – *Who is the ultimate Sovereign Leader of the entire universe!* Obviously, there is only one true source of the gift of leadership in our world – and that is God. As Shakespeare rightly said: *"Gold is still gold, whether it is in a fool's or a wise man's pocket!"* When it comes to leadership, we can have either "wise leaders" or "foolish leaders." There is a unified and bloody witness throughout secular history, Biblical history and contemporary events that unqualified leaders often rise to the top through might and the exercise of raw power. The fact still remains: *all truth is God's truth... all gifts are God's gifts...all leadership originates from God.* It matters not whether the recipient acknowledges God as the Source of his leadership gifts, his abilities still originate from the sovereign Hand of a gracious God. He may prostitute his leadership abilities through *selfish perversion* – or be manipulated in the expression of them through *satanic deception* – but his ability to lead still comes from God!

**Principle: *"Whether carnal or spiritual,
all leadership comes from God."***

With those thoughts in mind, let's look at a several helpful *definitions of leadership.*

1. A short definition of leadership is this: *"A leader is a person with followers."* In other words, *"If you don't have followers, you are not a leader!"* As someone said: The person who thinks he is a leader, but has no one following him, is just 'taking a walk!' If you are 'walking alone', then you are not leading. On the other hand, if you are a leader then you will have followers with you on your journey. But, *no followers – no leader!* D.E. Hoste, of the China Inland Mission, was once asked about the test of true leadership. After pausing a moment to reflect, Hoste replied: *"It occurs to me that perhaps the best test of whether one is qualified to lead, is to find out whether anyone is following!"*[3] How true!

2. A longer definition of leadership is: "A leader is a person who influences people. He motivates them to follow him toward a particular goal." One of the key distinguishing marks of leadership then is motivational influence. It takes influence to get people to follow you toward a particular goal.

3. I like the definition of *spiritual leadership* by John Piper:

   Spiritual leadership is knowing where God wants people to be and taking the initiative to use God's methods to get them there in reliance on God's power.[4]

Piper goes on to elaborate the uniqueness of *spiritual leadership* in contrast to what we might call *secular leadership*:

> *The answer to where God wants people to be is in a spiritual condition and in a lifestyle that displays His glory and honors His name. Therefore, the goal of spiritual leadership is that people come to know God and to glorify Him in all that they do. Spiritual leadership is aimed not so much at directing people as it is at changing people…if they don't change in their heart you have not led them spiritually. You have not taken them to where God wants them to be.*[5]

Piper reminds us that there is a world of difference – and an eternity of difference – between *spiritual leadership* and *secular leadership*. All true spiritual leadership is *Spirit-led leadership*, while the flesh dominates all secular leadership. Only *Spirit-filled leaders can exercise spiritual leadership!*

Oswald Sanders makes the same crucial point about the need of truly spiritual leadership in the Church:

> *…if the world is to hear the church's voice today, leaders are needed who are authoritative, spiritual, and sacrificial. Authoritative, because people desire leaders who know where they are going and are confident of getting there. Spiritual, because without a strong relationship to God, even the most attractive and competent person cannot lead people to God. Sacrificial, because this follows the model of Jesus. Churches grow in every way when they are guided by strong, spiritual leaders with the touch of the supernatural radiating in their service…Today those who preach with majesty and spiritual power are few, and the booming voice of the church has become a pathetic whisper.*[6]

4. Another very thoughtful and insightful definition of leadership is the one by John Haggai from his excellent book, *Lead On*:

> *Leadership is the discipline of deliberately exerting special influence within a group to move it toward goals of beneficial permanence that fulfills the group's real needs.*[7]

There are several carefully chosen words or phases in his definition that I want to highlight, just as Haggai does in his book:

"Leadership is the discipline…": This phrase reminds us that leadership is as much a learned discipline as it is an inborn behavior. Good leaders study and master the discipline of leadership.

"...deliberately exerting special influence...": This phrase is a reminder that there is no leadership without influence. Simply put: leadership is influence – nothing more, nothing less. The leader has a conscious awareness of his God-ordained ability to exert special influence on people. That special motivational influence is called leadership.

"...to move people toward goals...": This means that the leader must have a clear focus on his goals – and those goals must be both specific and measurable. If you can't define and measure your goals, then they are too vague to pursue. A leader's goals are designed to be stepping-stones to the fulfillment of his vision, or life mission. We will look more about the subject of goals later.

"...goals of beneficial permanence...": This phrase is a cardinal reminder that the goals he leads people toward are to be beneficial for the group. The goals are first for the good of the follower - rather than the benefit of the leader. The goals are to be permanent, enduring, and lasting in their results. That means that they have an impact for both time and eternity.

"...that fulfills the group's real needs": Whereas many worldly leaders abuse their followers, and intimidate or coerce them to unworthy and malevolent goals, a Biblical leader will always lead his people toward a goal that fulfills their real needs – not just their perceived needs. The meeting of real needs of real people in real life situations defines real leadership!

5. Let me share several other shorter definitions of leadership that are helpful and insightful (I have included even more definitions at the end of this chapter):
    *   *Leadership is knowing what to do next, knowing why that's important, and knowing how to bring the appropriate resources to bear on the need at hand. Whoever knows these three things will emerge as the leader, whether she or he is*

the positional leader, or the elected leader, or not! Now what is Christian Leadership? *How does that differ from* secular leadership? *Christian leadership is knowing what God wants done next, knowing why He wants it done, and knowing how to bring to bear the resources He would bring to bear on the need at hand.*[8]

- *The simplest definition of leadership I know is 'influence'. It is the ability of one person to influence others to his point of view. So, if you're supposed to be leading and no one is following, you're just taking a walk!...All good leaders have two important characteristics: first, they are going somewhere; second, they are able to persuade others to go with them. That puts motivation at the heart and soul of leadership.*[10]

- *Leadership consists of three things: Vision, Strategy, Motivation. Vision is seeing what needs to be done; strategy is figuring out how to do it; motivation is persuading others to join you in the effort. Anyone who does those three things is a leader.*[9]

WHERE LEADERS COME FROM

Having looked at some definitions of leadership, we now need to ask another crucial question: *"Where do leaders come from?"* There are two kinds of leaders: those who are leaders by *nature*, and those who are leaders by *nurture*. That means that some leaders are *born* – while many others are *built*.

1. ***Born Leaders:*** It is definitely true that some people are just natural *"born leaders."* By virtue of their birth, talents and personality, they are what we often call *"natural leaders."* For these people, leadership is as *natural* as breathing. It is what they were *born* to do. They just *naturally lead.* For them, leadership is *intuitive* and *unconscious.* without any forethought, training or preparation, they just naturally emerge as leaders in whatever sphere they are involved in – whether in sports, academics, economics, politics, or religion. Herman Cain makes this observation about one of the greatest American leaders of all time, Abraham Lincoln:

What better example of a born great leader than one of the most admired and respected presidents in our history, Abraham Lincoln. I do not recall ever reading that Lincoln took a leadership seminar. And even more amazing, Lincoln was viewed by his own advisors as nothing more than a gawky, second-rate country lawyer with no leadership experience.[12]

"I believe great leaders are born and good leaders are made."[11]
(Herman Cain)

---

2. **Built Leaders:** Other people are more *built leaders* than they are *born leaders*. This would be by far the larger category that most leaders come from. They have developed leadership skills through conscious effort, study, discipline and desire. For these people, leadership is more of a *learned behavior*. Their leadership skills have come more through *instruction* than through *intuition*. They have *learned leadership* through the mentoring of older mature leaders. For them, leadership is more of an external *example* they have followed – rather than an *existential* impulse they have expressed.

It is my firm belief that leadership skills can be both *caught* and *taught*. But if a person is going to be a good leader, whether they are *born leaders*, or *built leader*, they must be:

> Available
> Teachable
> Responsible
> Accountable

We can see a clear example of both of these types of leaders in the first twelve disciples chosen by Jesus. Some of them – like Peter, James and John – were more *natural born leaders*. But the majority of the rest of the twelve were not so much *natural leaders* as *nurtured leaders*. Through His mentoring, Jesus built them into the leaders He wanted them to be. We read about His *mentoring method of leadership development* in these verses from the Gospel of Mark:

"He...called *to Him* those He wanted, and they came to Him. He appointed twelve...that they might be *with Him,* and that He *might send them out* to preach" (Mark 3:13-14).

We can see here at least three phrases that distinguish His leadership training with the twelve. First, He called them *"to Him."* Secondly, they were to be *"with Him."* Thirdly, they would be trained *"by Him."* I believe that these three simple prepositional phrases – *"to Him...with Him...by Him"* – succinctly summarize Christ's style of leadership development. Simply put, His leadership training was *relationally based.* Jesus knew that the only way for His disciples to come to personal and spiritual maturity was in the context of *intense relationships.* Unlike other religious teachers of His day, Jesus was not just interested in *teaching them what He knew.* He wanted to go beyond that and *reproduce Himself in them.*

Principle:
"Jesus' leadership development was relational not institutional. He personally mentored men and women into ministry."

John Maxwell has often said: *"We teach what we know, but we reproduce what we are."*[13] Jesus did both in the lives of His followers. He *reprogrammed their minds with His thoughts;* and He *reproduced His heart in their heart.* Christ's mentoring model of leadership development was *relational... informal...oral...practical...concrete...mobile...transferable.* His emphasis was upon *learning by doing.*

---

*"We teach what we know,
but we reproduce what we are."*
(John Maxwell)

In contrast to our Western method of church leadership development, I think it is important to note that Jesus did not use the *institutional model* – although there were many available in the Judaism of His day. He was not interested in producing *academicians* but *apostles.* Jesus did not send His disciples off to some rabbinical school to be trained to lead His church. He used what I call the *incarnational instructional* model of leadership training. He called potential leaders alongside Him and "fleshed out" before them their instruction under every conceivable condition of life. *He modeled His message!* Today we largely depend upon the *institutional* model of Bible colleges, seminaries, and theological graduate schools to train and prepare church leaders. Although these institutions certainly have many good things to offer a Christian leader, Jesus largely trained, discipled, and mentored His men *"in the field."* He gave them practical *"on-the-job training."* His seminary was the *"learning laboratory of life."* His *method* of *mentoring* for *ministry* was the *marketplace!*

Principle:

"In training Christian leaders, Jesus used the *incarnational instructional model; He modeled His* *message to those He was mentoring."*

Gunter Krallman noted this about Jesus' mentoring method of leadership development:

> *An astute observer cannot help but recognize how immensely life-related, concrete and dynamic Jesus' leadership training mode was – and that He consciously shunned any tendency to formalize, structuralize or institutionalize it.*[14]

The local church should always be the spiritual epicenter for leadership development – not some academic theological institution. Bill Hybels, senior pastor of the Willow Creek Community Church, says: *"...the church is the most leadership-intensive enterprise in society."* In every other segment of society, the leader has an advantage over the follower – what some have called *"leadership leverage."* That simply means that in almost all other organizations, the leader by virtue of his *position* and *power* has leverage over the people under him. For example, in the military, the leader has a higher position and can "pull rank" on the soldiers under him. They have no choice but to obey and follow – or be court-martialed. In a business, the boss has the leverage of salary, benefits, perks. He has the power to "hire..."fire"..."promote"...and "demote." But in the church of Jesus Christ, that *"leadership leverage"* is not available. The followers are all *volunteers.* They cannot be coerced, forced, intimidated, or leveraged into following. The pastor must exercise leadership in its purest form. He must seek to influence the people to follow without the *leadership leverage* that the world uses: *promotion...position...power...prestige...privilege...perks... possessions.* He must *motivate them with love* and persuade them through the pure *passion of his vision!* If he cannot successfully exert leadership influence, the people simply will not follow.

CHRIST'S MENTORING MODEL

"Jesus went up on a mountainside and called to Him those He wanted, and they came *to Him*...that they might be *with Him* and that He might *send them out* to preach and to have authority to drive out demons." (Mark 3:13-19)

$$...To\ Him \quad \longrightarrow \quad (Mastery)$$
$$...With\ Him \longrightarrow \quad (Mentoring)$$
$$...By\ Him \quad \longrightarrow \quad (Ministry)$$

GENERAL LEADERSHIP CHARACTERISTICS

"We have different gifts according to the grace given us... If it is *leadership*, let him govern diligently..." (Romans 12:6, 8).

It has been my supreme joy now for over 35 years to disciple, teach and mentor young Christian leaders. In the earlier years of my life and ministry, I primarily focused on mentoring high school and college students. In those days, the subject of "Leadership Development" was not a widely known concept within the church. We just talked about the subject of *discipleship* – and even that was not widely understood or practiced.

As I began to disciple certain young people in their Christian lives, I quickly noticed that some of them had strong influence over their peers. They were the teenage "Pied Pipers," who always seemed to be center stage...out in front...leading the pack...setting the pace...initiating activities...speaking for the group. They had natural leadership skills – although often neglected or misdirected. These young leaders were about equally divided between guys and gals. Some were leaders in student body government, some in academics, some in social activities, some in athletics, and some in their churches. I began to reach out to them through various forms of "contact work." That meant hanging around with them after school, attending ball games, student body activities, going to social functions, taking them out for a pizza or burger and fries, inviting them into our home. As I developed relationships of trust, and built friendships with these teenagers, I increasingly focused in on the key young leaders. I tried to give them more concentrated time and attention.

During those early days of ministry, I certainly had no clear-cut "game plan" in mind for building Christian leaders. I just knew that some of the ones God had given me favor with had great leadership potential - and I wanted to capture and develop those abilities for the Kingdom of God. Other than the very practical spiritual nurturing I had received from my own two wise Christian parents growing up, my only other model of training people was the way in which *Christ discipled His disciples.* In just three short years, *He had spent enough time with the twelve to prepare them for the greatest leadership challenge in the history of the world - leading His church!*

"In three short years Jesus prepared His disciples for the greatest leadership challenge in history – leading His Church!"

One of my seminary professors was Dr. Robert Coleman. His lectures, which were later published, greatly impacted my thinking. His now renowned book is entitled *The Master Plan of Evangelism.* As the title indicates, it is a practical study in how our Master, the Lord Jesus, evangelized and discipled people. Dr. Coleman pointed out how Jesus spent most of His earthly life with just twelve men – not with the masses of people as Christians often think. Within the twelve, He had three to whom He gave more concentrated time and attention – and they were Peter, James and John. Within the three, He had one "soul mate" that He spent even more time with – and that was John the Beloved. I knew I could not improve on Christ's *Master Plan* of discipleship and leadership development. That understanding and relational approach became a vital part of my model of discipling…mentoring… leadership development.

Even though I did not have a "worked out and written down" plan, I did clearly understand from Christ's model that there were several essential ingredients to discipling people and building Christian leaders: *Selectivity, simplicity, time, discipline, focus, practicality,* and *life application.* With this relational plan in mind, I just "put some key young people in my hip pocket" - and virtually lived with them night and day. Together we faced almost every conceivable life situation – and in the process sought to apply God's Word and Spirit to that particular issue. Over time we squarely faced all of the perennial youth issues: parents...divorce...drinking...dating...sex...smoking...drugs...self-image...racism...prejudice...college...vocation...science...evolution...death...pain...suffering...heaven...hell, etc. We sought to create a totally safe environment of *unconditional love* where any question could be asked, any fear could be talked about, any doubt could be expressed, any sin could confessed, and failure could be faced. Through it all, we were trying to give them Biblical answers – rather than pat answers. We wanted to anchor them firmly in God's Word – not in our opinions. We sought to help them develop a holistic *Biblical worldview*. While these young people were constantly under my wing, I was by necessity hovering under God's gracious and strong wings (Ps. 36:7). As a result, we all grew spiritually, mentally, emotionally, and relationally together.

Principle:
"Leadership development is based upon selectivity, simplicity, time, discipline, focus, practicality, and life-application."

Thirty years later, it is a joy for me to report that the vast majority of those young people are still walking with the Lord. Many have become widely known Christian leaders, pastors, missionaries, youth workers, musicians, writers, educators, physicians, businessmen – active Christians in almost every profession. Some have been exalted by God to places of renown and influence that far exceed mine – which is "pay day" for Patt and me! Whether they are your *physical children* or your *spiritual children*, the greatest joy of parenting is to see your children do well – and even exceed you! The Apostle Paul said of such people he had won to Christ and discipled: **"You are my joy and crown"** (Phil. 4:1). He further said that they would be his confidence when he stood before the Lord Jesus to give an account for his life and ministry:

"What is our *hope*, our *joy* or the *crown* in which we will *glory in the presence of our Lord Jesus when He comes?* Is it not you? Indeed, you are our *glory* and *joy*...How can we thank God enough for you in return

for all of the *joy* we have in the presence of our God because of you?" (1 Thess. 2:19; 3:9)

I am humbled and awed over how God has graciously used our early fledgling efforts to raise up many faithful saints – and some wonderful Christian leaders! They only verify the truth of what Jesus told His first disciples: **"You did not choose Me, but I chose you and appointed you to go and bear fruit, and that *your fruit should remain"*** (Jn. 15 16).

Today, I continue to do what I have always done – *evangelize* the lost, and then *encourage, equip, enable,* and *empower* Christians. The only difference is that today my leadership development is primarily focused on key national leaders God has sovereignly linked me with around the world. Since those early years of discipling and mentoring American young people, I have taken time to do a lot of reading and studying on the subject of *leadership* – both from respected spiritual and secular writers. That ongoing study has greatly clarified my own thinking and continues to sharpen my approach to leadership development. I have also tried to pause and reflect over the things I have personally learned, experienced and taught about training leaders through the years. I have realized that mine has been far more of an *unconscious* and *unstructured relational approach* – than a *formalized* and *institutionalized* program of training leaders.

The principles I have written down in this book are the result of my past experience and current ministry of discipling and mentoring people – *interdenominationally, interracially,* and *internationally.* I have found these mentoring principles to be true and effective regardless of the *class, race, culture, sex, education,* or *age* of the people involved. Whether consciously or unconsciously – formally or informally – these principles have guided me in my lifelong ministry to help people move from where they are, to where God wants them to be. As a result, we continue to have the joy of seeing scores of bottled-up, insecure, inadequate, inferiority-ridden people – just like me – move toward their full potential for the kingdom of God!

In these following chapters, I want to look at a number of principles of leadership. Some writers would include more, others less. Regardless of the number used to describe leadership, *no leader perfectly embodies all of these characteristics!* There was only one Perfect Leader, and that was the Lord Jesus. He alone is the perfect Incarnation of all of the characteristics and virtues of *natural* and *supernatural* leadership. All other leaders fall far short of His perfect model. As a result, all leaders have their *strengths* and *weaknesses...assets* and *liabilities...abilities* and *inabilities...successes* and *failures*. As you study through this list of *"20 Principles of Leadership,"* do not become frustrated if you do not exhibit all of them. None of us do. I certainly do not! But use this list as a *leadership guide to growth*. Some of you reading this book will find that you just *naturally* exemplify certain characteristics of a good leader. However, in order to see other characteristics develop in your life, it will take a *supernatural* endowment by the Holy Spirit! Through the *Spirit* and the *Word*, you may learn some of these leadership characteristics rather quickly. For others to be manifested and matured in you, it will take a lifetime of disciplined *study* and *striving*. Either way, God wants you to develop and mature as a leader. So let's begin this study – and continue to play *"Follow the Leader."* It will be the leadership journey of a lifetime!

"There has only been one perfect Leader, and that is the Lord Jesus Christ!"

FURTHER QUOTATIONS ON LEADERSHIP

- *What are the keys to being a good executive? What does it require? 4 things:*

  > *Recognize talent*
  > *Organize the task*
  > *Galvanize the team*
  > *Mobilize the troops.*[15]

- *The altar of freedom is a thirsty altar. It requires either the sweat of our brows or the blood of our veins. If we would sweat more, we would bleed less. The altar of leadership has the same thirst.*[16]

Chapter 1

LEADERS ARE PURPOSEFUL

"We have different gifts, according to the grace given us.
If a man's gift is…leadership, let him govern diligently"
(Rom. 12:6-8).

When I use the word *purpose,* I am speaking of the single most distinguishing feature in a leader's life – *VISION!* Simply put, *leaders are people of vision.* They are *people of purpose.* Leaders are often spoken of as *visionaries.* They have a compelling *vision* that has resulted in a complete *revision* of their lives! It is their vision that makes them a "marked man" or "marked woman." It is *vision* alone that produces *virtue* and *value* in their lives. Their *vision* distinguishes them from the masses, and causes them to stand out from the crowd. *Vision is the foundation of all true leadership.* As J. Oswald Sanders noted:

> *Those who have most powerfully and permanently influenced their generation have been 'seers' – people who have seen more and farther than others – persons of faith, for faith is vision.*[1]

Principle:
"Leaders are visionaries. They have
a compelling vision that has caused a
complete revision of their lives."

"There's one thing worse than missing
your dreams. It's never to have had one."[2]
(Paul Powell)

An authentic vision includes *sight...insight...foresight...far-sight.* Therefore, every new church...new ministry...new agency...new institution... new invention...new endeavor...new business...new approach...new paradigm...new perspective...new break-through – is the result of *vision.* These radical changes do not happen accidentally, capriciously, or randomly. Every new thrust that is made, every new barrier that is broken, every new threshold that is crossed, is because someone had a *vision* and laid hold of it like a snapping turtle! They laid hold of it with untiring tenacity because it first laid hold of them with unrelenting pressure! Paul Powell described this crucial visionary aspect of leadership this way:

> *Vision has nothing to do with sight. It is a process of the mind. It is mental, not visual. It is seeing what everybody has seen but thinking what nobody has thought. The best leaders and the most powerful motivators have always been those with the ability to see today what others see tomorrow, to envision great things occurring in the future, and to see them happening in great detail.*

> *Ideas are the great moving force of history. For that reason, thinking is the single most important ingredient of leadership...we can never be free to do what we cannot think...You can mark this down, the difference between monumental littleness and greatness is not talent, nor charm, nor financial resources. The difference is vision. The great challenge of leaders, then, is to use their God-given and God-like ability to think and dream. To use their eyes for something more than just to keep from bumping into things. So if you are in a place of leadership, wake up and start dreaming. Take off your night cap and put on your thinking cap!*[3]

Powell concludes these thoughts with a cogent quote by D.K. Caldwell:

> *Big men think big; little men don't think!*[4]

Former President Richard Nixon made this observation:

> *All the really strong leaders I have known have been highly intelligent, highly disciplines, hard workers, supremely self-confident, driven by a dream, driving others. All have looked beyond the horizon.*[5]

That's why John Stuart Mill was correct when he said: *"One person with a dream is equal to a force of 99 who have only an interest."* Poet Carl Sandburg made the same point by saying: *"Nothing happens unless it is first a dream."*[6]

"Small dreams do not inflame the hearts of men."[7]
(Bill Bright)

It is *great visions and great dreams that create great leaders!* Also, *great visions attract great people.* That's why a leader tends to attract people proportionate to their vision. *Small visions attract small people; big visions attract big people.* Too many people, even Christians, *dream small dreams.* Paul Powell rightly observed this about many church leaders: *"Our preachers aren't dreaming. That's why the church is such a nightmare."*[8] There's a lot of painful truth about that observation of much of the church today!

"Make no little plans, for they
have no power to stir men's minds."[9]
(Paul Powell)

I believe that God wants us to be *big dreamers* for His kingdom and glory. If we can accomplish all of our dreams through our own human abilities…efforts…education…hard work – then they are probably not *"God-size dreams!"* Great leaders want to dream dreams that are so BIG that only God can accomplish them. That way only He gets the honor and glory through them. My friend Franklin Graham learned this lesson from one of his spiritual mentors, Bob Pierce. In his book *Living Beyond the Limits*, Franklin says this:

> *Possibly the greatest lesson I learned from Bob Pierce was something he called God room. This was a phrase he coined that simply means recognizing a need bigger than what human limitations can meet.*[10]

Principle: *"A leader attracts people*
proportionate to their vision."

There was an early Baptist preacher and writer in Texas by the name of J.B. Gambrell. He humorously made the same point about the relationship between the size of our vision and the size of the people we attract:

> *It is easier to do large things than little things. A great people cannot be rallied to little things. More people, a hundred to one, will join in a bear hunt than will turn out to kill a mouse!* [11]

Point well made! That's why former American President Theodore Roosevelt said:

> *Far better it is to dare mighty things, to win glorious triumphs, even checkered by failure, than to take rank with those poor spirits who neither enjoy much or suffer because they live in the great twilight that knows not victory nor defeat.*[12]

Spiritually speaking, this kind of *God-size-vision* only comes from God through His Holy Spirit. On the day of Pentecost, Peter acknowledged this radical alteration of their lives by quoting the Prophet Joel:

"Your sons and daughters will prophesy, your young men will see *visions*, your old men will *dream dreams*. Even on my servants, both men and women, I will pour out My Spirit in those days..." (Acts 2:17-18; Joel 2:28).

These verses remind us that we are never *too young* or *too old* to receive a life-changing vision from the Lord. A God-given vision does not come on the basis of our socio-economic standing, or sexual gender. *Spiritual visions are available to all of God's people!* Unfortunately, visions tend to come to those who are younger spiritually – and begin to fade-out and become more rare as a person ages. As John Piper says: *"It is tragic when age makes a man jaded instead of increasingly creative."* [13]

We can clearly see this leadership truth about vision expressed in Proverbs 29:18:

> **"Where there is *no vision*, the people *perish.*"** (KJV)
> **"Where there is *no vision*, the people are *unrestrained.*"** (NASV)
> **"For *lack of vision* a people *lose restraint*"** (*Tanakh*, Jewish Bible)
> **"Where there is *no revelation* the people *cast off restraint.*"** (NIV)

"Where there is *ignorance of God*, the *people run wild*." (Living Bible)
"When *people do not accept divine guidance*, they *run wild*"
(New Living Translation)

Without vision, there is *spiritual confusion, social disorder, diffusion of energy, rebellion of spirit* – even *anarchy*. A *vision vacuum* is one of the most dangerous and deadly situations for any person or for any society. John Maxwell says this about the necessity of vision:

> *Vision is everything for a leader. It is utterly indispensable. Why? Because vision leads the leader. It paints the target. It sparks and fuels the fire within and draws him forward. It is also the fire lighter for others who follow that leader. Show me a leader without vision, and I'll show you someone who isn't going anywhere.*[14]

Spiritually speaking, a vision comes from God. Since **"God is Spirit"** (Jn. 4:24), it follows that *a godly vision is spiritual by nature*. Spiritual vision has *virtue* simply because it comes from God – not from man. In his book, *Leading With Integrity*, Fred Smith makes this important distinction between *values* and *virtue:*

> *We talk about* values *because subconsciously we like to be in control;* we set values. Virtues, *however, hold their authority because they are not under human control but* come from revealed truth. *Our society could return to the values of our forefathers, and we could still have human values. When we return to* virtue, *we return to God.*[15]

That's a crucial distinction! That insight reveals the difference between much of *human vision* and *spiritual vision*. Human vision tends to be based on *human values*, while spiritual vision arises from *divinely revealed virtues*. Human vision sets forth a human agenda. Authentic spiritual vision sets forth God's agenda!

Since a spiritual vision is ethereal and non-tangible by nature, it must be both *visualized* and *verbalized*. A vision must first be clearly *crystallized* and *visualized* in the head of the leader before it can be clearly *verbalized* and *summarized* to the heart of the follower. Stephen Covey notes that *"All things are created twice."*[16] The first creation is in the mind and imagination of the leader, who in turn re-creates it in the mind of the follower. The vision must be a clear spiritual and mental picture in the heart and mind of the leader of what he sees himself doing – and others participating in. It is a clear understanding of God's will for his life, and for the life of the people he leads. The clearer the vision is to the leader, the more clearly he will be able to articulate it to his followers.

Principle:
"Vision must be crystallized, visualized,
verbalized, and summarized. It must first be
clearly crystallized and visualized in the head
of the leader; *only then can it be clearly verbalized*
and summarized for the heart of the follower."

In the final analysis, the leader *lives his life's vision.* He becomes inseparable from his vision. His vision produces *vitality* and *velocity* in his life. He thinks about it by day – and dreams about it at night! He mulches over it while he works, and mulls over it when he rests. Ultimately and continually, his vision compels him to action – and propels him to productivity. Vision sounds the death knell to complacency, inactivity, and a lack of involvement. It forces a person out of the bed...out of the shadows...out of the bleachers...out of passivity...out of inactivity... out of anonymity...out of mediocrity – and compels him to *seize the moment and lead!*

"Ideas won't keep; something
must be done about them." [17]
(Alfred North Whitehead, English philosopher
and mathematician)

Harvard Business School professor, John Kotter, says this about vision:

> *Vision plays a key role in producing useful change by helping to direct, align and inspire actions on the part of large numbers of people... The word 'vision' connotes something grand or mystical, but the direction that guides successful transformations is often simple and mundane.* [18]

Principle:
"A good vision has a certain elegant simplicity"
(John Kotter)

What he is saying is that even though in the *conception* stage, a vision may initially be something mental, mystical, ethereal, and abstract; the *application* of that vision to every day life must be very simple...basic... concrete...mundane...routine...ordinary. It is in the *communication* and *application* phase of a vision that things often break down between the visionary and the people. The desirable change does not take place. The result is frustration for both the leader and the follower. That's why Kotter says: *"A good vision has a certain elegant simplicity."*[19] Therefore, Kotter teaches his students that an effective vision must have at least six essential features:

Imaginable:	Through it people must be able to imagine what the future will look like.
Desirable:	It must appeal to the long-term interest of the people involved.
Feasible:	It must be realistic and attainable.
Focused:	It must be clear enough to provide guidance and decision making.
Flexible:	It must allow for individual initiative and changing conditions.
Communicable:	It is easy to communicate and can be successfully explained in a few sentences.

Principle:
*"A transformational vision first transforms the
thinking and living of the leader, who in turn
becomes the change agent to transform the thinking
and living of the follower."*

Kotter says that it is only when a vision has these essential characteristics that it will be a *'transformational vision'* resulting in the positive, needed, relevant transformation of people, businesses, organizations, society. Kotter also says that *"...major transformations are often associated with one highly visible individual."*[20] That's the leadership factor. If anyone in society is in the "business of transformation," it is the church of Jesus Christ! The pastors and church leaders should be the leading *'transformational leaders'* in society!

Vision first transforms the leader – who in turn transforms the followers through an effective communication of his vision. Just as his vision activates him and makes his life count for something, he wants it to bring the same transformation to the thinking and living of others. All of us – especially *"transformational leaders"* – live with a growing awareness of the brevity of life. There is a *sense of urgency* to make life count for something significant and eternal. That's why King David prayed to God:

> **"Show me, O Lord, my life's end and the number of my days; let me know how fleeting is my life. You have made my days no longer than the width of my hand; the span of my years is as nothing before You. *Each man's life is but a breath.*"** (Ps. 39:4–5).

As a result of this awareness of the shortness of his life, David was not *despondent* or *depressed* – he was *decisive*. He said: **"My heart grew hot within me, and as I meditated, the *fire burned*"** (Ps. 39:3). That's a description of the *white-hot passion of vision* burning in a person's heart and mind! It is the *fire of vision* that inflames a person to live for God – and *burn out* in the process if necessary! Only a Godly vision will inspire a person to make his life count for time and eternity! The only way we can live like that is through the *wisdom of God* rather than the *wantonness of man* during our brief sojourn through life. That's why Moses prayed: **"*Teach us to number our days aright, that we may gain a heart of wisdom*"** (Ps. 90:12)

According to John Haggai, this kind of vision comes from what he calls *"inspirational dissatisfaction."* Within the spirit of every person who emerges as a leader, there is a brooding *dissatisfaction* with the status quo – both within his own life and in the circumstances around him. This growing sense of *personal and vocational dissatisfaction* becomes his *inspiration* and *motivation* for change. As Haggai says:

> *"Inspirational dissatisfaction inspires*
> *a person to high attainment; despondent*
> *dissatisfaction paralyzes the action nerve,*
> *corrodes the spirit, and wrecks the life."*
> (John Haggai)

> *Without inspirational dissatisfaction, a person would make peace with the status quo, he would not see a need for change, could not grasp a vision of growth, and could not step out in faith. Inspirational dissatisfaction is an essential step to grasping a vision. Inspirational dissatisfaction inspires a person to high attainment.*[21]

This *inspirational dissatisfaction* becomes the stimulus for positive change… for decisiveness…for growth…for maturity…for leadership. Without it, a person can become morose, cynical, inert, depressed. As C.S. Lewis pointed out, all of us have an eternal longing that can never be fully satisfied in this life – because we were meant for eternity. God put this within us so that we would have that *inspirational dissatisfaction* that would compel us to *live on earth with an eternal purpose.* Without that, we lapse into what Haggai calls a *despondent dissatisfaction,* which he says *"… paralyzes the action nerve, corrodes the spirit, and wrecks the life."*[22]

Paul Powell made a similar observation in the conclusions of his great book on leadership:

> *The people who have made worthwhile contributions to civilization are those who have been* restless and dissatisfied *with the status quo…I wish the same* holy restlessness *for you…*It's the stuff that makes for a good leader.[23]

Concerning this desire – "holy restlessness" – to live for something higher than one's self, Richard Phillips rightly observed:

> *It is true that people will work for wages and are motivated by recognition and reward. But at the heart of working men and women is the longing – though oft forgotten and sadly despaired of – to participate in something greater than themselves, to belong to a cause that is meaningful and to share in a legacy that endures.*[24]

Recently a young woman wrote me about her current job. Even though she was very successful, with all of the accompanying economic benefits of her position, she was discontent – but with an *inspirational dissatisfaction!* Listen to her poignant words:

> *"...it's not that I don't enjoy my work, or quite frankly, the comforts and security of my cushy lifestyle. But I truly want to live my life in a way that counts for something. To offer a 'cup of cold water' in the name of Jesus, is something that absolutely thrills my soul – and that is what I am pursuing!"*

Vision is *transformational* and *life changing* – that's why it is absolutely foundational for all authentic leadership. It brings order out of chaos in his life. It gives *devotion, decisiveness,* and *direction* to living. It is vision that overcomes aimlessness, purposelessness, and drifting in life. It was the vision that God gave me shortly after graduate school that literally brought a *"new direction"* – a *divine direction* – to my life and ministry that I am still experiencing, exploring, enjoying, and expressing!

Principle:
"Leadership feeds on the vision of something great."[25]
(Richard Phillips)

Since vision is that which *defines, directs,* and *distinguishes* his life, a leader must be constantly sharpening the focus of his vision. As he sharpens his vision, *his vision sharpens him!*

Vision is what defines a leader's life and gives him purpose. Leaders increasingly become *one with their purpose.* A leader ultimately *loves* and *lives his vision.* It is the leader's *vision* or *purpose* that *defines* and *distinguishes* his life from others. It makes him or her *precise* and *decisive.* If the leader is not *precise in his purpose,* people will not follow. The more *precise the purpose,* the clearer the leadership. It is easy to see this defining purpose in the life of the Apostle Paul when he wrote:

"For to me to live is Christ..." (Phil. 1:21)
"I, Paul, apostle of Christ Jesus..." (Romans 1:1,
1 Cor. 1:1, Col. 1:1)
"This one thing I do..." (Phil. 3:13)
"Woe to me if I preach not the Gospel..." (I Cor. 9:16)

These verses are about incarnational theology. Paul could not separate himself from his vision and calling as an Apostle of Jesus Christ. This is a revelation and teaching that is unique to Christianity. The Bible tells us that Jesus Christ was **"The Word made flesh"** that came to earth to **"... dwell among us"** (Jn. 1:14). Just as Jesus gave living expression on earth of the true and living God, the leader is to give living expression of his vision. He is to incarnate…flesh out…live out his vision. A vision must be both verbalized and visualized. To quote Richard Phillips:

> *Here is a lesson for leaders. You cannot fake it. You have to be in order to do. In order to inspire the hearts of others, you must first have a passion for an ideal greater than yourself.*[26]

A leader's vision and purpose focuses and motivates him. It is a leader's vision that causes him or her to have a *strong work ethic.* One common characteristic to all successful leaders is their *passion for work.* They see work as a *blessing* rather than a *curse.* The French language has a good expression of this. They refer to this motivating vision or purpose of an individual's life as their *'raison d'être'* or *reason to be.* No leader who has matured in his vision has any hesitancy in answering what their *raison d'être* is.

> *"I've had my share of dreams and my share of nightmares. I have survived the nightmares because of my dreams."*[27]
> **(Dr. Jonas Salk)**

Vision also leads to suffering. A leader should be willing to *suffer* for his vision. If a vision can be fulfilled without sacrifice, then it is not a very worthy vision! If a vision is not worth giving your life for – then it is not a God-size vision! All true vision requires sacrifice – and the *greater the vision,* the *greater the sacrifice.* John Maxwell expresses it this way: "*A leader must give up to go up.*" He also goes on to say that, "*In order for a leader to stay up, he must give up even more.*"[28] Sacrifice for the vision is not a one-time experience – but a lifestyle. Like everything else worthwhile in life, sacrifice is both a *crisis* and a *process.* Leadership is based upon a continuous giving up of *your life…your time…your talents…your resources… your sleep…your free time – your all!*

Principle:
"A leader must give up to go up. And in order for a leader to stay up, he must give up even more.
(John Maxwell)

A leader's commitment to their purpose keeps other people's doubts... fears...uncertainty...lack of commitment...or opposition from *detracting* or *detouring* them. They keep *pressing on* toward their purpose – regardless of *how hard* the process...*how long* the journey...*how high* the mountain... *how deep* the valley...*how wide* the chasm...or *how great* the sacrifice. This determined focus of purpose and vision is seen in the life of Christ when He said: **"The Son of Man came to *seek* and *save* the lost"** (Luke 19:10). With those eleven words, Jesus summarized His life *mission statement!*

This redemptive purpose can also be seen in the life of Jesus as His earthly ministry neared its completion: **"As the time approached for Him to be taken up to heaven, *Jesus resolutely set out for Jerusalem."*** (Luke 9:5). There were many other cities where Christ could have gone – but it was in Jerusalem where His earthly destiny was to be consummated. This was the one city in the world where the prophets had foretold that the Messiah would suffer and die – so to Jerusalem He must go! His life vision could only be fulfilled in this ancient Holy City. He would let nothing or no one detour or detract Him from that final destination, neither the tyranny of Rome, the intrigue of the Jewish leaders, the fear of His disciples, the confusion of the masses nor the assaults of Satan!

"In every significant event there has been a bold leader, a shared vision, and most often, an adversary."[29]
(Fred Smith)

The Apostle Paul expressed the passionate pursuit of his purpose this way:

"Not that I have already obtained...I *press on* to take hold of that for which Christ Jesus took hold of me" (Phil. 3:12).

Every Christian leader can identify with those words of Paul. First, they all sense that they have not nearly **"obtained"**, or *"attained,"* the level of performance that they would like to achieve in the area of their calling. Secondly, as a result of this awareness, all leaders have an attitude of **"pressing on"** to new heights of achievement and attainment. There is a "divine discontent" that characterizes their lives. Their theme is expressed in two of the stanza of the old hymn *Higher Ground*:

> 1.   "I'm pressing on the upward way;
> New heights I'm gaining every day;
> Still praying as I'm onward bound,
> 'Lord, plant my feet on higher ground.'"

> 2.   My heart has no desire to stay,
> Where doubts arise and fears dismay;
> Tho' some may dwell where these abound,
> My prayer, my aim is higher ground.
> (Chorus)
> Lord, lift me up and let me stand,
> By faith, on heaven's table-land,
> A higher plane that I have found;
> Lord, plant my feet on higher ground."

"There are no big dreams with small price tags." [30]

(Paul Powell)

Leaders are always interested in going higher – scaling new heights of achievement. However, Biblical leaders know and acknowledge that it is God who **"...makes their feet like the feet of a deer."** It is the Holy Spirit that **"...enables him to *go on the heights"*** (Hab. 3:19).

**"...When God calls, He equips
with gifts and opportunities..."** [31]

(Fred Smith)

Biblical leaders have an acute sense that the Lord Jesus is sovereign in this high and holy calling that has gripped their lives. Every wise leader knows that it was the Lord Who took the initiative in their calling. They are not leading because of their *commitment* – but because of His *calling*. They know that it was Jesus who first **"took hold"** of them long before they surrendered and submitted to His calling upon their lives. Paul referred to the moment that the risen Christ arrested him on the Damascus Road as a **"heavenly vision"** (Acts 26:19) that resulted in a **"holy calling"** (II Tim. 1:9) upon his life. That heavenly vision became the purpose of his life from that moment on. Tragically, too many leaders in our world today have nothing higher or nobler than an "earthly vision" or a "worldly vision." It is God alone Who gives a **"heavenly vision!"** Perhaps few people have expressed this *paradox of leadership* better than A.W. Tozer:

> *A true and safe leader is likely to be one who has no desire to lead, but is forced into a position by the inward pressure of the Holy Spirit and the press of circumstances … There was hardly a great leader from Paul to the present day but was drafted by the Holy Spirit for the task, and commissioned by the Lord to fill a position he had little heart for… The man who is ambitious to lead is disqualified as a leader. The true leader will have no desire to lord it over God's heritage, but will be humble, gentle, self-sacrificing and altogether ready to follow when the Spirit chooses another to lead.*[32]

"The vision always precedes the resources.
Vision acts like a magnet – attracting, challenging,
and uniting people. It also rallies finances and
other resources. The greater the vision, the
more winners it has the potential to attract."[33]
(John Maxwell)

Whether one leads willfully or reluctantly, there is a growing oneness with their vision. There are scores of contemporary examples of American Christian leaders whose lives have become synonymous with their purpose. The very mention of their names automatically brings to mind the association of their life's calling. Here are just a few familiar examples:

Billy Graham	…Evangelistic Crusades
Cliff Barrows	…Music Ministry
Bill Bright	…Personal Evangelism
John Perkins	…Racial Reconciliation

Larry Burkett.....................Financial Ministry
Nicky Cruz........................Ministry to Gang Members
Josh McDowell....................Christian Apologetics
Ralph Winter.....................World Missions
Patrick Johnstone................Unreached People
Luis Bush........................AD 2000
John Haggai......................National Leader Training
James Dobson.....................Focus on the Family
Chuck Colson.....................Prison Ministry
Jack Van Impe....................Prophecy
R.C. Sproul......................Reformed Theology
Elisabeth Elliot.................Ministry to Women
John Maxwell.....................Leadership Development
Max Lucado.......................Inspirational Author
Frank Peretti....................Christian Fiction
Jay Adams........................Christian Counseling
David Seamands...................Emotional Healing
Beverly LaHaye...................Ministry to Women
Kay Arthur.......................Precepts Ministry
Chuck Swindoll...................Radio Bible Teacher
Bruce Wilkinson..................Walk Through the Bible
Ravi Zacharias...................Apologetics, etc.

If space and time permitted, this representative list of noted American Christian leaders could be greatly amplified by just as many national Christian leaders. Most of the leaders in this list are seasoned "senior saints" who have faithfully lived and ministered for decades. Some of them are in the final phases of their lives and leadership and some are already with the Lord. Since God will never be without a witness in any age, He is raising up another whole generation of younger leaders who will step out of the shadow of these older faithful leaders, and make their own impact for the kingdom of God. Scores of them are already distinguishing themselves in various areas of ministry.

In addition to these noted western Christian leaders, there are even more Christian leaders in other developing countries of the world who are just as known and important to God. Just as many of them live in so-called "developing countries," their spiritual leadership is also developing in both depth and breadth for God's Kingdom and glory. Even though many of them live and lead in Third World countries, their leadership is "first rate" and "First World" quality in every sense of the word! If space permitted, I could give the names of scores of these national leaders who are already having national and international impact as world-class Christian leaders. It has been my privilege to work with many of them personally around the world.

I have just shared this representative list of some popular American Christian leaders to demonstrate the point that a *faithful* and *focused leader* increasingly becomes one with his or her purpose. That's why FOCUS is so crucial in the life of a leader. Let me quickly share a few quotations about the importance of focus in leadership:

- *The focused life is the powerful life. The saints I have read seem to have a unified priority system. They are chiefly single-agenda individuals with a purity of purpose...When we focus and screw down the nozzle, we increase the force of the water...Once you decide what you want to do and the strategy that will accomplish it, then decision-making becomes simple. You do the things that advance the strategy and avoid the things that hinder it.*[34]

- *The ability to block out the unnecessary is the willingness to concentrate your resources for more impact, just as one can deliver a more forceful blow with the fist than with an open palm...the essence of focus is sacrifice. Leaders who cannot bring themselves to give up the unnecessary for the sake of the necessary do not possess the critical leadership characteristic of focus.*[35]

- *Effective leaders who reach their potential spend more time focusing on what they do well than on what they do wrong.*[36]

A leader must *stay focused* if he or she is going to be effective. To stay focused, a leader must live a life of *planned neglect.* He will have to *purposefully neglect some things in order to give his attention to other things.* To do that, a leader must constantly be *prioritizing* his life. In other words, he must constantly fight to keep *"first things FIRST!"* This is one of the greatest battles of every leader. The secondary and tertiary things constantly crowd out the things that should be in first place. This is certainly one of the lifelong struggles of my own life and leadership. I am constantly plagued by the *"tyranny of the urgent!"* It is so easy to spend my days *"hurrying BIG for little reasons!"* If we are not very careful, we can...

Let *other people's lack of agenda set our own agenda.*
Allow *their lack of schedule to interrupt our schedule.*
Permit *their lack of focus to blur our own focus.*
Allow *their lack of priorities to distort our own priorities.*
Allow *their lack of vision to destroy our own vision!*

Principle:
"Focus: the sharper it is, the sharper you are." [37]
(John Maxwell)

A man by the name of E.M. Gray has spent his life searching for the "Common Denominator of Success." He found that the single greatest factor common to all successful people was their secret of *"putting first things first."* [38] Let me share a couple of quotations and principles on this matter of *priorities* that I have found very helpful.

"Things which matter most must never be
at the mercy of things which matter least." [39]
(Goethe)

- *If you can determine what's really a priority and release yourself from everything else, it's a lot easier to follow through on what's important. And that's the essence of self-discipline.* [40]

- *You have to decide what your highest priorities are and have the courage – pleasantly, smilingly, non-apologetically – to say 'no' to other things. And the way you do that is by having a bigger 'yes' burning inside. The enemy of the 'best' is often the 'good.' Keep in mind that you are always saying 'no' to something. If it isn't to the apparent, urgent things in your life, it is probably to the more fundamental, highly important things. Even when the urgent is good, the good can keep you from your best, keep you from your unique contribution, if you let it... The key is not to prioritize what's on your schedule, but to* schedule your priorities. [42]

"The key is not to prioritize what's on your
schedule, but to schedule your priorities." [41]
(Stephen Covey)

Effective leaders are *people of purpose*. It is their *purpose that prioritizes their life and leadership*. Their purpose is to fulfill the vision that God has given them – and that *vision* becomes their *vocation*. Their vision adds *virtue, value, vitality, velocity* and *victory* to their lives!

Principle:

"When your vision becomes your vocation, it adds virtue, value, vitality, velocity and victory to your life."

FURTHER QUOTATIONS ON
PURPOSEFUL LEADERSHIP

1. VISION:

- *It's the leaders' job to establish the vision and values of the organization.*[43]

- *Worthwhile people are seeking to share a great purpose in life.*[44]

- *A legacy of vision: 'Creating and living an empowering mission statement has a significant impact on the way we spend our time. When we talk about time management, it seems ridiculous to worry about speed before direction, about saving minutes when we may be wasting years. Vision is the fundamental force that drives everything else in our lives. It impassions us with a sense of the unique contribution that's ours to make. It empowers us to put first things first, compasses ahead of clocks, people ahead of schedules and things...perhaps the most important legacy we can leave is vision.'*[45]

- *Vision is the best manifestation of creative imagination and the primary motivation of human action. It's the ability to see beyond our present reality, to create, to invent what does not yet exist, to become what we not yet are. It gives us capacity to live out of our imagination instead of our memory. If our vision is based on the social mirror, we make choices based on the expectations of others. It's been said that 'when man discovered the mirror, he began to lose his soul.' If our self-vision is no more than a reflection of the social mirror, we have no connection with our inner selves, with our own uniqueness and capacity to contribute. We're living out of scripts handed to us by others – family, associates, friends, enemies, the media.*[46]

- *Victor Frankl said we don't invent our mission; we detect it. It's within us waiting to be realized. Everyone has his own specific mission in life; everyone must carry out a concrete assignment that demands fulfillment. Therein he cannot be replaced, nor can his life be repeated. Thus, everyone's task is unique as his specific opportunity to implement it.*[47]

- *Vision is usually communicated most effectively when many different vehicles are used: large group meetings, memos, newspapers, posters, informal one-on-one talks. When the same message comes at people from six different directions, it stands a better chance of being heard and remembered, on both intellectual and emotional levels.*[48]

- *If you cannot describe your vision to someone in five minutes and get their interest, you have more work to do...A great vision can serve a useful purpose even if it is understood by just a few key people. But the real power of a vision is unleashed only when most of those involved in an enterprise or activity have a common understanding of its goals and direction.*[49]

- *A good board should spend 75% of its time talking about and creating the future, and only 25% of its time looking at (monitoring) the past...They must send most of their time looking forward through the windshield, not backward into the rearview mirror...All effective leaders do that. They spend lots of time thinking about the future and they encourage those around them to do the same...Dreams are a stimulant that keeps life fresh.*[50]

2.   IMAGINATION & DREAMS:

- *Everything that now is began as an idea, a thought in the mind of somebody. The universe, including man, began as a thought in the mind of God. And everything else as a thought in the mind of man...They saw it before it happened.*[51]

- *We use our imagination to keep the goal in mind, and our independent will to pay the price to achieve it. The power of these two endowments is formidable – it's the power of purposeful living.*[52]

- *All things are created twice...'Begin with the end in mind' is based on the principle that all things are created twice. There's a mental or first creation, and a physical or second creation to all things... Through imagination, we can visualize the uncreated worlds of potential that lie within us.*[53]

- *Dr. Charles Garfield has done extensive research on peak performers, both in athletics and in business. He became fascinated with peak performance in his work with the NASA program, watching the astronauts rehearse everything on earth, again and again in a simulated environment before they went to space...One of the main things his research showed was that almost all of the world-class athletes and other peak performers are visualizers. They see it; they feel it; the experience it before they actually do it. They begin with the end in mind.*[54]

- *Live your dreams. It must be borne in mind that the tragedy of life does not lie in not reaching your goals, the tragedy lies in not having any goals to reach. It isn't a calamity to die with dreams unfulfilled, but it is a calamity not to dream. It is not a disaster to be unable to capture your ideals, but it is a disaster to have no ideals to capture. It is not a disgrace not to reach the stars, but it is a disgrace to have no stars to reach.*[55]

- *When your dreams are your dreams then you can deal with the barriers that will inevitably get in your way. Some barriers you may choose not to remove, and some barriers are not removable at all. In either case, you find a way to go over, under, or around the barrier. If you live your dreams then barriers are setbacks and not permanent detours. Barriers are timing delays but not cancellations of your journey...Anyone can dream but not every embraces their dreams. To embrace your dreams is to want them badly enough that you are willing to work hard enough and long enough to reach them. When you run into detours along the way or experience setbacks, the passion inside of you gives you the strength to pick yourself up again, shake the dust off your feet, and keep on going.*[56]

- *Dreams that touch one child and make a difference in that child's life may one day touch millions – or even change the world. And just as only God knows how many apples there are in an apple seed, only He knows how many people will be touched by your good deeds.*[57]

- *God pity the one-dream man. When you run out of dreams you run into trouble as a leader.*[58]

- *...tyranny is a beast that devours itself, whether in nations or in corporations. And history is a tale that is always written on the living hearts of human beings, a drama played out in a world ruled by a just God. So dreams remain alive long after the tyrants are gone...*[59]

3. **FOCUS & PURPOSE:**

- *The focus of the mandate must be specific and clear so that everyone knows exactly what is meant by it. In fact, it should* not be possible to interpret a mandate except in a narrow sense. That discipline enables the leader to set boundaries...When a leader is sure of the mandate, he or she can create a more effective leadership team. One can discipline and evaluate people in the light of the mandate... Selection is largely determined by the mandate...If someone is not moving the mandate forward by his or her activity, then that activity should be stopped...A mandate gives a leader the ability to define the leadership he needs.[60]

- As leaders think about the mandate for their particular organization, they should remember that the simplest way it can be accomplished is the most effective. Organizations tend to let what they do become too complicated...There are only two questions you need to answer starting out: Number one: 'What are you really trying to do?' Number Two: 'What is the simplest way you can do it?'...Albert Einstein once said that whatever God does, He does in its simplest form. And how can we improve on that?[61]

- ...have the courage...to say 'no' to other things. And the way you do that is by having a bigger 'yes' burning inside.[62]

- ...I heard...Rev. Dr. Nigel McPherson, use some thought-provoking words to define happiness: "something to love, something to do, and something to hope for."...If one of Reverend McPherson's "somethings" is missing, you have a happiness deficiency that only you can fill...[63]

- Drucker's understanding of business is also humane. He has never accepted profit as a goal for any enterprise. Rather, profit is a necessity — for without an adequate margin of profit, business cannot survive, or if it survives, cannot grow and innovate. Profit is always a means to an end, never an end. Nor does business, in Drucker's mind, exist to make and sell things. Business exists to meet human needs...you have to define what needs you will meet, and how...[64]

- ...people who are cause-oriented. Those with double agendas are like those with double-mindedness, against which the Scripture warns. When we focus and screw down the nozzle, we increase the force of the water...Once you decide what you want to do and the strategy that will accomplish it, then decision-making becomes simple. You do the things that advance the strategy and avoid the things that hinder it...[67]

- Drucker preaches incessantly that leaders must find out what their own unique contribution can be. He applies the sermon to himself, *taking two weeks every year to evaluate what he has done and to plan for the coming year...*[68]

4.   PRIORITIES:

- *...the leader must carefully select priorities. He or she must thoughtfully weigh the value of different opportunities and responsibilities. The leader cannot spend time on secondary matters while essential obligations scream for attention. A day needs careful planning. The person who wants to excel must select and reject, and concentrate on the most important items.*[69]

- *To live, to love, to learn, to leave a legacy: Doing more things faster is no substitute for doing the right things.*[70]

- *The key is to consistently do whatever builds your strength in these areas and increases your capacity to live, to love, to learn, and to leave a legacy. An hour a day spent "sharpening your saw" creates the "private victory" that makes public victories possible.*[71]

- *...people first, things second. It's leadership first, management second. It's effectiveness first, efficiency second. It's purpose first, structure second. It's vision first, method second.*[72]

- *It's incredibly easy to get caught up in an activity trap, in the busy-ness of life, to work harder and harder at climbing the ladder of success only to discover it's leaning against the wrong wall. It is possible to be busy – very busy – without being very effective...*[73]

- *How different our lives are when we really know what is deeply important to us, and, keeping that picture in mind, we manage ourselves each day to be and to do what really matters most. If the ladder is not leaning against the right wall, every step we take just gets us to the wrong place faster...*[74]

- The key is not to prioritize what's on your schedule, but to schedule your priorities...[75]

- *...Often the pressure a spiritual leader feels comes from assuming tasks that God has not assigned; for such tasks the leader cannot expect God to supply the extra strength required...*[76]

- *We express our values by our choices...*[77]

- *When we believe that God engineers our circumstances, He sets our priority...*[78]

~~~~~~~~~~~~~~~~~~~~~~~~~~~~~~~~~~~

Chapter 2

LEADERS ARE PROPHETIC

"He gave some to be apostles, some to be prophets, some to be evangelists, and some to be pastors and teachers, to prepare God's people for works of service, so that the body of Christ may be built up…"
(Eph. 4:11-12).

From the above verses, we can clearly see that the role of *prophet* is one of the five-fold leadership gifts Christ gave to His Church. While not every church leader is called to be a *prophet*, every authentic leader, sacred or secular, has a prophetic dimension to his life and leadership.

It is a *vision* that causes a leader to be *prophetic* by nature. A prophet is a person who sees what other people *do not…cannot…*or *will not see*. That *prophetic insight* into the future may be either *natural* or *supernatural* in origin, as we will shortly see. Either way, *prophetic insight* always calls for a major *paradigm shift in people's thinking and living – beginning with the leader!*

Principle:
"Prophetic insight always calls for a major paradigm shift in people's thinking and living beginning with the leader."

Prophets have an ability to see into the *immediate* or *distant future*, and then communicate that *futuristic vision* to the present population. Through their visionary insight, *they cause the future to intersect the present* – usually resulting in a radical change of direction for many people. When the prophetic vision has been successfully communicated, it usually brings about a radical shift in people's *worldview* – which is *the way they view life*. It is only *prophetic insight* that changes *people's sight*. Understandably, most people view their present condition through the lenses of their past experiences. It is only the prophetic voice that impacts a person's present worldview with the future rather than the past. Whereas *historians are past oriented, visionaries* are *future oriented.*

People with a historic *perspective view the present through the past.* As the turn-of-the-century philosopher George Santayana wrote in *The Life of Reason:* "*Those who cannot remember the past are condemned to repeat it.*"

Visionaries, on the other hand, *view the present through the future.* Their maxim would be: "*He who does not see the future will live only for the present, and thereby forfeit their future.*"

There are many kinds of prophets in the world: *social prophets, economic prophets, business prophets, educational prophets, political prophets, scientific prophets, environmental prophets, entertainment prophets, religious prophets.* Both history and contemporary experience painfully remind us that there are also many *false prophets* in all of these realms! Whether well intentioned or willfully deceitful, many of these so-called *"prophets"* – along with their *"prophetic insights about the future"* – prove to be totally wrong. As a result, they are discredited, while many of their followers are deceived.

It is because of the prevalence of these many kinds of visionaries... seers...soothsayers...prophets, that *futurology* has become a very popular and growing "science." Since the dawn of human history, mankind has always tried to devise ways to see beyond the veil of the present and peer into the future. Most of these futuristic methods were either *superstitious* or *satanic* in origin and nature.

Today, more and more educated and enlightened people are trying to move the study of the future from the realm of the mystical, ethereal, nebulous, cultic, superstitious, hocus-pocus – to a legitimate science. On the one hand, people are trying to remove the crystal balls, Ouija boards, Tarot cards, signs of the zodiacs, and prophetic slight-of-hand from forecasting the future. They want to make it a legitimate analytical science. They want to permanently separate the *physical* from the *meta-physical*…the *spiritual* from the *scientific*…the *empirical* from the *experiential.*

On the other hand, many more people – through fear, alienation, loneliness, and disillusionment – are turning away from the impersonal realm of science, and back to the realm of the mystical and superstitious. Because of this desire to probe into the future, millions in the West are in pursuit of the transcendent, ethereal, and non-material realms for guidance. As a result, astrologists, fortunetellers, psychic, mediums, clairvoyants, palm readers, spirit guides and mystics have never been in more demand! They can now be dialed up on the telephone, clicked onto through the Web Page, or turned to on the television! There is a revival of cultic superstition sweeping many segments of society in the so-called enlightened West.

For many people in the scientific, social, economic, and business realms, *futuristic thinking is a legitimate science.* Through their detailed study and analysis of social behavior, buying and spending habits, economic trends, market shifts, environmental changes, etc – they make projections about the future. These futuristic projections are made so that governmental organizations, economic institutions, and businesses can better prepare for coming changes. History has shown that only the organizations, institutions, and businesses that can adapt to change *have any future.* The rest over time become extinct – just like the dinosaurs! Both national and international change is taking place in this electronic age of cyberspace at a faster rate than ever before in history. Our world is increasingly interconnected as a global community with a world economy. Many organizations, institutions and businesses that cannot downsize…tool-up…transition to…make the shift…adjust to the new paradigm, will be left behind in either bankruptcy or obsolescence.

Religion, just like all other segments of human existence, is radically influenced by the changing times. They either adapt their *message* and their *method* to the ever-changing human conditions – or stagnate into irrelevance. Because of their inability or unwillingness to change, many religions have become little more than spiritual relics from the past – "theological dinosaurs" that can only be studied in museums. Tragically, some expressions of Christendom fall into this category – as the empty cathedrals of Europe testify. *It is only the prophetic voice that keeps any religion from spiritual atrophy!*

Principle:
"It is only the prophetic voice that keeps organizations from obsolescence, institutions from becoming antiquated, and religions from spiritual atrophy."

Understandably, *Christianity by its very nature is prophetic.* In fact, it is the only faith that is authentically prophetic. Our faith neither originated from man nor Satan but from God. It did not have its origin in time – but in eternity, where *past, present,* and *future* are non-entities. Because God exists outside of time - past, present and future are the same to Him. All other human beings are encapsulated in time. God is not. He sees all three of these human "time zones" as *simultaneous* – rather than *sequential.* Since God created time, He is superior to time and transcends it. From His vantage point in eternity, He is "above"…"outside of"…"beyond time" as we experience it. Only the true and living God is the *"Alpha* and the *Omega…the First* and the *Last…the Beginning* and the *End"* (Rev. 1:8, 17, 21:6). That's why God alone can say: **"I make known the *end* (future) from the *beginning* (history), from ancient times, what is still to come"** (Isa. 46:10).

Christianity is a *prophetic faith* because it is inspired by a *prophetic book* – the *Bible!* Great portions of the Bible are correctly referred to as 'Prophetic Books.' These "major prophets" and "minor prophets" foretold future events by the *inspiration of the Holy Spirit.* The vast majority of these prophecies have already come to pass with a precision and accuracy that could not in any way be orchestrated or manipulated by man. *Fulfilled prophecy is one of the greatest proofs for the divine inspiration of the Bible!* Hundreds, even thousands, of years in advance, Biblical prophets spoke to man about future events on behalf of God. In God's perfect time, those prophecies have been fulfilled in minute detail. Those hundreds of fulfilled prophecies should be enough to convince even the greatest skeptic of the *divine inspiration* and *accuracy* of the Bible! As Peter wrote:

> **"You must understand that *no prophecy of Scripture came about by the prophet's own interpretation.* For *prophecy never had its origin in the will of man,* but *men moved by the Holy Spirit spoke from God*"** (II Pet. 1:20-21).

It was only because they were speaking for God that these men were known as *prophets.* Even though the purpose of this chapter is not to do an in-depth study of the subject of prophecy, we need to pause and understand a few defining things about *Biblical prophecy.*

Sometimes the prophets spoke about events that were in the *immediate future,* or in the *distant future* – or both. This kind of prophecy is best described by the word *'foretelling.'* They *foretold* coming future events that they could not possibly have any knowledge or understanding of through human reasoning or study.

At other times, they were giving God's *prophetic interpretation* on contemporary events and how those events would affect their future. This kind of prophetic word is best described by the word *"forth-telling,"* or *"telling forth the word of God."* Through no study or investigation of their own, the prophets could reveal and *tell-forth* divine revelation and interpretation of current events.

It is crucial to remember that *every future-oriented prophecy in Scripture is set within the context of a practical exhortation for present living.*

Biblical prophecy is never a *"pie-in-the-sky-by-and-by"* message! It is God's authoritative message to His people while they are living in their present situation. Through prophetic proclamation, He tells them about how their willful choices and contemporary life-style will impact their future – both for time and eternity! Prophecy is not so much *pietistic* as it is *practical.*

As a result of their prophetic *"thus saith the Lord",* most prophets were not very popular with their contemporaries! They were commissioned by God to tell the people things that they did not want to hear. The prophets almost always called the people to a *radical change of thinking with a corresponding radical change of lifestyle* – which is what *repentance* means! The Greek word for *repentance* is the verb *metanoeo*, which means *"to think again; to change your mind."* This *rethinking* was to result in a *redirection* of one's life. The prophetic message of *repentance* has never been very popular because of its call to *change your beliefs* so that you can *change your behavior*. Jesus said to the resistant religious leaders of His day: **"...you kill the prophets and stone those sent to you..."** (Mtt. 23:37; c.f. 5:12).

Paul Powell wrote: "I cannot give you a formula for success, but I can give you a formula for failure – *try to please everybody."* [1]

The unpopularity of speaking prophetically is one of the reasons that *prophetic leadership* is still not popular today – whether in the world or in the church! But authentic leadership is not a call to popularity. It is a call to *obedience* to a 'heavenly vision'...a higher calling...a compelling inner voice...a holy compulsion...a vision for the future that must be shared – regardless of the cost. Let the verbal or physical stones fly, a prophetic visionary cannot easily be silenced! Unfortunately, a prophetic leader is often not fully appreciated until long after he is dead and gone. Sometimes it takes years, even decades or centuries, for his vision of the future to be realized, and his reputation to be vindicated. That's why Charles Cowman wrote:

> *Often the crowd does not recognize a leader until he has gone, and then they build a monument for him with the stones they threw at him in life.*[2]

"The man who leads the orchestra must turn his back on the crowds."
(Thomas Jefferson)

It is because of the initial unpopularity of a prophetic vision for the future that visionary leaders are often ridiculed and rejected. *Suffering, pain,* and *sacrifice* go along with visionary leadership. *Prophetic leadership often leads to self-sacrifice and persecution.* But it does not stop there. If the communication of a prophetic vision leads to persecution for the visionary, it also usually results in some *pain* to the followers. That's why there is so often *short* or *long-term pain* involved in the communication and implementation of a prophetic vision. Harvard Business Professor, John Kotter, has observed:

> *Vision refers to a picture of the future with some implicit or explicit commentary on why people should strive to create that future...Vision serves to facilitate major changes by motivating action that is not necessarily in people's short-term self-interests. The alterations called for in a sensible vision almost always involves some* pain...*A good vision helps to overcome this natural reluctance to do what is often painfully necessary by being hopeful and therefore motivating.*[3]

Principle:
"Prophetic vision often leads to long-term persecution for the leader, and short-term pain for the follower."

Prophetic leadership integrity necessitates that *the leader must be the first one to take the lead in the implementation of the futuristic vision.* He must never call others to make changes in preparation for the future that he is not willing to make first. He must take the initiative to live out...flesh out...incarnate...demonstrate the *prophetic paradigm shift.* The leader must not only *speak prophetically,* he must also *live prophetically!* As a leader, he must *practically incarnate his message for people to see.* To express it more plainly, a leader must *walk the talk.* He must not only *lead by exhortation,* he must also *lead by example.* As Harvard Business School's John Kotter writes:

> *Often the most powerful way to communicate a new direction is through behavior...When they see top management acting out the vision, a whole set of troublesome questions about credibility and game playing tends to evaporate...We call such behavior 'leadership by example.' The concept is simple. Words are cheap, but action is not. The cynical among us tend not to believe words but will be impressed by action...In short: Nothing undermines the communication of a changed vision more than behavior on the part of key players that seems inconsistent with the vision.*[4]

Again, if there is going to be *leadership integrity,* the one out front must not only *speak prophetically,* he must also *live prophetically!*

Principle:
"A leader must speak prophetically and live prophetically. He must practically incarnate his message."

As we have already seen, prophetic thinking and living often cause a leader to be out-of-step with the people. It puts him ahead-of-his-time in his thinking; and out-in-front of the pack in his living and leadership. That's why a prophetic leader "marches to a different drummer" – and the cadence of the music beckons from the future rather than echoes out of the past. This bucking of the tide swimming against the current… standing against the prevailing wind is often socially, relationally and emotionally painful.

Many times it requires the leader to *stand alone* and *go it alone*. As a result, he may lose respect…lose friends…lose business associates…lose his job…lose his finances…lose his security – even lose his life. But if he loses his vision, he loses his reason to live! Until his prophetic paradigm is validated and accepted, his message is not popular. For a time – and sometimes a long time – he is not seen as *politically* or *socially correct.*

> **"A leader must have 3 qualities: *head, heart,* and *guts.*"** [5]
> **(President Richard Nixon)**

His vision of the future radically threatens the present…the accepted wisdom…the status quo…business as usual…normal procedure…the popular way of doing things…the party line – whether in business, economics, education, science, politics, or religion. Virtually every great leader in history has had to go through periods of ridicule, rejection, character assassination, vilification, suffering. Thus the *pain of prophetic leadership!*

Principle:
"There is always pain in prophetic leadership – both for the leader and for the follower."

It is the reality of sacrifice that causes many to shirk away from prophetic leader-ship. That's why many so-called "leaders" would rather submit to group pressure...play to the crowd...march in step with the masses... sing the group songs...parrot the party platform...chant the hollow slogans...live by majority vote – than be different. They choose to be *popular leaders* rather than *prophetic leaders*. They end up *speaking for man* rather than *speaking for God*.

Principle:
"Popular leaders speak for man;
prophetic leaders speak for God."

The *pain barrier*...the *popularity pull*...the *fear of rejection*...the *possibility of suffering* are prophetic leadership issues that cannot be avoided. That's why Jesus said that we should **"...count the cost"** of following Him (Lk. 14:28; KJV). In his book, *The Other Side of Leadership*, Eugene Habecker writes:

> Leadership is a fairly high-priced calling *and persons are advised not to rush headlong into it unless, after counting the costs, they are persuaded that God has still called them into such a position. Perhaps the attitude should be one of a reluctant but willing servant.*[6]

In my opinion, one of the greatest books on leadership was written by the late Oswald J. Sanders, entitled *Spiritual Leadership*. In it he has much to say about the pain and suffering that almost always accompany authentic spiritual leadership. He exhorts the would-be Christian leaders to spend much time pondering the words of the Lord Jesus to James and John about the cost of leadership. As you will recall, in their youthful enthusiasm and spiritual naiveté, they were confident of their readiness to take their places of leadership shoulder-to-shoulder with the Lord Jesus. One would lead from His right, and the other would lead from His left! Jesus sobered their thinking with a penetrating question about the suffering that inevitably goes along with true spiritual servant leadership: **"Can you drink the cup I drink or be baptized with the baptism I am baptized with?"** (Mk. 10:38). With that question in mind, let me share a couple of quotes from Sanders about *suffering leadership*:

- *"True leaders must be willing to suffer for the sake of objectives great enough to demand their wholehearted obedience..."*[7]

- *"To aspire to leadership in God's kingdom requires us to be willing to pay a price higher than others are willing to pay. The toil of true leadership is heavy, and the more effective the leadership, the higher it goes."*[8]

Sanders also quotes Samuel Zwemer, who founded one of Christianity's earliest missions to Muslims – and faced much suffering in the process. Zwemer pointed out: *"...the only thing Jesus took pains to show after His resurrection were His scars."*[9] Sanders concludes that:

> *Scars are the authenticating marks of faithful discipleship and true spiritual leadership...Nothing moves people more than the print of the nails and the mark of the spear. Those marks are tests of sincerity that none can challenge, as Paul knew well. **"Let no one cause me trouble,"** he wrote, **"for I bear on my body the marks of Jesus"**[10]* (Gal. 6:17).

Authentic spiritual leadership is *prophetic* by nature. It is oriented toward *receiving* and *revealing God's perspective of the future.* Prophetic leadership does not primarily come from a study of current events...popular trends...prevailing theories...majority polls...or statistical analysis – but from a *study of the Bible.* Prophetic insight does not come from *human reasoning* but from *divine revelation.* It is only when a leader peers into the future through the lenses of Holy Scripture that he can have an accurate diagnosis of current events – and an absolutely trustworthy forecast of coming world events. It is only the *Spirit of God* who can reveal to the *spirit of man* through the *Word of God* what is in store for the *people of God.* Whether in the world or in the church, whether individually and collectively, prophetic leadership is desperately needed in our world today.

Prophetic leadership has one ear tuned to the *spirit of the age,* and the other tuned to the *Spirit of God.* He lives in two worlds simultaneously – one *earthly,* and the other *heavenly*...one *corporeal,* the other *spiritual*...one *seen,* the other *unseen*...one *temporal,* the other *eternal.*

In conclusion, one of the greatest needs in our world today is for authentic *prophetic leadership!* If this is true for the world – how much more it is true for the church! More than any other organization or institution in society, the church of Jesus Christ is to be characterized by *prophetic leadership.*

Christians are to be the incarnation of God's prophetic paradigm for the world. We are to demonstrate in our individual lives...marriages...family relationships...jobs... expenditure of money...use of time...recreational activities – the values of God's Kingdom. The ethics of Christ's *Sermon on the Mount,* are to be lived out in our living rooms, bedrooms, classrooms, storerooms, locker rooms and boardrooms. The church is to be a microcosm of the kingdom of God – a collective expression in time of God's future coming world order. For that to increasingly take place, individually or collectively, there must be *authentic prophetic leadership.*

FURTHER QUOTATIONS ON
PROPHETIC LEADERSHIP

1. PAIN & SACRIFICE:

- *SELF-SACRIFICE: This part of the cost must be paid daily. A cross stands in the path of spiritual leadership, and the leader must take it up...*[11]

- *A. W. Tozer wrote:*

  A true and safe leader is likely to be one who has no desire to lead, but is forced into a position by the inward pressure of the Holy Spirit and the press of {circumstances}...There was hardly a great leader from Paul to the present day but was drafted by the Holy Spirit for the task, and commissioned by the Lord to fill a position he had little heart for...The man who is ambitious to lead is disqualified as a leader. The true leader will have no desire to lord it over God's heritage, but will be humble, gentle, self-sacrificing and altogether ready to follow when the Spirit chooses another to lead."[12]

- *God can and does magnify such* gifts offered in faith. *After all, it was one little boy who gave his lunch to Jesus, but with it God fed an entire multitude. He asks us merely to give what we have to offer, and to trust in Him for the harvest.*

  Consider the names we will never see in this history, names of men and women who had the same opportunity to act with valor but let it pass by, who kept their provisions for themselves instead of taking them out to David in his flight, who stayed on the fence forever. These are the ones who remained nobodies. These small heroes we do see are just a few out of tens of thousands, but they were the few who remembered, who understood, and who gave of themselves when it counted. And so they each became a somebody, and even now we remember them with honor...[13]

2. STANDING ALONE:

- *Harry Truman, who embodied moral courage, once said: "How far would Moses have gone if he had taken a poll in Egypt? What would Jesus Christ have preached if He had taken a poll in the Land of Israel? What would have happened to the Reformation if Martin Luther had taken a poll? It isn't polls or public opinion of the moment that counts. It is right and wrong and leadership."*[14]

• *Moses paid the price for his leadership – alone on the mountain, alone on the plain, misunderstood and criticized...The Old Testament prophets were lonely men. Enoch walked alone in a decadent society as he preached judgment. His compensation was the presence of God. Jonah was alone in vast Nineveh, a heathen city of a million souls. The loneliest preacher today is the person who has been entrusted with a prophetic message ahead of the times, a message that cuts across the temper of the age...Gregarious Paul was a lonely man, misunderstood by friends, misrepresented by enemies, deserted by converts. How poignant are his words to Timothy:* **"You know that everyone in the province of Asia has deserted me"** *(2 Timothy 1:15).*

"Most of the world's greatest souls have been lonely," wrote A.W. Tozer. "Loneliness seems to be the price a saint must pay for his saintliness." The leader must be a person who, while welcoming the friendship and support of all who offer it, has sufficient inner resources to stand alone...[15]

Chapter 3

LEADERS ARE PEOPLE-ORIENTED

"A new command I give you: Love one another.
As I have loved you, so you must love one another.
By this all men will know that you are My disciples,
if you love one another"
(John 13:34-35).

Leadership is about people – nothing more, nothing less. Good *leadership skills* are based upon good *people skills*. The better a person's people skills, the better his leadership skills.

From start to finish, *the leadership calling is a people calling*. Spiritual leaders are called to give their lives to *people*, not *programs*. First and foremost, leaders are committed to *individuals* – not to *institutions*. If this principle is true for leaders in general, how much more true is it for spiritual leaders. That's why Jesus called Himself a *Shepherd*, and referred to the leaders He trained in the same way. **"I am the good shepherd,"** Jesus said (Jn. 10:10, 14).

Shepherds have one primary focus – their sheep. They *love their sheep... abide with their sheep...live for their sheep...enjoy their sheep...work for their sheep...feed their sheep...protect their sheep* – and if necessary, *die for their sheep.*

Because of this life-long focus by the shepherd on his sheep, you cannot separate *shepherd leadership* from *servant leadership*. The shepherd by definition is one who "serves the sheep" – even unto death. As Jesus said: **"the good shepherd lays down his life for the sheep"** (Jn. 10:10).

The sheep do not exist for the shepherd, but the shepherd exists for the sheep. Neither one is independent of the other. There is an *inter-dependence* and *mutualism* between the shepherd and the sheep.

Their *existence, survival* and *prosperity* are intertwined. As one goes, so goes the other.

> The healthier the sheep, the healthier the shepherd.
> The more prosperous the sheep, the more prosperous the shepherd.
> The more successful the sheep, the more successful the shepherd.
> The more the sheep grows, the more the shepherd grows.

For that kind of health, growth, maturity, and prosperity to take place among the sheep, the shepherd must *toil night and day!* His shepherding leadership skills are never off duty. Through every circumstance, the shepherd strives to intimately *know his sheep.* They are not an impersonal, abstract, nameless, faceless herd to him. They are a group of unique individuals. The better he individually knows them, the better he can lead them. Once again, Jesus set the perfect example of shepherd leadership. As He describes the role of a true shepherd leader, we can see His *intimate relationship* with His sheep:

> **"...the sheep listen to his voice. He calls his own sheep by name and leads them out. When he has brought out all his own, he goes on ahead of them, and his sheep follow him because they know his voice...I have come that they may have life, and have it to the full...I am the good shepherd, I know My sheep and My sheep know Me...I lay down My life for the sheep"** (Jn. 10:2-16).

The longing for *intimate relationship* is one of the deepest and most abiding longings of the human heart. Tragically, *most people go through their entire lives without a single intimate relationship,* not with their family...their spouse...their friends...their business associates – not even with fellow church members, or ministry partners. They live and die in *lonely isolation!*

They may have many acquaintances – even a few friendships – but few, if any, intimate relationships. That's because *knowing takes time*. Intimacy requires a growing *transparency* on the part of both the leader and the follower. The only thing that will move a person to drop their defenses... masquerades...role playing and become increasingly transparent with another human being is *unconditional love*. There is only one source for that kind of love in the universe and that is Jesus Christ. It is called *agape*, and is the *self-giving-God-kind-of-love*. Only Christ's unconditional love for us will motivate us to unconditionally love another person – especially after we have seen their immaturities...faults...failures...fears!

Principle:
"Intimacy is the deepest longing of the human heart. Yet few leaders allow themselves to be known intimately; nor do they ever get to know their followers intimately. But the more intimately he knows them, the better he can lead them."

We cannot get to know another person quickly. Relationship building requires the "Four T's": *time, talking, transparency* and *testing*. Only as we take the time to really *know people* can we really *love them*. The principle is this: *"loving is based upon knowing; and knowing takes time."*

Principle:
"Loving is based upon knowing. The more intimately we are known, the more intimately we are loved, and the better we can lead."

Many shepherd leaders are unwilling to give that much time, talking, transparency, and testing to their followers. Instead, they build *superficial relationships...functional relationships...project-based relationships...goal-oriented relationships...business-related relationships...church-based relationships* – but not real *covenant relationships* based upon Christ's *unconditional love*.

In John 10, we can see and hear how this deep human need for intimacy is being emotionally met through Christ's relationship with His sheep. His knowledge of His sheep is seen through the fact that *He knows each of their names.* In addition, He knows each of their individual *voices* – just as they know His. He knew the bleat of each sheep, and whether it was a bleat of hunger…a bleat of thirst…a bleat of fear…a bleat of frustration…a bleat of hurt…a bleat of contentment. That takes a lot of *shepherd leadership listening!*

Principle: *"Relationship building and intimacy take 4 things: time, talking, transparency, and testing. Without them leaders will only build functional relationships, not covenant relationships based in Christ."*

It is a basic principle: *"The better we listen, the better we can lead."* American president, Woodrow Wilson, said: *"The ear of the leader must ring with the voices of the people."*[1] In his book, *Leadership is Common Sense*, Herman Cain says this about the importance of listening leadership:

> *People always want to feel that you genuinely listen to what they say, even if you decide not to pursue their idea. People want to feel they contribute to something successful, and that you as leader appreciate their contribution even if no one else understood their impact.*[2]

Effective leadership is based upon *listening* and *loving* – because *listening is the first act of loving!* It was only because Christ first *lovingly listened,* that He could also *lovingly lead.* As He lovingly listened to His sheep, He knew exactly where they needed loving and leading. He could then give them the decisive and loving leadership that they needed and desired by **"…going ahead of them"** so that they would **"…find pasture"** and **"…have life abundantly."** That's a description of true *shepherd leadership!*

Principle:
*"The better we listen, the better we can love; and
the more we love, the better we can lead. Listening,
loving, and leading are inseparable."*

We can see the difference between *effective spiritual leadership*, and *efficient worldly leadership*. There is a crucial difference here between being an *efficient leader* as opposed to being an *effective leader*. Many leaders are *efficient* – but they are not *effective*. What is the difference? Stephen Covey explains:

> *While you can think in terms of efficiency in dealing with time, a principle-centered person thinks in terms of* effectiveness *in dealing with people…you simply can't think efficiency with people. You think* effectiveness with people, *and* efficiency with things.[3]

We may become very *efficient* in organizing people…managing people… manipulating people – without ever really effectively relating to them as *people!* You can manage them like a cog in a machine…move them around like a pawn on a chessboard…check them off like a line item on your 'to-do' list – and never get to know them as individuals. *Efficiency* can be very impersonal, while true *effectiveness* flows out of intimate relationships!

There is another great contrast between worldly leadership and kingdom leadership. *In the world greatness is determined by how many people serve you* – not by how many people love you. The more people who revolve around you…answer to you…serve you…do your bidding…meet your needs, the greater you are deemed to be. However, *in the Kingdom of God, greatness is determined by how many people you serve* – and *serving is the proof of loving.* It is a totally different *leadership paradigm.* In the Kingdom of God, there is a *radical shift of axis from self to others.* For this leadership shift to take place, *pride* and *ego* have to be *laid low!* This egotistical self has to be crucified with Christ…wrapped in the shroud of *self-denial*…and buried in the grave of *self-surrender!* Otherwise, the spiritual leader becomes a *carnal walking corpse of self-centeredness!* Richard Phillips warns about the exaltation of self in his book, *The Heart of an Executive:*

> *When a person rises in position, as happens to leaders in the church, the tendency to pride also increases. If not checked, the attitude will*

disqualify the person from further advancement in the kingdom of God, for "...the Lord detests all the proud of heart" (Prov. 16:5). These are strong and searching words! Nothing aggravates God more than conceit, the sin that aims at setting the self upon a throne, making of God a secondary figure. That very sin changed the anointed cherub into the foul fiend of hell.[4]

The first battlefield for every spiritual leader is the inner battle over the throne-room of the heart. That's always the last prideful stronghold to fall! The great question is: *"Who will supremely reign there – Christ or self?"* Psychotherapist Sheldon Kopp noted the universal primacy of this inner struggle when he wrote: *"All the significant battles are waged within self."*[5] Tragically, self oftentimes wins the "battle of the heart" in the life of the leader. The result is always the same – leadership tainted with ego and tarnished by selfishness.

The philosopher Plato stated: *"The first and best victory is to conquer self."* But the only problem with his philosophical analysis of the human condition is that *self cannot conquer self!* Pride will never willfully surrender first place. Self-seeking will *never* step down from the throne. Ego will never capitulate to another. Selfishness will never serve others. No! Self cannot conquer self. *Only Christ can conquer self* and He does so through *crucifixion.* The Apostle Paul expressed it this way through his own experience of dying to self:

> **"I have been *crucified with Christ* and I no longer live, but Christ lives in me. The life I live in the body, I live by faith in the Son of God, Who loved me and gave Himself for me"** (Gal 2:20).

Jesus turned leadership upside-down – or rather right side up! Sin had inverted leadership and made it self-serving. *Jesus exalted leadership by causing it to take the lowest position!* He made the route to leadership greatness the exact opposite of the world's route. He taught His disciples whom He was mentoring for future spiritual leadership:

> **"...whoever wants to become *great* among you must be your *servant,* and whoever wants to be *first* must be your *slave* –** just as the Son of Man did not come to *be served,* **but to *serve,* and to *give His life as a ransom for many"* (Mtt. 20:26-28).

This lesson of servant leadership was an exceedingly hard one for the disciples to learn. Just like us, their pride and egos constantly took over – causing great friction among them! All of us are familiar with the occasion when His disciples were arguing among themselves over who was the greatest one among their ranks. As we listen to their heated argument, and Jesus' response, we can clearly perceive the difference between *worldly leadership* and *spiritual leadership*.

> **"In this world the kings and great men order their people around, and yet they are called 'friends of the people.' But among you, those who are the greatest should take the lowest rank, and the leader should be like a servant. Normally the master sits at the table and is served by his servants. But not here!** *For I am among you as one Who serves"* (Lk. 22:24-27; NLT & NIV).

Jesus succinctly summarized true spiritual leadership with this paradigm: **"The *greatest* among you will be your *servant"*** (Mtt. 23:11). The late Dick Halverson, Chaplain to the United States Senate, often said: *"All progress in Christ is measured downward."* The world thinks that the route to greatness is upward – not downward. But Christ demonstrated that it was *downward* to the lowest place of a servant – even a suffering and dying servant. Paul summarized Christ-like leadership this way:

> **"Your attitude should be the same that Christ Jesus had. Though He was God, He did not demand and cling to His rights as God. He made Himself nothing; He took the *humble position* of a slave and appeared in human form. And in human form He obediently *humbled Himself* even further by dying a criminal's death on a cross"** (Phil. 2:5-8; NLB).

Principle:
"If you want to lead on the highest level, be willing to serve on the lowest level."[6]
(John Maxwell)

We can clearly see through the life of Christ, that *humility* is the true mark of *spiritual maturity* and *spiritual greatness!* Not in *upward mobility* but rather in *downward mobility.* Notice the steps downward Jesus took from His heavenly exalted position as the Second Person of the eternal Godhead. He stepped down from heaven to earth...from God to man... from man to a servant...from a servant to a criminal's death! That's true downward *servant leadership* from *total exaltation* to *total humiliation!*

Principle:
"Since all progress in Christ is measured downward, humility and servanthood is the mark of spiritual maturity."

In the world, *the followers serve the leader.* But in the Kingdom of God, *the leader serves the follower.* This is not *natural leadership* – but rather *supernatural leadership.* Living for others is not natural to our sinful, self-seeking, self-serving prideful egos. In our fallen spiritual condition, we all want others to serve us, rather than us serve them. That sad fact is seen in the eternal "war between the sexes" in marriage...political strife in nations...racial, tribal and ethnic strife among people...student-teacher conflict in schools ...employer-employee conflict in business... management-labor conflict in industry...pastor-parish conflicts in the church.

Oswald Sanders poignantly writes about this difference in leadership style between the world and the body of Christ:

> *True greatness, true leadership, is achieved not by reducing men to one's service but in giving oneself in selfless service to them. And* that is never done without cost. *It involves drinking a bitter cup and experiencing a painful* baptism of suffering. *The true spiritual leader is concerned infinitely more with the service he can render God and his fellow men than with the benefits and pleasures he can extract from life. He aims to put more into life than he takes out of it.*[7]

Authentic spiritual leadership is recognized by a *people-focus* in general, and a *servant-people-focus* in particular. In the world, leadership is oriented around *position* and *power.* In the Kingdom of God, leadership revolves around *people.* Worldly leadership often *uses* and *abuses* people for the purpose of the leader. They *manipulate* and *intimidate* the follower for the purpose of the leader. In the Kingdom of God, servant leaders *mentor* and *motivate* the followers for their own good – and for God's glory.

When a leader loses his *people-focus*, he loses his ability and integrity as a true leader!

The greater his love for people, the greater his leadership will be!

Principle:

"When a leader loses his people-focus, he loses his leadership-focus. The greater his love for people, the greater his leadership will be."

FURTHER QUOTATIONS ON
PEOPLE-FOCUSED LEADERSHIP

1. SHEPHERDS:

- *...Being a shepherd is exhausting. For one thing, the shepherd leads the flocks out into lands filled with danger: predators, hostile weather, starvation, and disease. For another, sheep are just about the most inept followers imaginable. Besides being plain stupid, they are easily panicked and annoyed and debilitated. Unable to defend themselves against wolves, they also need protecting from themselves; sheep are notorious for wandering off good pastures or away from sources of water, for destroying what good grass is available, and for placing themselves in one irretrievable situation after another...*[8]

- *...The shepherd lives among the sheep. He identifies with them in his heart and takes note of them on his weekly planner. The shepherd shares the hardships the sheep must face, the risks and the dangers as well. Indeed, the shepherd stands among the sheep both figuratively and literally, leading through personal presence and intimate acquaintance...*[9]

- *...The shepherd is the servant of the sheep; it is their growth and nurture that define his task and set the agenda for his success...*[10]

- *...the shepherd-executive...lays it down for the sheep. She spends herself for their sake. He can be trusted and believed in because he sacrifices himself for their sake...*[11]

2. RELATIONSHIPS:

- *Nurture self-accountability and self-government. It's important to realize that we are not ultimately responsible for the development of anyone else. We can never really change someone; people must change themselves. But we can help. We can be a resource. We can nurture, encourage, and support. We can be a leader/servant.*[12]

3. EFFICIENCY & EFFECTIVENESS:

- *Efficiency is "getting more done in less time." It makes good sense. We get more done. We reduce or even eliminate waste. We're streamlined. We're faster. We're leveraged. The increase in productivity is incredible. But the underlying assumption is that "more" and "faster" is better. Is that necessarily true? There's a vital difference between efficiency and effectiveness. You may be driving down the highway, enjoying great traveling weather, and getting terrific mileage. You may be very efficient. But if you're headed south down the California coast on Highway 101 and your destination is New York City — some three thousand miles to the east — you're not being very effective...While you can be efficient with things, you can't be efficient — effectively — with people.*[13]

4. SERVING:

- *Life is like tennis — you have to serve well if you are going to win.*[14]

- *Leadership does not exist for the benefit of the leader, but for the benefit of the people he leads. Leadership is an opportunity to serve.*[15]

- *Self-advancement is not a proper goal for the spiritual leader...*[16]

- *True greatness, true leadership, is found in giving yourself in service to others, not in coaxing or inducing others to serve you...*[17]

- *..."servant" is the essential image of the Christian religion. The Son of God became the servant of God in order to do the mission of God. That image provides the pattern for mission societies, churches, and individual believers to fulfill their God-given mission...*[18]

- *N. Eldon Tanner has said, "Service is the rent we pay for the privilege of living on this earth."*[19]

- *...one of the early pioneers of the American West, Bryant S. Hinckley, said: "Service is the virtue that distinguished the great* *of all times and which they will be remembered by. It places a mark of nobility upon its disciples. It is the dividing line which separates the two great groups of the world – those who help and those who hinder, those who lift and those who lean, those who contribute and those who only consume. How much better it is to give than to receive. Service in any form is comely and beautiful. To give encouragement, to impart sympathy, to show interest, to banish fear, to build self-confidence and awaken hope in the hearts of others, in short – to love them and to show it – is to render the most precious service.* [20]

5. PRIDE:

- *The bottom line is, don't take yourself too seriously. You can't take your work too seriously, but you can take yourself too seriously…Keep a sense of humor. Those who can't laugh at themselves leave the job to others.*[21]

- *…pride also describes one of the most destructive paradigms in life…A prideful person is essentially competitive in nature, constantly seeking to elevate himself or herself above others. In the words of C. S. Lewis:*

"Pride gets no pleasure out of having something, only out of having more of it than the next man…It is the comparison that makes you proud; the pleasure of being above the rest."

…Pride is the ultimate emotional parasite. There is no deep joy, no satisfaction, no peace in it because there's always the possibility that someone else is better-looking or has more money, more friends, a bigger house, or a newer car.

Pride is insidious because it pollutes meaning and purpose. It dulls, ignores, and even dethrones conscience. As C. S. Lewis observed, "Pride is a spiritual cancer: it eats up the very possibility of love, or contentment, or even common sense." *It eventually leads to hate, envy, and war.*

Prideful people get their security from how far up the ladder they are compared to others, rather than whether or not their ladder is leaning against the right wall. They feel worthwhile when they see people beneath them. The reward, the focus, is being ahead...even if it means being ahead in the wrong things... The antidote for the poison of pride is humility – the humility to realize that we're not an island, that the quality of our lives is inseparably connected to the quality of the lives of others, that meaning is not in consuming and competing, but in contributing. We are not laws unto ourselves, and the more we begin to value principles and people the greater will be our peace...[22]

6. HUMILITY:

- *Humility is the hallmark of the spiritual leader...*[23]

- *It takes humility to seek feedback. It takes wisdom to understand it, analyze it, and appropriately act on it. But it truly is the lunch of champions.*[24]

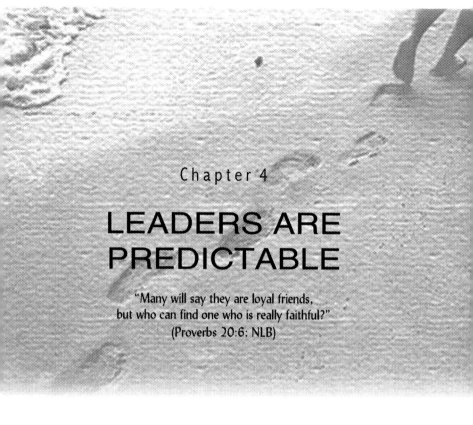

Chapter 4

LEADERS ARE PREDICTABLE

"Many will say they are loyal friends,
but who can find one who is really faithful?"
(Proverbs 20:6: NLB)

As we saw in our last chapter, *leaders must be people-oriented* rather than *program-oriented*. They must have a heart for *building individuals* rather than a head for *building institutions*.

The *people-building business* – whether in parenting, industry, or ministry – is based upon *predictability. Just as an unpredictable parent will produce an unpredictable child; an unpredictable leader will produce unpredictable followers.* Every child needs to be able to predict his parent's behavior in order to develop *emotional security*. Without emotional security a child will not healthily develop physically, mentally, socially, or spiritually. In the same way, a follower needs to be able to expect the same predictability from his or her leader. Whether in children or in followers, *unpredictability always produces emotional insecurity*. If a parent or a leader is unpredictable, unstable, inconsistent, erratic, constantly changing like the weather, there will be confusion and insecurity in the followers.

Principle:
"Predictable leaders produce predictable followers.
Unpredictable leaders produce unpredictable
followers."

Predictability in the life of a leader is essential for a sense of security and well-being among those who follow him. Just as a wife should be able to expect predictability from her husband – or a child should be able to expect predictability from his parents – *a follower should be able to expect predictability from his leader.* This *consistency of life* is an essential ingredient of effective leadership.

Every would-be leader should strive to develop a consistent predictable lifestyle. It is in the *daily disciplines of life* that great leadership virtues are nurtured. It is the example of *consistency* that builds leadership integrity – one block at a time. It is *daily predictability* – not the *passion of a moment,* that lasting leadership comes from. As Aristotle said: *"We are what we repeatedly do."* Therefore, *excellence in any field of endeavor is not an act of the moment, but rather the habit of a lifetime.*

Principle:
"We are what we repeatedly do." (Aristotle)

That means that *no young leader will ever be any greater in the future than his or her preparation for greatness now.* There is no substitute for the *daily disciplines* of a consistent lifestyle. Even though we all need some spontaneity in life, it is consistency and predictability that equip us for the long haul of life and leadership. The daily disciplines of prayer, Bible Study, meditation, reading, writing, working, exercising, serving, giving – are all essential for well-rounded spiritual leadership development.

Principle: *"A person is never any greater in the future than their preparation for greatness now."*

The importance of *preparation for leadership* cannot be overly emphasized. Good leaders do not just suddenly step on the stage of life and take control. They spend a lifetime of faithful preparation for leadership. When the strategic moment arises, they will be ready to "seize the opportunity" and give the needed leadership. In this preparation stage, they must be like an athlete in training for an Olympic competition…a musician preparing for his debut performance…an orator preparing for his first speech…a doctoral candidate preparing for his oral examination…a young preacher studying for his first sermon. Achievement in any area that comes *too quickly* or *too easily* is almost always corrupting. As Thomas Paine rightly observed: *"That which we obtain too easily, we esteem too lightly."*[1] God does not quickly exalt any person to a position of leadership. He first tests and tries him through the furnace of affliction…the fires of adversity…the hostility of the wilderness…the humiliation of failure…the heartbreak of disappointment.

Principle: *"That which we obtain too easily, we esteem too lightly."* (Thomas Paine)

It is in this *season of preparation* that a young leader needs to establish a life-style of consistency and predictability that will make him a trustworthy leader. This is the time for establishing *holy* and *healthy habits* that will result in *holistic living and leading.* It is the time for *building up your spiritual reservoir, storing up Biblical information, clarifying your theology, sharpening your mind, refining your people skills, polishing your speaking abilities and developing emotional stability.*

Oswald Sanders wrote this about the daily grind of leadership preparation:

> …*the cost of every great achievement…is not paid in a lump sum.* Achievement is bought on the time-payment plan, with a new installment required each day. *Fresh drafts are constantly being drawn, and when payment ceases, leadership wanes.*[2]

Herman Cain wrote about the benefits of developing wholesome habits, when he said: *"Concepts, principles, instructions, or values which are internalized can be applied spontaneously and repeatedly."*[3] When we habitually store up healthy habits in our life, we can *spontaneously* and *unconsciously* draw upon them as needed the rest of our lives. But we cannot *draw out* what we do not first of all *put in!*

Leadership predictability is like the computer with which I am writing this book. It has many different programs stored up in its memory chips. I can with a "click," call upon any number of programs to help me in my writing. Every one of these programs is absolutely predictable. Just as long as I follow the directions in the various menus, they will always perform predictably. Imagine my confusion and frustration if every time I clicked on a particular icon on my tool bar it would do something different! I would quickly become frustrated and cease to use my computer! I would go back to the older and slower, but *predictable*, method of writing by hand. In the same way, followers eventually quit following erratic, unstable, unpredictable leaders!

If every leader is honest with himself, he will readily confess that neither *consistency* nor *predictability* is a part of his nature. As well intentioned as we may be, we are all *inconsistent...erratic...unpredictable*. Christian leaders have an advantage over worldly leaders. We can draw from the nature of God – Who is always consistent and predictable. One of the greatest attributes of God is His *unchangeableness*. This divine attribute is theologically known as the *immutability* of God. He *has not...does not... will not change.* Only God can say with absolute integrity: **"I the Lord *do not change"*** (Mal. 3:6; c.f. Num. 23:19; Heb. 7:21). That's why the Apostle James could confidently say that God our heavenly Father: **"...does *not change*** like shifting shadows"** (Ja. 1:17). Likewise, the writer of Hebrews could with absolute certainty point to the Lord Jesus, and affirm: **"Jesus Christ is the same *yesterday* and *today* and *forever"*** (Heb. 13:8).

In addition to the example and inspiration of the immutable character of God, the Christian leader can also draw upon the person and power of the Holy Spirit to build consistency and predictability in his life and leadership. Three of the fruit of the Holy Spirit are **"...patience... faithfulness...and self-control"** (Gal. 5:22). It is when we do not have those virtues growing in our life that our leadership becomes inconsistent, erratic, and unpredictable. To lead others, we constantly need *patience* and *faithfulness*. To lead ourselves, we constantly need *self-control*.

Principle:
"To lead others we need patience and faithfulness. To lead ourselves, we need self-control."

Oswald Sanders wrote this about the necessity of the Holy Spirit for a life of spiritual leadership:

> To be filled with the Spirit is to be controlled by the Spirit. The Christian leader's mind, emotions, will and physical strength all become available for the Spirit to guide and use. Under the Spirit's control, natural gifts of leadership are lifted to their highest power, and sanctified for holy purposes. Through the work of the... ungrieved and unhindered Spirit, all the fruits of the Spirit start

to grow in the leader's life. His witness is more winsome, service more steady, and testimony more powerful.[4]

Sanders then poignantly concludes:

The filling of the Spirit is essential for spiritual leadership. And each of us is as full of the Spirit as we really want to be.[5]

Principle: *"Each of us is as full of the Spirit as we really want to be."* (Oswald Sanders)

Regardless of the level of his life in the Spirit, every leader from time to time faces circumstances beyond his control. These unforeseen events interrupt his schedule...alter his plans...modify his timetable...change his itinerary...redirect his focus. However, these unforeseen changes should be the *exception* - not the *norm*, for his pattern of leadership. Predictability should be his pattern of leadership – not a constant change of priority, emphasis, and direction.

Like all good leaders, the Apostle Paul sometimes had to change his schedule. Things outside of his control altered his plans. When this happened, he did all he could to explain the change. He knew that without a clear explanation, his followers would become confused...disoriented ...frustrated...disappointed...disillusioned with his leadership. This perceived instability on the part of Paul would also give ammunition to his enemies to undermine the credibility and integrity of his Apostolic leadership. More than that, Paul also knew that some young Christians would project upon God the instability and unfaithfulness they thought they saw in him. When he had to change his plans to visit the Christians at Corinth, he took pains to write and explain the change to them:

"I planned to visit you on my way to Macedonia and to come back to you from Macedonia, and then to have you send me on my way to Judea. When I planned this, did I do it lightly? Or *do I make my plans in a worldly manner* so that in the same breath I say, 'Yes, yes' and 'No, no?' But as surely as *God is faithful*, our message to you is not 'Yes' and 'No.' For the Son of God, Jesus Christ, Who was preached among you by me and Silas and Timothy, was not 'Yes' and 'No,' but in Him it has always been 'Yes.' For

**no matter how many promises God has made, they are
'Yes' in Christ. And so through Him the 'Amen' is spoken
by us to the glory of God"** (II Cor. 1:16-20).

Leaders must *say what they mean,* and *mean what they say.* Too many Christian leaders and followers are like many politicians – *they say one thing and do another.* They give their word on an issue, knowing that they will not follow-through on what they have said. They say "*Yes*" when they really mean "*No,*" and vice-versa. They make promises and commitments that they have no intention of fulfilling. When the *performance* does not match the *promise* – integrity is lost. That's why I have always been challenged by the definition of integrity that says: *"Say what you really think, and do what you say you are going to do."* That's the kind of leadership integrity that produces *predictability* and *credibility* – and results in *confidence* and *security* in the life of the follower.

Principle:
*"The law of predictability says: Speak what you
really believe. Say what you are going to do —
and do what you say."*

FURTHER QUOTATIONS ON PREDICTABLE LEADERSHIP

1. CONSISTENCY:

- *The law of the harvest governs; we will always reap what we sow – no more, no less...*[6]

- *Do not fear...for fear is the enemy within our own walls, more devastating than any siege weapons outside. Fear causes us to abandon our strongest weapons, to deviate from our plans and principles...*[7]

2. DISCIPLINE:

- *There is responsibility in privilege. Leaders need to hold themselves to a stricter discipline than is expected of others. Those who are first in place must be first in merit...*[8]

- Integrity *is more a matter of the will than of feelings. Certainly feelings are important, for without feelings we become mechanical. We are not able to connect with others or to feel empathy or compassion. Feelings energize us. They are great implementers but poor leaders.* Our will must control our feelings...[9]

3. PREPARATION:

- *PREPARATION AND MOTIVATION...inspired and properly prepared...*[10]

- *David's triumph resulted from preparation and practice. No one had watched, much less applauded, on those lonely nights when he fended off mountain lions and drove away the wolves...*[11]

4. HABITS:

- *"We are what we repeatedly do. Excellence, then, is not an act, but a habit."* - Aristotle...[12]

- *Knowing that we are responsible – "response-able" – is fundamental to effectiveness and to every other habit of effectiveness...*[13]

- *"The successful person has the habit of doing the things failures don't like to do," he (E. M. Gray) observed. "They don't like doing them either necessarily. But their disliking is subordinated to the strength of their purpose."*[14]

- ***Mental Habits That Support Lifelong Learning***

  Risk taking: *Willingness to push oneself out of comfort zones*

  Humble self-reflection: *Honest assessment of successes and failures, especially the latter*

  Solicitation of opinions: *Aggressive collection of information and ideas from others*

  Careful listening: *Propensity to listen to others*

  Openness to new ideas: *Willingness to view life with an open mind* [15]

- *The young man of leadership caliber will work while others waste time, study while others snooze, pray while others daydream.* Slothful habits are overcome, whether in thought, deed, or dress. *The emerging leader eats right, stands tall, and prepares himself to wage a good warfare.*[16]

- *Leaders who betray their basic values, who brush aside the principles they publicly espouse, pay a heavy cost with the passage of time. With every compromise of principle, the principle itself has less power over us. Before long a pattern emerges, ultimately solidifying into a habit.* Further down the line, the habit becomes ingrained and a new aspect has alloyed itself into the character. *Our lives are this way. We are constantly engaged in the work of making and remaking ourselves – like it or not – by means of the choices we make day to day...*[17]

Chapter 5

LEADERS ARE POSITIVE

"Rejoice in the Lord always. I will say it again: Rejoice!
Whatever is true, whatever is noble, whatever is right,
whatever is pure, whatever is lovely, whatever is admirable
– if anything is excellent or praiseworthy – think about such things"
(Phil. 4:4-8).

In this attribute of leadership we are talking about *attitude*. This represents the *positive mind-set* of the leader. Usually the single biggest difference between the people who are the leaders and the ones who are the followers is *attitude*. Life after life and leader after leader have clearly proven that *attitude* is far more crucial to success in life than *aptitude!* Simply put, it is *attitude* more than *aptitude* that determines *altitude!* You can have all of the *aptitude*, or *ability* in the world, but if you have a *negative, defeatist, critical, faultfinding attitude*, you will not succeed in life. Your leadership *altitude* will flop rather than fly - if you have a bad attitude. Good leaders are never *negative* people. They almost always have a *positive personality* – which is the *"winning attitude!"*

Principle: *"Attitude more than aptitude
determines altitude."*

Because they are *people of purpose*, good leaders are basically *positive* people who win the allegiance of others. Only a *positive purpose* is worthy of giving your life for – which is what makes the Christian faith and life so appealing. It is "Good News" because its message is centered in the cross of Jesus Christ – which is the biggest positive or "plus sign" in history! Only the cross of Jesus Christ *crosses out* all of the other negative selfish and self-centered motivations for living and leading. A Biblical leader finds his *positive purpose* in the *Christ-centered* and *cross-centered* life. As we saw in the preceding chapter, Paul expressed this kind of *exchanged life* in these words:

> **"I have been crucified with Christ and I no longer live, but Christ lives in me. The life I live in the body, I live by faith in the Son of God, Who loved me and gave Himself for me"** (Gal. 2:20).

The more a leader has been liberated from the *"self-life"* through the *"crucified life,"* the more he will be qualified to lead others – and the more others will be drawn to follow him.

It is important to remember that people are not generally drawn to, or motivated by, a *negative person* or a *negative purpose* – unless they are spiritually and socially sick individuals! However, history has demonstrated that there can be a *vision vacuum* that allows a sick person with a negative vision to rise to power. Both Holy Writ and secular history record the stories of evil leaders who led people toward the fulfillment of negative goals: Pharaoh, Jeroboam, Ahab, Pilate, Nero, Hitler, Mao Tse Tung, Idi Amin, Pol Pot – only to mention a few of the tyrants of history. The list of satanically inspired demigods and egotistical maniacs who became leaders is almost endless! The historic record is dripping with the blood of millions who were destroyed by the sick visions of sick leaders! But before they could lead people to the accomplishment of their negative goals, they had to first convince and brainwash the people into believing that those negative goals were indeed positive – and therefore good for them and their country. In the absence of a positive benevolent vision, people can be deceived and seduced by a malevolent one! That's why godly leadership is so desperately needed in our world today!

People are looking for someone positive to follow because they already feel so much negativity in their own hearts and minds. Most people are also immersed in an environment that is negative, repressive and hostile – whether in their marriage, family, neighborhood, or jobs. Many desperately long for a positive leader who will lead them out of their hopelessness, and give them a vision that is worth living for – and if necessary, dying for.

A good leader certainly does not ignore the realistic negative facts and factors in life. Even though a wise leader does not ignore negative factors, he never allows them to shatter his vision and destroy his purpose. Every wise leader clearly recognizes that there are many *problems in life.* However, while others become crippled and inept before a particular life problem – or run away from it in fear – a good leader squarely faces the problem and works out a viable solution. *Good leadership* is based upon *good problem solving.* (We will look at this more under the chapter *"Leaders are problem-solvers".*) Oftentimes it is the timely solving of a problem that separates and marks out the leader from the rest of the people.

While others become crippled by the problem, the *leader becomes challenged, motivated, and energized by the possibility!* Leaders tend to focus more on the *opportunity* than they do on the *opposition.* It is not that they are blind to the problems that may exist – or ignorant of the opposition they may face. Mature Biblical leaders do not fall into the folly of either the *"Power of Positive Thinking,"* or *"Possibility Thinking"* that is largely humanistically based. Their positive thinking is based upon the doctrine of *Providence* – which means *"the benevolent guidance of God."*

Christian leaders choose to believe that God is a sovereign God Who has all power to accomplish His purposes; but that He is also a benevolent God whose purposes for mankind are good and gracious. Their focus is more on the promises that come from God than upon the problems that confront man. They strongly believe the Biblical promise: **"Everything is possible for him who believes"** (Mk. 9:23).

Principle:
"While others are crippled by the problem,
leaders are energized by the possibilities."

In the natural world, leaders clearly understand that they are inadequate for most of the tasks of Christian leadership that they face. They also know that if they only *attempt the possible,* they will get the credit for whatever is accomplished – and God will be robbed of the glory! But when God accomplishes the *impossible* through them, there is no way they can take credit! God receives the glory that He alone deserves! Christian leaders have learned to increasingly focus on the *sovereignty of God…the Lordship of Christ…the power of the Spirit…*and the *authority of Scripture.* That's where their confidence lies – not in themselves, but in Him. When confronted with a problem, their hearts reverberate with the words of Christ: **"With man this is *impossible*, but *with God all things are possible*"** (Mtt. 19:26).

Most worthwhile things of eternal value are *impossible* for us because we are *impotent*, or *powerless*. That's why Jesus said: **"Apart from Me you can do nothing"** (Jn. 15:5). But while we are *impotent*, God is *potent*. That's why we speak of God as *omnipotent*, or *all-powerful*. Paul learned and affirmed that truth when he wrote: **"…it is God who works in you to *will* and to *act* according to His good purpose…I can do everything through Him Who gives me strength"** (Phil. 2:13; 3:13).

This is where the *"Faith Factor"* comes into play. It is the single BIGGEST plus factor in the life of a Biblical leader! He has learned this important Biblical principle: *"God honors faith because faith honors God."* One of the most crucial verses for his life and leadership is Hebrews 11:6, which says:

> ***"Without faith it is impossible to please God*, because anyone who comes to Him must believe that He exists and that He rewards those who earnestly seek Him."**

When God is the sole object of our faith, the *impossible becomes possible!* Not because of us – but because of Him. *God puts no limitations on faith – because faith puts no limitations on Him.* The opposite is also true: *"Faithlessness limits God."* It is our *little faith* – or *lack of faith* – that is the limiting factor in the equation. One day Jesus was confronted with two blind men who desired sight. Humanly speaking, this was an absolutely *impossible situation!* Jesus asked them what He often asks Christians and leaders who face impossible situations: **"Do you believe that I am able to do this?"** They affirmed their faith in Him and said: "Yes, Lord." Then Jesus touched them and said: ***"According to your faith* will it be done to you"** (Mtt. 9:27-29). Therefore, it is "…according to our *faith"* that God works in our behalf. We can either have "mountain moving faith" or "molehill moving faith!" It's up to us! As Richard Phillips wrote: *"Faith inspires what riches and rewards could never motivate."*[1] If all we want to ever see God do in and through our lives is what is *possible*, we will never have the joy of watching Him do the *impossible!* Faith never leaves us where we are. It always takes us to a new level of achievement because it is focused on God. That's why Biblical leaders want God to give them a vision that is so BIG that only He can accomplish it!

Principle:
"God honors faith because faith honors God."

Authentic Biblical faith focuses exclusively on God and makes Him...His Word...and His Spirit the center of everything. Faith allows God to fully be Who He is and accomplish all that He wants to do. As a result, God alone receives the glory that He fully deserves. Be well assured, *God's perfect will – will be done!"* It will happen *with us –* or *without us!* Biblical leaders are just selfish enough to want to experience the joy and thrill of being a small part of what God is doing in His universe! That can only happen *by faith!* Faith is the greatest *positive* factor in the life of any leader. That's why the spiritual leader wants to *live by faith...love by faith...lead by faith.* He also wants to take every opportunity to build faith in the life of his followers. As Oswald Sanders wrote: *"Faith builds faith. Pessimism dismantles faith. The spiritual leader's primary task is to build the faith of others."* [2]

"The spiritual leader's primary task is to build the faith of others." (Oswald Sanders)

While not ignoring the *problems,* the Biblical leader sees the *possibility* and appropriates *God's power* to accomplish *God's purpose.* He helps others reach the *potential* for which they were created.

Principle:
"Leaders face the problems, but focus on possibilities and appropriate God's power so that others may reach their potential."

Leaders are *"providential possibility thinkers"* who focus on the inherent *possibility* while others focus on the apparent *problem!* They have the *ability* to see the *possibility in the problem* that others cannot see...will not see...or are unwilling to pay the price that it will cost to transform the problem into a possibility. It is the difference between what a buzzard and a hummingbird see as they fly over a field. One sees the dead carcass – while the other sees the flowers! The buzzard smells rotting flesh – while the hummingbird smells the nectar! It all depends upon the perspective.

Good leaders have learned to look for life – rather than dwell on death. They focus on *possibilities* rather than *problems...opportunities* rather than *opposition...victories* rather than *defeats*. We see this spirit of "realistic optimism" in Paul when he described his ministry at Ephesus:

> **"I shall remain in Ephesus until Pentecost, for a *wide door for effective service has opened to me*, and there are many who *oppose* me"** (I Cor. 16:8-9).

In this situation at Ephesus, Paul could have either focused on the "... **wide door for effective service...opened to me**"; or he could have focused on the reality that "...**there are many who oppose me.**" He was certainly not ignorant or naïve about the very real *opposition* that awaited him on the other side of that "...**wide open door for effective service.**" He already "...**bore on his body the marks of Jesus**" (Gal. 6:17) as a result of often walking through such open doors of opportunity into the face of violent opposition! He was willing to pay the *price of pain* in order to *seize the opportunity!* Paul's life and leadership is a challenging example of a person who chose to focus on the *opportunity* rather than upon the *opposition*. As a result of that timely leadership decision, a vibrant church was born at Ephesus – perhaps one of the greatest churches he ever birthed! Without it, we would not have the *Book of Ephesians* – oftentimes called the *"Queen of Epistles,"* which gives us the highest New Testament teaching on the church! It has always been true: *"The greater the opportunity, the greater the opposition* – but also the *greater the outcome."*

Principle: *"The greater the opportunity, the greater the opposition – but the greater the outcome."*

As John Piper has rightly said: *"Spiritual leaders are optimistic not because man is good but because God is in control."*[3] Earlier I referred to this mindset as *"Providential thinking"* because it is *God-centered thinking* rather than *man-centered thinking.* Thinking that is based on a wrong view of man will ultimately lead to disillusionment, depression, despair, and defeat. Focusing on God will lead to a *supernatural optimism* – even if one is not naturally optimistic! Spiritual leaders constantly remind themselves of Romans 8:28: **"For God works all things together for good for those who love Him and are called according to His purpose."**

> *"Spiritual leaders are optimistic not because man is good but because God is in control."* (John Piper)

Every leader must keep positively focused on his vision through the dual prisms of Romans 8:28 – and the sovereignty of God. Without that perspective, his life and leadership become *naturally negative.* As a result of that wrong mind-set, everything becomes distorted by negativity – and all of life then goes out of focus! By contrast, a proper heavenly vision becomes *the positive purpose* and *passion* of a leader's life that helps him reach his *potential* – while leading others to that same goal.

Leaders are basically *positive people.* They have come to understand and live by the *"paradigm of plenty"* rather than by the *"paradigm of paucity."* As author Stephen Covey says, the *paradigm of plenty* believes that there is *"...plenty out there for everybody"*[4] – rather than barely enough to go around. In contrast to the *paradigm of plenty*, he explains the opposite negative mentality this way:

> *Most people are deeply scripted in what I call the* scarcity mentality. *They see life as having only so much, as though there was only one pie out there. And if someone were to get a big piece of the pie, it would mean less for everybody else. The* scarcity mentality *is the* zero-sum paradigm of life.[5]

Covey describes how this *scarcity mentality* tends to work itself out in the minds and hearts of leaders:

> *Often, people with a* scarcity mentality *harbor secret hopes that others might suffer misfortune – not terrible misfortune, but acceptable misfortune that would keep them "in their place." They're always comparing, always competing. They give their energies to possessing things or other people in order to increase their sense of worth...It's difficult for people with a* scarcity mentality *to be members of a complementary team.*[6]

When I first began to minister in Haiti over 30 years ago, I learned about this *scarcity mentality* through the thinking and lives of the people there. Haiti is one of the poorest countries in the world – and definitely the poorest country in the Western Hemisphere. In that poverty-stricken Caribbean island, there is a widely believed Haitian Proverb that says: *"God is a good Provider – but a poor Divider!"* I believe that this is one of the great lies of the devil that has trapped millions in Haiti in both spiritual and physical poverty for generations! While I do not want to be either simplistic or reductionistic, it is safe to say that much of the physical poverty in Haiti is the direct result of this negative unbiblical thinking. This mind-set wrongly portrays God as a *God of favoritism with limited resources.* When a population – rulers and people alike – believe in the *scarcity mentality,* they will seek to reap and rape all they can from their surroundings when and while they can. There will be little or no thought about how their taking will affect the lives and futures of others around them. They will just fight and scrap to get as big a piece of the dwindling pie as they can – for as long as they can! They will live for the moment with little thought or forethought about tomorrow. This *paucity mentality* is the paradigm that many poor people around the world live – or rather *exist* by. It is only the light of the Gospel that liberates people from the darkness of this negative worldview.

Principle: *"The belief that 'God is a good Provider but a poor Divider' is a satanic lie that impoverishes our living and leading."*

In contrast to this negative *"pauper mentality,"* Stephen Covey describes the opposite mentality as follows:

> *The* abundance mentality, *on the other hand, flows out of a deep inner sense of personal worth and security. It is the paradigm that there is* plenty out there and enough to spare for everybody. *It results in the sharing of prestige, of recognition, of profits, of decision-making. It opens possibilities, options, alternatives, and creativity.*[7]

Effective leaders are people who live by the *positive paradigm of plenty!* They do not live by the *paucity mentality* that always fears that there is not enough to go around. They believe that there is "enough supply to meet the need." There are enough resources to go around. They do not have the *"pauper mentality"* – but rather the *"plenty mentality."* They have learned this positive mind-set by looking at both the *natural* and *supernatural* realms. In the realm of nature, it is easy to see this *principle of plenty.* God designed His creation in such a way that there is *abundance from every seed planted.* Generally, neither seeds nor fruit reproduce on a "one-to-one ratio" but on a "one-to-many ratio." From a single grain of corn, multiple ears are produced – with each ear having hundreds of grains of corn. From one apple there are many seeds. The abundance mentality is not as concerned with *"how many seeds there are in an apple"* – but rather *"how many apple trees there are in an apple!"* One perspective sees an apple with a few individual seeds. The other perspective sees an *orchard full of apples!*

This same principle is true in the spiritual realm. The Bible reminds us that the true and living God is not a *God of scarcity* – but rather a *God of plenty.* He is not a *God of limited resources* but of *unlimited resources.* Because God knows no lack, He does not have to carefully "dole out" His heavenly supply so as not to run out! No! He is not a God Who has to "cut His pie of resources" in ever thinner and thinner slices so as to make it go around. He is *abounding in love, mercy and grace!* The Apostle Paul expressed God's abundance this way:

> **"In Him we have redemption through His blood, the forgiveness of sins, in accordance with the *riches of God's grace* that He *lavished on us...* "** (Eph. 1:7-8).

With similar words, the Apostle John reminds the Christian of God's abounding love toward His children:

> **"See how great a love the Father has *lavished on us,* that we should be called children of God"** (I Jn. 3:1).

In reality, the true and living God is the only One **"...Who is able to do *immeasurably more than all we ask or imagine,* according to His power that is at work within us..."** (Eph. 3:20).

God has revealed and demonstrated the *principle of abundance* in both W*ho He is* and in *what He does.* We can clearly see this principle expressed in both the *natural* and *supernatural realms.* Spiritual leaders have learned to lay hold of and appropriate that principle through *faith!* Effective Christian leaders live and lead by this *positive paradigm.* In doing so, they have made one of the major shifts of axis in life from the *paradigm of paucity* to the *paradigm of plenty.* Their thinking has been eternally shifted from the *scarcity mentality* to the *abundance mentality.* They can rejoice in God's abundant blessing upon others without fear that someone else's gain is their loss.

Effective Christian leaders are *people with an attitude* – but it is a *positive attitude!* Because they realize how decisive the attitude is, they constantly monitor their own attitude in order to keep it positive and upbeat. They are ever alert to keep pessimism and negativity from getting a foothold in their thinking. Through the example of their life and leadership, they do all they can to make positive "attitude adjustments" in the thinking of their followers. They know that every single person they will ever attempt to lead "...*has an attitude.*" The only question is: "*What kind of attitude do they have?*" Do they have a *problem attitude* or a *positive attitude?* Do they have a *pessimistic attitude* or a *possibility attitude?*

The greatest leadership challenge is leading an attitude change in the thinking of people. Understanding this important principle of leadership, Fred Smith succinctly wrote: "*Speak to change attitudes.*"[8] When you *change attitudes,* you totally *change behavior.* Since all *action springs from attitude,* you can only *change the action by changing the attitude.*

Principle: "*The greatest challenge of leadership is leading a change in attitude. Only when you change attitude do you change actions.*"

FURTHER QUOTATIONS ON
POSITIVE LEADERS

1. ATTITUDE:

- *Samuel Johnson observed: "The fountain of content must spring up in the mind, and he who hath so little knowledge of human nature as to seek happiness by changing anything but his own disposition, will waste his life in fruitless efforts and multiply the grief he proposes to remove."[9]*

- *"I learned very early in life never to take counsel of my fears." (General George Patton)[10]*

- *Negative thinkers and pessimists never inspire or motivate anyone except to negativism and pessimism.[11]*

- *In 1940, Winston Churchill did by himself turn the tide of history. His shoulders held the sky suspended. He saved his country and the course of human freedom. In the War Room from which he directed the war, he kept a piece of cardboard on which were printed these words: "Please understand there is no pessimism in the house and we are not interested in the possibilities of defeat; they do not exist."[12]*

- *Maybe more important than ability is attitude. Herb Kellehher, president of Southwest Airlines, says, "We look for attitude... we'll train you on whatever it is you have to do, but one thing Southwest cannot change in people is inherent attitudes.[13]*

- *The pessimist sees the difficulty in every opportunity and the optimist sees the opportunity in every difficulty.[14]*

- *Golfing legend Jack Burke, Jr., in advising one of his star pupils...to always keep a positive attitude, said, "Keep your head up. Everything in the world with its head down gets eaten. Chickens, hogs, cows. Every time you see a leopard, his head is up, isn't it? You don't see any leopards getting eaten, do you? No gloomy guy, dragging around, looking at his shoe tops, ever won anything worth winning."[15]*

- *...the Law of Magnetism really is true: who you are is who you attract...*[16]

- *No one can live on a level inconsistent with the way he sees himself. You may have observed that in people. If someone sees himself as a loser, he finds a way to lose. Anytime his success surpasses his security, the result is self-destruction. That's not only true for followers, but it's also true for leaders...*[17]

- *Insecure leaders are dangerous – to themselves, their followers, and the organizations they lead – because a leadership position amplifies personal flaws...*[18]

- *Most people like to win, to be on a winning team, or to be a part of a winning effort. The desire to win inspires people, and a leader who projects a winning attitude or winning ways attracts people who want to win. No one that I know wakes up in the morning hoping their day will be a failure...*[19]

- *A prominent psychiatrist once told me that America's second greatest sin, after refusing to delay gratification, is transference, at the heart of so much of the victim syndrome. Those who feel they are victims generally expect more than they are due...*[20]

- *As Viktor Frankl discovered in the death camps of Nazi Germany:*

  "We who lived in concentration camps can remember the men who walked through the huts comforting others, giving away their last piece of bread. They may have been few in number, but they offer sufficient proof that everything can be taken from a man but one thing: the last of the human freedoms – to choose one's attitude in any given set of circumstances, to choose one's own way.

  "And there were always choices to make. Every day, every hour, offered the opportunity to make a decision, a decision which determined whether you would or would not submit to those powers which threatened to rob you of your very self, your inner freedom; which determined whether or not you would become the plaything of circumstance..."[21]

- *Discouragement is literally dis-courage-ment − a lack of courage…It comes when we have no vision, when we live with imbalance, when we fail to achieve our goals. It comes when we get lost in the urgent, limited perspective of the day, when we fail to act with integrity in the moment of choice. It comes when our thinking is competitive and scarce, when win-lose interactions fill our lives and our environment with backbiting, politicking, and comparative thinking.*

  Discouragement is being lost in the woods without a compass or an accurate map. It's discovering that many of the maps people hand us lead us farther away from where we really want to go.

  Courage, on the other hand, comes as a result of knowing there are principles, of fulfilling our needs and capacities in a balanced way, of having clear vision, balance between roles, the ability to set and achieve meaningful goals, the perspective to transcend the urgency of the moment, the character and competence to act with integrity in the moment of choice, the abundance mentality to function effectively and synergistically in the interdependent reality. Courage comes from the heart, and being in touch with the heart creates hope. [22]

- ### *Tale of Two Attitudes*

  The Christian leader or businessperson must keep in mind that the power of negative thinking is just as great as the power of positive thinking. Negative thinking is one of Satan's most effective tools. If he can cause you to form negative thoughts and attitudes, he knows he will get negative results from your actions… [23]

- *Pessimism and leadership are at opposite ends of life's attitudes. Hope and optimism are essential qualities for the servant of God who battles with the powers of darkness over the souls of men and women. God's ideal servant is optimistic until every part of God's work is done…Are you reasonably optimistic? Pessimism and leadership do not mix…* [24]

- *Cynicism has no integrity. Cynicism often properly evaluates* the present, but it has no hope for the future. As Christians we are not without hope for the future. Christians believe in the possibility of the future. Our responsibility is to make a difference, not to drop out...[25]

- Family life expert Denis Waitley... "The winner's edge is not in a gifted birth, a high IQ, or in talent. The winner's edge is all in the attitude, not aptitude. Attitude is the criterion for success."[26]

- "The greatest discovery of my generation is that human beings can alter their lives by altering their attitude of mind." – William James, Psychologist... A successful man is one who can lay a firm foundation with the bricks others have thrown at him." – David Brinkley, Television Journalist.[27]

- The question is not "Is the speech a good one?" but "Is it an effective one?" Speak to change attitudes and behavior...[28]

- Attitudes and values are best learned by modeling within the mentoring relationship. You can learn mathematics, literature, science, and a wide variety of things from a textbook, from a computer, or from a lecturer. But it is difficult to learn in a classroom setting how to have a new attitude toward a person or a situation. Attitudes are best learned by watching someone you admire and respect model those attitudes...[29]

- Gratitude is one of the most fragile emotions. The Scripture praises the sacrifice of thanksgiving. Until we are grateful for what we have, how can we deserve to have more?[30]

- Envy is the magnifying glass through which we look at the faults of others.[31]

- **The Value of a Good Attitude**

    Definition: "An attitude is an inward feeling expressed by an outward behavior."

Synopsis of an Attitude

1. *It is the "advance man" of our true selves.*
2. *Its roots are inward, but its fruit is outward.*
3. *It is our best friend...our worst enemy.*
4. *It is more honest and more consistent than our words.*
5. *It is an outward look based on past experience.*
6. *It is the thing that draws people to us, or repels them.*
7. *IT IS NEVER CONTENT UNTIL IT IS EXPRESSED.*
8. *It is the librarian of our past.*
9. *It is the speaker of our present.*
10. *It is the prophet of our future.*

FIVE ATTITUDE AXIOMS

1. *Our attitude determines our approach to life.*
2. *Our attitude determines our relationship with people.*
3. *Our attitude is often the only difference between success and failure.*
4. *Our attitude at the beginning of a task will affect its outcome more than anything else.*
5. *Our attitude can give us an uncommonly positive perspective.*

ATTITUDE: Chuck Swindoll

"The longer I live the more I realize the impact of attitude on life. Attitude, to me, is more important than facts. It is more important than the past, than education, than money, than circumstances, than failures, than success, than what other people think, say, or do. It is more important than appearance, giftedness or skill. It will make or break a company, a church, a home. The remarkable thing is we have a choice every day regarding the attitude we will embrace for that day. We cannot change our past...we cannot change the fact that people will act in a certain way. We cannot change the inevitable. The ONLY THING we can do is play on the one string we have, and that is our attitude. I am convinced that life is 10% what happens to me and 90% how I react to it." [32]

2. FAITH:

- *...our understanding of God is at the center of our beliefs about all other things...*[33]

- *Providence is God's intervention for the good of those who trust Him...*[34]

- *The Christian leader's ability to think positively is greatly influenced by his concept of God. In fact, our goals are in direct proportion to the size of our God. We never trust God for more than we think He will do. One of the great tragedies is that God stands ready to do far more than we can think, pray, or dream. This is evident when we read, 'Now glory be to God who by His mighty power at work within us is able to do far more than we would ever dare to ask or even dream of – infinitely beyond our highest prayers, desires, thoughts, or hopes' (Eph. 3:20, LB).*[35]

- *Hebrews 11 tells us that it was faith that kept Noah in sync with God. When the skies were still clear, Noah got on board, didn't he?...Faith leads to action...*[36]

3. SCARCITY & ABUNDANCE:

- *Satan always tries to convince the Christian leader or manager there are not enough resources to accomplish the job. People involved in resource planning should keep in mind that if the plans are in accordance with God's will for the individual and/ or organization, He will provide the resources to accomplish the activities.*[37]

- *Most people are deeply scripted in what I call the Scarcity Mentality. They see life as having only so much, as though there were only one pie out there. And if someone were to get a big piece of the pie, it would mean less for everybody else. The Scarcity Mentality is the zero-sum paradigm of life... Often, people with a Scarcity Mentality harbor secret hopes that others might suffer misfortune – not terrible misfortune, but acceptable misfortune that would keep them 'in their place.' They're always comparing, always competing. They give their energies to possessing things or other people in order to increase their sense of worth...It's difficult for people with a Scarcity Mentality to be members of a complementary team...The Abundance Mentality, on the other hand, flows out of a deep inner sense of personal worth and security. It is the paradigm that there is plenty out there and enough to spare for everybody. It results in sharing of prestige, of recognition, of profits, of decision-making. It opens possibilities, options, alternatives, and creativity...*[38]

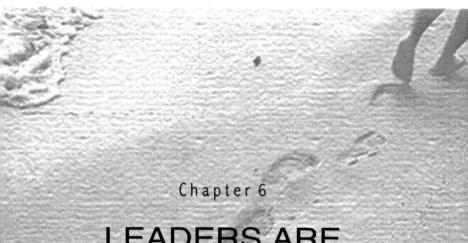

Chapter 6

LEADERS ARE PASSIONATE

"Never be lacking in zeal, but keep your
spiritual fervor in serving the Lord"
(Rom. 15:11).

Good leaders are inevitably passionate people. Effective leaders are always characterized by a high level of *zeal...enthusiasm...zest...vitality.* This *priority of passion* is one of the most universally defining characteristics of leadership. A leader's passion is one of the things that quickly distinguish him from other less passionate people. The fact that he exudes *passion in his personality* is one of the attractive attributes that draw people around him.

Unfortunately, too many people go through life rather *dispassionately* – they are just not very excited about *anything!* As a result of this lack of passion, many people feel their lives are about as exciting as a bowl of warm Jell-O! Because they have a low level of passion and little purpose, their lives have settled down to the lowest common denominator of bland...tasteless...colorless...purpose-less...aimless... offense-less *middle-class mediocrity!* There is just not much excitement there! They are not really *living* – they are just going through the motions of life. Rather than "making time," they are just "marking time" – much less *"...redeeming the time"*(Eph. 5:16).

Secretly many of those very same people have a deep inner longing for something or someone to come along and arouse their smoldering passions! Many are like Rip van Winkle – slumbering their way through life in their own little dormant Sleepy Hollow. Others are like "Sleeping Beauty," awaiting the *kiss of passion* and *purpose* to arouse them from their cosmic coma – and give them a new lease on life. In the business realm, such people are often referred to as "sleepers." Many of them will live and die that way unless they are awakened by a good leader with a great purpose and great passion!

Principle:
"Fear not that your life will come to an end,
but that it will never have a beginning!" [1]
(John Henry Newman, British Theologian)

Effective leaders are always *marked by passion.* There is absolutely *no substitute for passion in leadership.* Nothing else can take the place of passion in the life of a leader – neither age…nor education…nor degrees… nor experience…nor money…nor position…nor power. *There is nothing that will compensate for a lack of passion in leadership.* Passion produces what nothing else can in the life of a leader – *achievement.*

Principle:
"A leader with great passion and few skills always out performs a leader with great skills and no passion." [2]
(John Maxwell)

Noted leadership guru, John Maxwell, is *passionate about passion!* He expresses it this way: *"Passion is the first step to achievement."* [3] Concerning the priority of passion in the life of a leader, Maxwell quotes noted author Napoleon Hill, as saying: *"The starting point of all achievement is desire."* If you are going to be an effective leader, you've got to *know what you want.* You must have a *"desire that drives you!"* In spiritual terms, you must have a white hot "holy passion" that inflames you! Passion is absolutely necessary for leadership – whether one is leading in the home…in the church…in politics…or in the military. The famous military Field Marshal, Ferdinand Foch, observed: *"The most powerful weapon on earth is the human soul on fire."* [4] John Wesley told his young preachers: *"If you will get on fire for God – people will come from miles around to watch you burn!"* There is a lot of truth in that. People are not interested in following a leader with the enthusiasm of a melting icicle! John Maxwell correctly summarizes it this way: *"Your desire determines your destiny."*[5] Small desires *produce small destinies* – while *great desires produce great destinies!*

"The most powerful weapon on
earth is the human soul on fire."
(Field Marshal Ferdinand Foch)

Understanding the importance of passion in life, consultant Bobb Biehl poses this question to leaders who seek his council: *"What is your passion today?"*[6] Those five little words crystallize the crux of leadership. That's *the* crucial question for every would-be leader. Early in the leadership process, a leader must get in touch with his or her passions. Simply put: "if his passions are *low*, his leadership will be *slow!* If her passions are *high*, her leadership will *fly!"* It is also true that a leader will *lose* if his passion is *diffused* – because his followers will be *confused! Diffused leaders* produce *confused followers*. There is a direct relationship between a *diffusion of the passion of the leader*, and the *confusion of the passion of the follower*. There is a basic principle that says: *"An ambiguous heart sends out an ambivalent flow."* If the leader is ambiguous about his vision…his purpose…his dream…his desire, it will be reflected through ambivalent signals going out from his life. *The more focused the passion of the leader – the more focused the passion of the follower*. A focused passion in the life of a leader is like the focused heat of a welder's torch – it can cut through almost any obstacle or opposition!

Principle:
"If your passions are low, your leadership will be slow.
If your passions are high, Your leadership will fly!"

Early in the life of every leader, he must ask himself: *"What am I really passionate about?"* Until the answer to that question is crystal clear in the leader's mind, it cannot become compellingly clear in the mind of the follower. We can express this leadership question in more extreme terms this way: *"What am I willing to die for?"* In other words, if it came right down to it, *What in life would I as a leader not stop doing – regardless of the cost? What cause or purpose for me is greater than all possible negative consequences?* In his book, *The Heart of an Executive*, Richard Phillips asks:

> *Is there anything you are willing to go down in flames for? When it comes right down to it, is there anything to which you are more committed than self-preservation?*[7]

Phillips concludes:

> *To be a somebody you must be willing to display personal loyalty at great cost, to stand up in the face of danger, in defense of what the past has achieved, to step off the sidelines and offer yourself to something greater than yourself...Leadership feeds on the vision of something great.*[8]

There is a flip side to the issue of giving yourself to a cause that is greater than you. It is a question of *ownership*. In other words, *does the cause own me* or *do I own the cause?* Many leaders started out compelled by a great cause. Gradually, they started acting like the cause was their own private property. It increasingly belonged exclusively to them. They began to speak about the "common cause" with personal possessive pronouns. In the Christian realm, leaders sometimes speak about the "cause of Christ" with phrases like: "my vision"..."my spiritual gifts"..."my church"..."my people"..."my"..."my"..."my!"

When this happens, Richard Phillips warns: *"It is only a small step from the commitment of yourself to a cause, to the commitment of the cause to yourself."*[9] When any leader treats the vision or cause with an exclusive spirit, others soon lose interest. There's no longer any real place for them in the vision. The cause has ceased to be inclusive. As the leader's ego has increased, the followers have been decreased. They have been shrunk down to being the helpless and hapless slaves of the leader's ego. They have become little more than nameless and faceless pawns that are *used...abused...*and reduced to *refuse* by the leader. They have become "cannon fodder" that are expendable for the leader's cause! At the end of the day, there is nothing in it for them. They gave themselves to the leader's cause – but the cause gave them nothing in return. At that point, the *passionate cause* has been reduced to an exclusive *personal cause*. This *personification of purpose* in one person is very dangerous. Exclusive authority and centrality of leadership is one of the chief characteristics of cultic groups. A *possessive* *leader* soon becomes a *paranoid leader*. As a result, he cuts himself off more and more from people. He distances himself from his followers. His inner circle gets smaller and smaller – until it is finally reduced to a majority of one! At that point, he will no longer share power...share authority... share control...share responsibility...share resources...share profits...share praise...share *anything!* His passion has now become a *personality cult!* Secular and spiritual history is full of tragic examples of such *perverted passion* in the hands of *paranoid leaders*. The story of their lives and leadership are littered with the lives of broken, disillusioned, destroyed followers!

There is a timely warning here in our discussion of passion that must also be heeded. When the cause becomes the sole passion of the leader, others soon give up their ownership in it. They walk away. That's because the followers don't want the leader to achieve *alone*. They want to have a real sense of *partnership* and *ownership* in the vision. Along with the leader, they too want to cross the finish line...make the goal...share the success...experience the victory...celebrate in the winner's circle! Richard Phillips writes this about what I call *exclusive victories* as opposed to *inclusive victories*:

> *Your triumph is not itself inspiring to anyone but you. It is the triumph of the cause, of the faith, of the quest and the calling that electrifies the hearts of followers.*[10]

Even though both secular history and Biblical revelation are full of examples of *perverted passion* – leadership still cannot go far without it. In spite of the inherent dangers in it, *it is still impossible to lead without passion*. However, the greatest passion is *purified passion!* Only when leadership passion is *broken by God...purified by the Holy Spirit...enlightened by Holy Writ*...and *cleansed of ego* is it worthy to follow!

Principle: *"Self-sacrifice is the acid test of our passion"*[11] (Fred Smith)

For decades, Fred Smith has been a respected leadership advisor in the secular world, and leadership mentor in the Christian world. He has written some of the most helpful insights on *passion* that I have ever read. In his great book, *Leading With Integrity*, Smith gives us a very balanced definition of passion. I believe as leaders understand and apply this definition of passion in their lives, there will be balance. Here is his definition:

Passion is concentrated wisdom with high energy in the pursuit of meaning.[12]

The key phrase here is *"concentrated wisdom with high energy."* This is the balance that leadership must have in order to be sustained with dignity and integrity. In this definition, there is *"concentrated wisdom"* – or *purpose;* plus "high energy" – or *passion.* When there is a *purified* and *passionate purpose* in the life of a leader – *it concentrates his energy.* It *focuses his life.* It *galvanizes his resources.* Without that focus, his leadership passion becomes *confused* and *diffused.* He is no longer a focused *spot light* – but rather a diffused *flood light.* Fred Smith amplifies this need of focus this way:

> *The advantages of passion are multiple. It brings purpose, unity, intensity, concentration assuring accomplishment. It gives intentionality to life. Passion gives depth, keeping us from the shallowness of mediocrity.*[13]

I love that little phrase that Smith uses when he says that passion *"…gives intentionality to life!"* Passion means that you live your life *intentionally* rather than *randomly.* Instead of just *drifting* through life, you are *directed* and *driven* through life. Every Christian leader lives with a *divine intention* that motivates and concentrates his life. He has an *intentionality* to his life that produces *inspiration* in the lives of others. That *intentionality* is what sharpens his life and causes him to want to stay on the "cutting edge" of what God is doing in the world. That *passionate intentionality* in his life also gives him the ability to attract others to the cause. It is only that *divine passion* that keeps the leader and follower from settling down in the *"shallowness of mediocrity!"* That's why Fred Smith concludes:

> *Every effective leader is imbued with passion. An accomplishment is often in direct proportion to the amount and intensity of the leader's passion. Passion is contagious for followers.*[14]

Principle:
"*In leadership, focused passion accomplishes much more than scholarly intellect.*" [15]
(Fred Smith)

Dr. Ramesh Richard agrees with the importance of *concentration* and *focus* in the life of the leader. He warns leaders: *"If you have multiple passions, you'll be ripped to pieces internally, resulting in a fragmented, random life."*[16]

Once again, *diffusion* produces *confusion* – both in the life of the leader and in the follower. A *fractured passion* in the leader results in a *fragmentation of passion* in the life of the follower.

Principle:
"*You can never lead something you don't care passionately about.*" [17]
(John Maxwell)

We can clearly see that you cannot separate *passion* from *vision*. For the leader, *it is the vision that is the source of his passion*. And, *the greater the vision, the greater the passion!* Fred Smith wonderfully expresses this relationship between *passion* and *vision* – and shows us how it practically works itself out in the corporate life of an organizations:

> *The clearer the vision, the more focused the passion. If the vision becomes blurred, the passion becomes dissipated and weakened. In an organization where everyone buys into and fully understands the passion and purpose, all effort is unified with high energy. An organization without passion is a car without gasoline, a rocket without fuel. Two organizations may have the same general vision, but the one with the deeper passion will have the greater accomplishment. A pure passion turns the ordinary into the extraordinary.* [18]

Principle:
"*A great leader's courage to fulfill his vision comes from passion, not position.*" [19]
(John Maxwell)

Noted church consultant, Lyle Schaller, echoes the same thing about *passion* and *vision:*

> *If a pastor does not have a passion for the mission, he can forget the rest of leadership. A passion to make a worthwhile difference is indispensable to effectiveness. Passion and vision need to work together. Passion energizes vision, and vision disciplines the passion. The clearer the vision, the greater the passion. The closer*

we get to the goal, the more it demands of us and the more it means to us.[20]

"Passion energizes vision, and vision disciplines the passion."
(Lyle Schaller)

Leaders are energized by their purpose. Simply put, *vision produces vitality!* Influential leaders are always *passionate about their purpose*. It is their passion that ignites other people's passion. Effective leaders are *passionately positive* and *positively passionate!*

Principle:
"Vision produces vitality. Leaders are passionately positive and positively passionate."

King David revealed the source of his passion in life when he exclaimed: **"The joy of the Lord is my *strength"*** (Psalm 118:24). Unquestionably, David was the greatest king in Israel's history – and certainly one of the greatest leaders of all time. He had a passionate ability to bring people together and unite very diverse groups under his leadership. Even though he struggled from time-to-time with disappointment, discouragement, despondency, and depression – *as every leader does* – joy ultimately won out. David did not have joy because his leadership challenges were easy. He faced every conceivable leadership problem and every challenge imaginable! Because his joy was centered in God, *his strength had a divine base.* David's life and leadership remind us that even though circumstances change – God does not. Wise leaders like David have come to understand the difference between *happiness* and *joy.* Since this is such an important life and leadership issue, let's pause to distinguish one from the other.

The English word *"happiness"* comes from the root *"hap"* - from which we get the word *"happen."* The word *"happen"* means: "to occur by chance or without plan." Therefore, the word *"happiness"* means: "favored by circumstances, lucky, fortunate." It in turn comes from the word *"happenstance."* We can see that *happiness is circumstantial.* If the circumstances are positive and the environment is favorable, there is *happiness*. But if the circumstances are negative and the environment is unfavorable, there is *unhappiness*. Since *happiness is based upon happenstance* – it changes like the weather!

Joy, however, is not based upon happenstance or circumstance. *Joy, comes from the Lord!* It is one of the fruit of His Holy Spirit. Because of this fact, the Christian leader has the consistency of an internal weather pattern produced by the "joy of the Lord." The *spiritual leader* has an advantage over the *worldly leader*. The *happiness* of a worldly leader is held hostage by *happenstance* and *circumstance*. His external environment largely controls his happiness and dictates his moods. By contrast, the *joy* of a spiritual leader is centered in an unchanging God. He has a consistent internal environment produced by the *joy* of the indwelling Holy Spirit.

In this telling little verse, King David reminds us of the source of his leadership strength – "the joy of the Lord!" Few things are less appealing to leader and follower alike than *"joyless leadership!"* With that in mind, the writer of Hebrews exhorts church members:

> **"Obey your leaders, and submit to them; for they keep watch over your souls, as those who will given an account. *Let them do this with joy* and not with grief, for this would be unprofitable for you"** (Heb. 13:17; NASV).

When it comes to joy in life and leadership, the writer of Hebrews also reminds us of the example of the Lord Jesus. Neither His life nor His leadership was lived out in a largely receptive atmosphere. Few circumstances surrounding His life were positive. The *happenstances* and *circumstances* of His life were generally very *hostile* and *hard!* Even though His life was *hard*, Jesus did not become *hard*. He was not motivated by *happiness* – but by *joy*. Hebrews reminds us how Jesus responded to negative and hostile circumstances – even when the shadow of a rugged cross loomed before Him. We read that **"...for the *joy* set before Him endured the cross, scorning its shame..."** (Heb. 12:2). Neither *pain* nor *shame* could take away Christ's joy. It was only because He kept focused on the *results of His passion*, that He could **"...endure the cross"** and **"scorn its shame."** That's the fruit of joy! Those are responses that happiness can never produce.

As a result of their *passion*, leaders are almost always both *energetic* and *enthusiastic people* – even in the face of adversity. As we will see in a later chapter, leaders have often been naturally endowed with a lot of physical energy. However, their real energy is more *supernatural* than *natural*. Their energy and vitality come from the "joy of the Lord" and from the power of the indwelling Holy Spirit – not from their own human energies. The Apostle Paul reflected this when he compared his works to others: **"I worked harder than all of them,"** Paul said, **"yet not I, but the grace of God that was with me"** (I Cor. 15:10). In saying this, Paul was not boasting, just stating facts!

Good leaders are not casual, laid-back, easy-going, passive people. By nature they tend to be passionate in almost everything they do! For them, passion is not so much an *experience of the moment* – but a *lifestyle*. Many people have momentary passion, which doesn't last long. Their passion is fickle – it is turned on and off…it goes up and down…it runs hot and cold. By contrast, good leaders have *persistent passion*.

Someone rightly observed that the world today is being led by *tired men!* It could also be said that: *"Much of the Church is being led by tired pastors!"* Too many Christian leaders become tired out…worn out…burned out when they try to lead through the limited resources of the flesh. Every Christian leader must learn to live by the *passion of love* and by the *power of the Holy Spirit!* To sustain his leadership, a leader must have a *passionate love* for his calling – and a *divine power* to sustain it.

Principle:
"No one can be successful unless he loves his work."[21]
(David Sarnoff, CEO of RCA)

Just as their energy is both natural and supernatural, a leader's enthusiasm must be an *enlightened enthusiasm*. Their enthusiasm has to be *enlightened by God's Word* and *illumined by God's Spirit*. That's what the word *"enthusiasm"* teaches us. It comes from the Greek word *en-theos* which is composed of the two words: *en*, or "in," and *theos*, which means "god." It is only "God within" that produces authentic *enthusiasm!* As we would expect, *Godly enthusiasm* always results in a striving for *excellence* for God's glory!

Principle:
*"Enlightened enthusiasm coupled with energy always
results in the pursuit of excellence."*

Every leader must always remember that, if he is not *enthusiastic* about his vision, no one else will be! One of the most successful football coaches of all time was the late Vince Lombardi. He often told his players and fellow coaches: *"If you are not fired BY enthusiasm – you will be fired WITH enthusiasm!"* He knew that there was no excuse for either an unenthusiastic coach or unenthusiastic football player. He clearly understood the psychological dynamic that *"enthusiasm runs downhill!"* Enthusiasm must begin with the coaching staff if it is going to infect the players. Therefore, Lombardi taught and demonstrated the principle: *"Enthusiasm produces enthusiasm!*

Principle:
*"Enthusiasm runs downhill. Therefore, enthusiasm at
the top produces enthusiasm at the bottom."*

Because of the importance of *passion* and *enthusiasm,* a leader must move people's *hearts* before he tries to move their *heads!* Harvard Business School's John Kotter says that in leadership *"...both head and heart are required."* He tells his students:

> *After seventeen or more years of formal education, most of us know something about using our heads, but little about using our hearts.*[22]

Contrary to popular opinion, man is not the rational, cognitive creature that he likes to think that he is. In reality, people are moved and governed far more by their passions and emotions than they are by their minds and reason. Fred Smith wisely points out:

> *Every fact is preceded by a feeling and if we rightly employ our discernment, we can affect the facts by understanding the feelings that precede the facts.*[23]

Honest observation of human nature confirms that we always tend *to "lead with our hearts"* rather than *"lead with our heads."* Effective leaders soon learn this about themselves and about others. As a result, they do not try to base their leadership solely on an intellectual, cerebral, reasoned approach. They seek to lead with a balance of *heart* and *head.* Good leadership seeks to both *inflame the heart* – as well as *inform the head!* John Maxwell summarized this balance through this principle: *"To lead yourself, use your head; to lead others, use your heart!"* [24]

"What people want most from an admired leader is someone who can ignite the 'fire in the belly!'" [25]

(Herman Cain)

As we have already seen, the Bible is not silent on this whole issue of passion in life and leadership. Let me share a couple of good verses that remind us of this *spiritual passion* that must exude from an authentic Biblical leader.

The Apostle Paul reminds us to **"Never be lacking in *zeal* but keep your *spiritual fervor* serving the Lord"** (Romans 12:11). The word here for "spiritual fervor" is the word *zeontes.* It comes from the root word, *zeo,* meaning "to boil." The word is used only twice in the New Testament. In this passage, and again in Acts 18:25, Apollos is described as a leader who **"...spoke with great *fervor...*"** Apollos, like Jeremiah of old, had **"...fire in his bones"** (Jer. 20:9)!

***"For Christ's love compels us,* because we are convinced that One died for all, and therefore all died"** (II Cor. 5:14). The word Paul uses here for "compels" or "constrains" (KJV) is the word *sunecho.* It means: *"to hold together, confine, secure, hold fast."* Paul reminds us that it is nothing short of the *agape* love of Christ that *compels...constrains...confines* us. It is the love of Christ within him that "holds fast" the leader to his vision and purpose. It is *agape* that is the source of his *passion!* It is only because the love of Christ holds the leader fast, that he in turn holds fast to his vision.

Agape love is increasingly the source of the passion in the life of every authentic Biblical leader. Just as God's self-giving love was Incarnate in

Christ and the defining passion of His life, it is also to be the *defining passion* of every authentic Christian leader. People are far more influenced by *how much we love* than they are impressed by *how much we know!* Leaders need to learn that they can far better *influence through their love* than they can *impress through their knowledge.* They emphasize *loving* over *knowing.* People will not remember how much we *knew* – but rather how much we *loved!*

Principle:
"In the final analysis we are what we love."[26]
(Richard Phillips)

A basic principle of leadership is this: *"It is not until love is felt that the message is heard."* It is only when love is *verbalized* and *visualized* by the leader that people are compelled to follow. That kind of *incarnational love* must oftentimes be *vulnerable,* or sensitive and susceptible to others. Also, the very nature of agape love is that it is *vicarious,* or willing to *suffer with* others – as well as suffer *for* others. Agape is both a *sensitive love* and a *suffering love.*

Principle:
"It is not until love is felt that the message is heard. Therefore, agape love must be verbal, visual, vulnerable and vicarious."

In conclusion, it is because of this *loving passion* that Christian leaders are committed to *excellence* rather than *mediocrity.* Leaders tend to have a natural *"passion for excellence."* Leaders also understand that *excellence* always takes *effort.* True excellence is never achieved effortlessly! As a result, leaders are never satisfied with what is "average…ordinary… usual…normal…acceptable." While others may want to *"do just enough to get by"* – leaders want to *"do whatever it takes to fly high!"* As John Maxwell says: *"Highly competent people always go the extra mile. For them, good enough is never good enough."*[27]

Principle: *"No one can do the minimum
and reach his maximum potential."*[28]
(John Maxwell)

Tragically, our Western society has increasingly become satisfied with mediocrity – in almost all areas of life. In his book entitled *Excellence*, John Gardner poignantly writes this:

> *An excellent plumber is infinitely more admirable than an incompetent philosopher. The society which scorns excellence in plumbing because plumbing is a humble activity – and tolerates shoddiness in philosophy because it is an exalted activity – will have neither good plumbing nor good philosophy. Neither its pipes nor its theories will hold water.*[29]

Gardner's rather humorous observation about *excellence in plumbing* and *mediocrity in philosophy* points out the fact that our society has often confused *success* with *excellence*. Success is based upon the attainment of certain cultural goals – whether that is measured in number of cows, acreage owned, or in the amount of blue chip stock in one's portfolio. Calibrated that way, success is achievable only for a select few. On the other hand, *excellence can be achieved by everybody* – but only if they are willing to "go for it!" In his book entitled *Christian Excellence*, Jon Johnston contrasts the difference between *success* and *excellence* this way:

> *Success bases our worth on a comparison with others. Excellence gauges our value by measuring us against our own potential. Success grants its reward to the few but is the dream of the multitudes. Excellence is available to all living beings but is accepted by the few. Success focuses its attention on the external...Excellence beams its spotlight on the internal spirit...Success encourages expedience and compromise, which prompts us to treat people as means to our ends. Excellence cultivates principles and consistency.*[30]

It is obvious that Christians – especially Christian leaders – should be pursuing *spiritual excellence* rather than *worldly success!*

As a result of this *desire to excel,* the effective leader continues to push himself towards *excellence* – while others around him may be characterized by *excuses*. It is a growing spiritual passion for God's glory that motivates Biblical leaders to live by the ideal of *"EXCELLENCE FOR CHRIST!"* They are seeking to do the very best they can...where they are...with what they have – for God's glory. It is this *supernatural passion* that more and more refines their *natural passion* – and frees them from *excuses... procrastination...blame-shifting...rationalization...mediocrity* – and general *low-level living!*

Principle:
"A true leader loves excellence."[31]
(Fred Smith)

This passion for spiritual excellence increasingly spills over into other areas of a leader's life – which is why good leaders generally strive to excel in *everything they do.* They usually have learned from painful personal experience that when they lose passion in one area of life, it soon erodes their passion in other areas of life. The central passion that *defines* and *refines* a leader's life is their *passion for God.* It is only a *passion for God* that produces a *Godly passion!* Only a *Godly passion* will purify, balance and sustain all of the other passions of life!

Principle:
"Energy coupled with enlightened enthusiasm results
in 'Excellence for Christ.'"

FURTHER QUOTATIONS ON
PASSIONATE LEADERSHIP

1. PASSION:

- *More than 50 percent of all CEOs of Fortune 500 companies had C or C- averages in college. Nearly 75 percent of all U.S. Presidents were in the bottom half of their school classes. And more than 50 percent of all millionaire entrepreneurs never finished college. What makes it possible for people who might seem ordinary to achieve great things? The answer is passion. Nothing can take the place of passion in a leader's life.*[32]

- *There is no substitute for passion. It is fuel for the will. If you want anything badly enough, you can find the will power to achieve it The only way to have that kind of desire is to develop passion.*[33]

- *Leadership demands a strong will – not a selfish or stubborn will, but a determined will to do what needs doing. By will we overcome our yen for pleasure and our satisfaction with mediocrity.*[34]

- *How do you motivate?*
  ① *Challenge motivates*
  ② *Enthusiasm motivates*
  ③ *Judgment motivates*
  ④ *Integrity motivates*
  ⑤ *Caring motivates*
  ⑥ *Communication motivates*
  ⑦ *Participation motivates* [35]

- *Who motivates you? Who motivates the leader? The answer is: no one. I'm self-motivated. A leader's motivation is the result of spontaneous combustion. They set themselves on fire. They have a fire within that drives them, compels them. That's why they are leaders. So if you can't ignite yourself, you can't ignite another.* [36]

- *Too many times when people get in positions of leadership they start to rest on their laurels. They get to the top and stop!... At that point, the three "I" sins usually show up: indifference, ignorance, and indecision. Sometimes people settle down so hard they flatten out...Effective leaders have to learn how to survive success. Surviving success means staying hungry and not resting on your laurels. So whatever you do in life, don't stop starting. Once you've reached a goal, set yourself another.*[37]

2. JOY:

- *...the joy of the Lord is actually a fruit of the Holy Spirit, and is therefore a radiant condition of the soul.* [38]

- *We participate in His joy through acts of worship, praise, prayer, and song, in witnessing to the saving grace of God and in helping others.* [39]

- *...joy is an attribute of God Himself. It brings with it pleasure, gladness, and delight. Joy is merriment without frivolity, hilarity without raucousness, and mirth without cruelty...Joy radiates animation, sparkle, and buoyancy....it draws from a deep spring that keeps flowing long after the laughter has died and the tears have come...Joy is not a sentimental word. It has a clean tang and bite to it, the exhilaration of mountain air. It blows away the dustiness of our days with a fresh breeze...*[40]

- *...the Psalms are not dirges or wails; overwhelmingly they are the exuberant outpouring of writers who are literally kicking up their heels, so excited are they to discover the redemptive love of Almighty God. "Shout for joy!" "Praise Him with the clash of cymbals." "Praise Him with tambourine and dancing." "Make music to Him." "Praise Him, sun and moon." "Extol the Lord." "My heart leaps for joy."* [41]

- *Elisabeth Elliot reminds us that "obedience always leads finally to joy."* [42]

3. ENTHUSIASM:

- *"You can do anything if you have enthusiasm." (Henry Ford)*[43]

- *Enthusiasm is the yeast that makes your hopes rise to the start.*

Enthusiasm is the sparkle in your eyes, the swing in your gait, the grip of your hand, the irresistible surge of will and energy to execute your ideas.[44]

4. HEART & HEAD:

- The only true king is the king of hearts. *Here is the greatest calling for the executive, and the greatest challenge, too: to master his own heart so as to inspire the hearts of others...*[45]

- *...how often it is that God makes alive our hearts by first breaking them. He makes us wise by exposing the extent of our propensity to folly...*[46]

- *...the heart is where leadership takes place; it is born there and there it dies as well...*[47]

- *...it is not ability, not experience, not position that separates the champions from the scoundrels; it is the heart that makes the difference, then and now, the heart that distinguishes between faithfulness and treachery, truth and façade, purpose and petty opportunism. A great chasm lies between these descriptors; on one side stand the eagles, while on the other side the vultures circle...*[48]

- Leadership, like greatness, is born in the heart. *David was great for what he loved and for what he hated. It was his heart that held him fast in times of trouble and his heart that brought him triumph. This too is God's great message through David for every leader who seeks His approval: "Man looks at the outward appearance, but the Lord looks at the heart."...*[49]

- *Ours is a generation infatuated first with the mind, and then with the working hands. Yet both the mind and the hands are under full control of the heart...*[50]

- *It is in the heart that every battle is won or lost, and so the heart is always primary...*[51]

- *...wisdom is a marriage – a synergy – of heart and mind.*[52]

- *The key to motivation is motive. It's the "why." It's what gives us the energy to stay strong in hard moments. It gives us the strength to say "no" because we connect with a deeper "yes!" burning inside...Doing the right thing for the right reason in the right way is the key to quality of life, and that can only come through the power of an educated conscience that aligns us with vision, mission, and true north.*[53]

- *Martin Luther claimed that he "never did anything well until his wrath was excited, and then he could do anything well."*[54]

- *John R. Mott counseled leaders to "rule by the heart. When logic and arguments and other forms of persuasion fail, fall back on the heart-genuine friendship."*[55]

- *"Never be lacking in zeal, but keep your spiritual fervor, serving the Lord." Harrington Lees translates this verse: "Not slothful in business, kept at boiling point by the Holy Spirit, doing bondservice for the master...".... "Kept at boiling point by the Holy Spirit"...Verse 11 holds out the alluring possibility of living "aglow with the Spirit." We need not go off boil if the Spirit is the great central furnace of our lives...*[56]

- *...both head and heart are required in this exercise. After seventeen or more years of formal education, most of us know something about using our heads but little about using our hearts. Yet all effective visions seem to be grounded in sensible values as well as analytically sound thinking...*[57]

5. LOVE:

- *The late Dr. Hans Selye, in his monumental research on stress, basically says that a long, healthy, and happy life is the result of making contributions, of having meaningful projects that are personally exciting and contribute to and bless the lives of others. His ethic was "earn thy neighbor's love."*[58]

- *(Dr. Ramesh Richard) "First in life, decide on your passion. What is your first love? If you have multiple passions, you'll be ripped to pieces internally, resulting in a fragmented, random life.* If anything other than the Lord Jesus Christ is your first love, you will fall into idolatry." *Christ is the focus of passion, insuring integrity of leadership...*[59]

- *God goes beyond tolerance. He loves. Tolerance ultimately is a total disconnect. Love is a total connection. Tolerance is apathy toward others. It may even be controlled hostility. To tolerate is passive, to love is active. Love doesn't ignore the other for its own convenience. It disciplines, it suffers, it challenges, it corrects. The Scripture tells us that God's correction is evidence of His love...Likewise; the Christian obligation is not self-righteous judgment but self-sacrificing love. The implications of complete tolerance for the social order are chaos and decadence. This was pointed out in Judges: 'Everyone did what was right in his own eyes.' Tolerance is in the end social hypocrisy. A lasting community cannot be built on it. Love, not apathy, is the glue that holds a group together.* [60]

6.   **EXCELLENCE:**

- *As Gandhi observed, "One man cannot do right in one department of life whilst he is occupied in doing wrong in any other department. Life is one indivisible whole."*[61]

- *Integrity in the Moment of Choice: Quality of life depends on what happens in the space between stimulus and response.*[62]

- *Between stimulus and response, man has the freedom to choose... there is a gap or a space between stimulus and response, and... the key to both our growth and happiness is how we use that space...I began to stand in that gap and to look outside at the stimuli. I reveled in the inward sense of freedom to choose my response ...*[63]

- *The typical goal that binds individuals together on guiding change coalitions is a commitment to excellence, a real desire to make their organizations perform to the very highest levels possible. Reengineering acquisitions and cultural change efforts often fail because that desire is missing. Instead, one finds people committed to their own departments, divisions, friends, or careers...*[64]

- *...Willa A. Foster remarked, "Quality is never an accident; it is always the result of high intention, sincere effort, intelligent direction and skillful execution; it represents the wise choice of many alternatives."*[65]

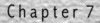

Chapter 7

LEADERS ARE PERFECTIONISTS

*"Not that I have already...been made perfect, but
I press on to take hold of that for which Christ Jesus took hold of me...
I do not consider myself yet to have taken hold of it.
But one thing I do: forgetting what is behind,
and straining toward what is ahead, I press on toward the goal
to win the prize for which God has called me..."
(Phil. 3:12-14).*

Like the Apostle Paul, growing spiritual leaders are always *pressing on toward perfection*. Effective leaders by nature are people who are *driven to do things well*. You might say that they have a *passion for perfection!* They generally have a low tolerance for poor performance...sloppiness...or half-heartedness – in themselves or in others around them. Because they constantly *push themselves toward perfection*, they often prayerfully push others in that same direction. That's why Paul prayed for some of his beloved Christian friends: **"Our prayer is for your *perfection"* (II Cor. 13:9). Likewise he exhorted these same Christians in his benediction: "Finally brothers...Aim for *perfection*...be of one mind, live in peace. And the God of love and peace will be with you"** (II Cor. 13:11).

Paul wanted Christians to always *"...aim for **perfection.**"* Did that mean that they would always achieve it? Certainly not! Paul was not teaching the doctrine known as *Christian Perfection*. This is a doctrine held by many Christians, and teaches that a person can become spiritually perfect in this life. I believe that is an erroneous doctrine that is not based on sound Biblical exegesis. Personal experience proves to any honest person that none of us can perfectly achieve perfection in this life. Only Christ did that. While we can *will it*, we cannot achieve it. We can desire it, but not attain it. However, we should still *desire it…aim at it…focus our hearts on it…strive for it…push ourselves toward it* – all the while resting in the knowledge that every Christian has the *imputed perfection of the Lord Jesus.* Because of grace we are clothed in the righteousness of Christ. As a result, we stand before God as *perfect in Christ.* That's known as *positional perfection* – or spiritual perfection that is based upon our spiritual position *"…in Christ Jesus"* (I Cor. 1:30). We are *positionally perfect,* but *practically imperfect!* While God sees us as perfect in Christ, others see us as imperfect. If you have any doubts about your imperfection, ask your spouse or children about it. They will quickly dispel any delusions of perfection in your life! It is the "performance gap" between our *positional perfection* in Christ, and our *practical imperfection* in life, that every serious Christian is always trying to narrow. As long as we are in this body of clay, we will live with the tension between *what now is* and *what is yet to come…*between Christ's *perfect work* and our *imperfect work…*between *His perfection* and our *imperfection…*between *His performance for us* and our *performance for Him.*

As we have already seen, this spiritual tension between *positional perfection* and *practical perfection* was a tension that Paul lived with all of his life. He honestly confessed that he had not yet "…been made perfect." Yet it was clearly a spiritual goal that he was aiming at…pressing on for…straining toward… suffering for. As he said: **"All of us who are *mature* should take such a view of things…Only let us live up to what we have already attained"** (Phil. 3:15-16). This is what Paul called **"walking *worthy* of our calling"** (Phil. 1:27; Eph. 4:1; Col. 1:10; I Thess. 2:12).

There is a pithy old proverb that says: *"If you aim at nothing, you will hit it every time!"* It is far better to *aim at perfection* and fall short of the mark, than aim at nothing and hit the bull's eye! When we do not aim at perfection, we tend to settle down into *bland mediocrity.* We become stunted in *spiritual immaturity.* Like the children of Israel, we live out our lives in the *wilderness of carnality* – rather than in God's *Promised Land, which* is **"…flowing with milk and honey"** (Ex. 3:8).

Principle:
*"It is far better to aim at perfection and miss the mark;
than aim at nothing and hit the bull's eye!"*

Perfection of character was the passion of Paul's life – not a *perfection of performance.* His desire was to be personally more and more conformed to the image of Christ every day. *Spiritual maturity,* or *Christ-like character* and *conduct,* were also the passion of Paul's mentoring ministry. In fact, Paul said that it was the job description of every Christian leader worth his salt. He was to do everything possible to bring new Christians to spiritual maturity. Listen to these words:

> **"It was He who gave some to be apostles, some to be prophets, some to be evangelists and some to be pastors and teachers, to prepare/equip God's people for works of service, so that the body of Christ may be built up until we all reach unity in the faith and in the knowledge of the Son of God and become *mature,* attaining to the whole measure of the fullness of Christ"** *(Eph. 3:11-13).*

He wrote almost identical words to the churches of Colossia:

> **"We proclaim Him, admonishing and teaching everyone with all wisdom, so that we may present everyone *perfect in Christ.* To this end we labor, struggling with all His energy which so powerfully works in me"** *(Col. 2:28-29).*

The Apostle Paul had a *passion for perfection!* He not only pushed himself toward the spiritual perfection of maturity in Christ; he did everything possible to take others with him on that same journey toward Christ-likeness. This was the passion and purpose of Paul's life and ministry. It should also be the model for other serious spiritual leaders to follow.

For the Christian leader, this need and drive to *do things well* is not something that is super-spiritual...vague...idealistic...ethereal...or nebulous. It is highly practical. This *passion for excellence,* this *pursuit of perfection,* this *motivation toward maturity* is expressed in the mundane...ordinary... everyday things of life and leadership. It generally causes a leader to do things like keeping his study and work area neat and orderly. Admittedly, that may be different things to different people! But however they may define *order*, effective leaders must have it before they can be creative and "get the job done." They tend to believe in the maxim: *"A place for everything, and everything in its place."* That means:

A writer must know where his resources are.
A builder must know where his materials are.
A mechanic must know where his tools are.
A chemist must know where his chemicals are.
A doctor must know where his instruments are.
An inventor must know where his raw materials are.
A cook must know where his ingredients are.
A musician must know where his instruments are.
A leader must know where his people are.
A shepherd must know where his sheep are.
A Bible teacher must know where his notes are.
A pastor must know where his parishioners are.

If you can't find what you need to do your work, you will waste a lot of time, energy and effort looking for things. That is time that could be more profitably spent on creativity rather than on searching for misplaced resources.

Our *external environment* is a projection of *our internal environment*. A person tends to project upon their external environment the condition of their internal environment. If they feel sloppy, untidy, disorganized, confused on the inside – they will project that on the outside. Teenagers and adolescents who are struggling with *who they are* often produce a very sloppy living environment. Their personal identity crisis is also often reflected in their dress – which usually reveals a confusion of who they are *individually, sexually,* and *vocationally.*

Leaders have solved the identity crisis of adolescence. They know in their inner being that God created them to lead and influence others. It is that conviction that has increasingly brought *order* and *orderliness* to their lives. Their external work environment reflects the order of someone who knows who he is, and where he is going in life. I believe it is a true leadership principle that *purpose produces a desire for perfection.*

Principle:
"Purpose in the heart inspires plans in the head –
which result in the pursuit of perfection with the
hands."

Most leaders are frustrated by a lack of *order* and *cleanliness* in either their living or working environment. It would be safe to say that most leaders have an *ardor for order!* When that is not there, they have a need to *"bring order out of chaos"* before they do anything else. Before they can give "marching orders" to others, they must first bring order to their own lives. Otherwise, the disorder and confusion around them stifles their creativity. A necessary part of good leadership is *"bringing order to one's own private world."* Generally speaking, if a person cannot bring order to his own *private world*, he will not be able to bring it to his *public world.* People are not inclined to follow leaders who are unorganized – or have that appearance.

When leaders perform a task, they seldom do just enough to get by. They seek to do the job the very best they can. They clearly understand that a job that is done poorly is a reflection upon their leadership integrity. Even more, they understand that *doing any job poorly is a dangerous work ethic!* Effective leaders never tolerate the *cancer of sloth* in what they do. Their striving to do a job the very best they can is to meet an internal standard of perfection – rather than just to meet the requirements of some external standard of job performance. Their drive for perfection is more of an *internal motivation* than an *external expectation.*

That's why effective leaders do their best – *even when no one is watching!* Since they are their own greatest critics, they need not have the eyes of others upon them to motivate them to do their best.

Principle:
"A leader's passion for perfection is more of an internal
motivation than an external expectation."

Paul warned servants, or employees, not to do a good job only when their masters were watching.

> "Servants, obey your earthly masters in everything; and do it, *not only when their eye is on you and to win their favor*, but with sincerity of heart and reverence for the Lord. Whatever you do, work at it with all your heart, as *working for the Lord, not for men*, since you know that you will receive an inheritance from the Lord as a reward. *It is the Lord Christ you are serving*" *(Col. 3:22-24)*.

He gave equal exhortation to the master, or employer. Just as Paul instructed Christian servants to do their job well regardless of whether their masters were watching; he reminded the masters to be fair and just – because God was always watching!

> "Masters, provide your slaves with what is right and fair, because you know that you also have a Master in heaven" *(Col. 4:1)*.

Spiritual leaders are *internally motivated toward excellence.* They have an *intrinsic passion for perfection.* They work with an acute awareness that the eyes of the Lord are always upon them. They are seeking to please Him first and foremost in everything they do. Their highest motivation is to hear Him say: **"Well done, good and faithful servant"** (Matt. 25:21). In their striving toward perfection, they are not trying to *appease God* – but rather to *please God.* One motivation is positive and healthy, while the other is negative and unhealthy. A person will try to *appease* a God that they feel is harsh…angry…over-bearing…unfair…unjust. On the other hand, they will live to *please* the God Who has perfectly accepted them in Christ Jesus – and loves them with an everlasting love! That's the kind of *unconditional love and acceptance* that motivates *healthy living* and *healthy leading.* First and foremost, it is the Lord that they are serving through their leadership gifts – not man. They are not just working for their *earthly welfare* – but for an eternal **"Well done!"** However, the paradox is that *our leadership before man is no better than our lives before God.*

If leaders have a motto in this area, it is this: *"Anything that is worth doing, is worth doing right."* They know that if they do the job right the first time, they will not have to come back and repeat the effort. Effective leaders have an understanding of the importance of *conservation of time, energy* and *effort*. When a job is done right in the first place, there is no need to waste time, energy and effort in repeating it.

Principle:
"Pleasing God rather than appeasing God is the highest motivation for happy living and healthy leading."

The positive side of this perfectionist characteristic is that *leaders generally excel in their jobs*. Doing a job well is one of the greatest emotional satisfactions for a leader. He gets a lot of "psychic joy" over a *job well done* – whether it is preparing a speech...giving a report...planning a strategy...organizing a job...carrying out a task...washing a car... mowing his lawn...or plowing his garden.

The down side of this perfectionistic inclination is that it can easily *control the leader* – rather than *cultivate the leader*. He becomes a *perfectionist* to the degree that he can never ever please himself. Even worse, neither can other people ever please him – whether it is his spouse, children, or employees. A growing discontent emerges. A critical spirit often takes over. He passes out far more *criticisms* than he does *compliments*.

He becomes so focused on perfection that he *always sees the flaws*. He increasingly focuses on the imperfections in himself...in what he does... in others around him...in what they do. The perceived imperfection he always sees and feels, robs him of the joy of personally completing a task with a sense of satisfaction. This often can be traced back to the person's childhood – and a parent who could never be pleased with their child's performance. Nothing was ever quite good enough. Grades should have always been higher. Performance should have always been better. They should have always achieved more than they did. Rewards and praises seldom ever came. As a result, the child grew up with an obsessive drive toward achievement. They are constantly trying to satisfy that compelling inner voice of their parent who was always demanding more achievement and better performance. This can become a sick drive toward perfection that can literally "drive them crazy!" While all grown on the outside, their stunted and unfulfilled inner child drives them throughout life. People like this who become leaders tend to be *slave drivers* rather than *servant motivators*.

Good conscientious leaders can easily cross the mental and emotional line into *perfectionism*. If they have not found healing and balance in this desire and drive to excel, it will mar their leadership skills with a growing negativity. They will never be satisfied with *any* job. They become *obsessed* by the unrealistic expectations they place upon themselves – and upon others around them. This can easily degenerate into a personality disorder known as *obsessive-compulsive behavior*. They can never bring *finality…closure… completion* to a task because there is always something more that they feel can and should be done. An *obsessive-compulsive leader bent on perfection* will ultimately damage or destroy every interpersonal relationship he touches!

This perfectionism to the extreme makes it difficult for many leaders to turn over a task to others. Their perpetual dissatisfaction will prevent them from ever fully relinquishing the reins of leadership to others. They always feel that they can do the job a little better. They find it difficult to fully give up control. They become "control freaks!" Nothing is ever fully completed until they themselves have put on the final "finishing touches!"

One of my mentors, Dr. David Seamands, taught me an important principle in this area early in my life and ministry. He said:

> *"J.L., one of the hardest things you will often have to MAKE yourself do is to sit back and sometimes watch the job be done second best. Whether in parenting or discipling, you can often step in and do the job quicker and better because of your training and experience. However, if you always do that in the lives of your children – or with the people you are mentoring – you will stunt their spiritual and emotional growth."*

That was very wise and seasoned advice I have never forgotten. Even though I have not always perfectly applied that principle, I believe it with all my heart. This wise friend and mentor knew that by nature I was a perfectionist – with strong obsessive-compulsive tendencies! He also knew my natural inclination to "take the lead" in most situations. I have often had to MAKE myself back off and let others "try their wings." In mentoring others, I have learned that, if I always "take the lead," and have the "final say" on every issue, I will frustrate the leadership gifts of others. I would stunt their growth as growing young leaders. *Wise parents* and *wise leaders* must not only allow, they must encourage others to take the lead. It is an emotional truism that says: *"If we always do for others what they can do for themselves, we create an emotional cripple."* In the process we also destroy their individual initiative.

Whether in our *physical children* or our *spiritual children*, we must encourage them to "try their wings...leave the nest...move out of their comfort zone...step out of our shadows...take control...take the lead." Even though they may falter and fail – just as we do – we must encourage them to "move out" and "move up" for God. That's the joy of parenting – physically and spiritually!

Principle:
"When we do for others what they are capable of doing for themselves, we ultimately destroy initiative and produce an emotional cripple."

A motivation towards perfection is a very good leadership quality – but only as it is kept in balance by *realistic expectations*. Every leader should strive to do his very best at everything he does. He should seek to motivate others to do the same. However, he also must learn both *balance* and *priority* in this.

He must first learn to *balance perfection with reality* – a lesson I am still learning! A leader's desire to do things well must be constantly tempered with the reality that *there was only one perfect person who ever lived – and that was Jesus Christ!* His work alone is the one that is stamped with perfection and marked by completion. All of the rest of us will by nature often do many things poorly.

Leaders must also learn to *temper their perfectionism with priorities*. Not all things are of equal importance. Not all things should receive the same amount of time, energy and effort. To strive to do things well that affect people is important. To strive to develop spiritually and please God is our highest calling. But to be driven toward perfection in non-people things can easily become sick and distorted. I know of men who can never finish washing their car until every water spot is gone. I know women who can never rest until every speck of dust is cleaned from their homes. And yet many of these same people who have such obsessions with material things, tolerate very bad habits in their lives – and in the lives of their children. Many people in the Western world become obsessed with clothes and externals. Before they will step out of the house, everything must be perfectly matched and stylishly coordinated. Yet many of these same people show little or no concern over how they look on the inside to God.

We must learn to put the emphasis where it belongs. *We must put first things first.* We should strive for perfection in the things that are eternal – and learn to give less attention to things that are only temporal.

Jesus said: **"Be perfect as your heavenly Father is perfect"** (Matt. 5:48). He said this at the end of the Sermon on the Mount in which He was teaching about ethics, morals, and interpersonal things that have to do with our character. Ultimately, only these things determine our eternal destiny. In the areas of the spirit, we should constantly strive toward perfection through the power of the Holy Spirit. In the things that are only temporal and short-lived, we should not become obsessed.

As good leaders, we should always seek to be good stewards of our time, energy and efforts by seeking to do our best in everything we do. But if we do not have our priorities straight, we will put the emphasis in the wrong place. We may achieve a degree of perfection in things that will one day be reduced to ashes in the fire of God's judgment. It is then that we will wish that we had sought more for the spiritual perfection of Christ-likeness!

As Paul said, the world has only seen one model of perfection – and that is the Lord Jesus (Eph. 4:12-13). When Paul said we should strive for *maturity*, he used the word *teleios*. It is often translated as *"perfect"* in the New Testament. Something that is *teleios* is *"anything that has reached its desired end. It is something that has arrived at the end for which it was created."*

Wise leaders always strive for *perfection* in everything they do. First and foremost, they want to increasingly achieve a *spiritual* and *moral perfection of character* that will add true integrity to their lives and leadership. As an external manifestation of their inner pursuit of perfection, they seek to excel and do well in everything they do. While they must learn to be tolerant and realistic about their own imperfections and inabilities, they must NEVER tolerate imperfections of character in their own lives! Through humility and repentance, they must constantly bring those areas of moral imperfection under the scrutiny of the Spirit and the Word.

Principle:
"Perfection of character and conduct is the highest calling of leadership."

FURTHER QUOTATIONS ON PERFECTION IN LEADERSHIP

1. ORDER & ORGANIZATION:

- *Mark Twain said, "The secret of getting ahead is getting started." The secret of getting started is breaking your complex, overwhelming tasks into small, manageable tasks, and then starting on the first one.* [1]

2. HARD WORK:

- *All good leaders carry their own bags. They get up earlier, stay later, work harder, give more and go farther than anyone else. Leadership, they know, requires long days and sleepless nights.* [2]

- *"Success is a ladder that cannot be climbed with your hands in your pockets" (American Proverb). The ladder of leadership can't either. It takes both hands and hard work.* [3]

- *If you snooze – you lose. If you snore, you lose more.* [4]

- *What are the traits of a hard-working leader?*
  Let me name four:
  - o *A leader must be energetic*
  - o *A leader must be enthusiastic*
  - o *A leader must be optimistic*
  - o *A leader must have a sense of urgency* [5]

- *There is simply no substitute for hard work. Hard work will make up for almost any other deficiency you might have. There is no elevator to success in leadership. You must take the stairs.* [6]

3. PERFECTIONISM:

- *We accept the responsibility for our own excellence. We don't blame shoddy performance on someone else; we're not lifted up by praise we don't deserve. Criticism or praise from others is secondary to our own connection with conscience.* [7]

4.   MATURITY:

- *On the maturity continuum,* dependence *is the paradigm of* you – you *take care of me;* you *come through for me;* you *didn't come through;* I blame you *for the results.* Independence *is the paradigm of* I – I *can do it;* I *am responsible;* I *am self-reliant;* I *can choose.* Interdependence *is the paradigm of* we – we *can do it;* we *can cooperate;* we *can combine our talents and abilities and create something greater together. Dependent people need others to get what they want. Independent people can get what they want through their own effort. Interdependent people combine their own efforts with the efforts of others to achieve their greatest success...* [8]

- *...your growth will be* evolutionary, *but the net effect will be* revolutionary... [9]

- *How often am I willing to pray, "Lord prosper me financially in proportion to my spiritual maturity"?* [10] Chapter 9, p. 128.

5.   INTEGRITY:

- *When we fail to act in harmony with our inner voice, we begin to build a wall around the conscience that blocks its sensitivity and receptivity. As C.S. Lewis observed, "disobedience to conscience makes conscience blind."* [11]

- *...In the words of Dag Hammarskjold, "You cannot play with the animal in you without becoming wholly animal, play with falsehood without forfeiting your right to truth, play with cruelty without losing your sensitivity of mind. He who wants to keep his garden tidy doesn't reserve a plot for weeds...* [12]

- *...it is painful to observe, then and now, men and women placed in the executive's chair – a seat of possibility and meaning and importance – only to squander it all over tawdry ambition and shortsighted gain. How hard it is to see the servant's place taken by the charlatan...* [13]

- *The counterfeit leader is reprehensible in the extreme, just as burdensome to the heart of God as he is to the backs of men...[14]*

- *...when real leadership disappears people will always follow those who simply look the part, regardless of their motives and real qualifications. And that is why our organizations are so full of false executives today...[15]*

~~~~~~~~~~~~~~~~~~~~~~~~

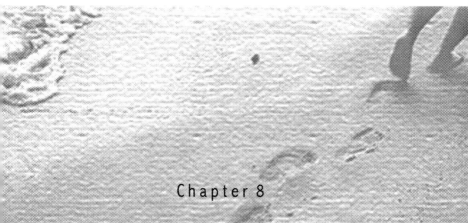

Chapter 8

LEADERS ARE PERCEPTIVE

"Give your servant a discerning heart to govern your people and to distinguish between right and wrong"
(I Kings 3:9).

Good leaders must be *discerning* and *perceptive* of the dynamics around them. Leaders have a keen perception of their environment. They are always seeking to "get a handle" on their immediate situation so they will know where to take hold. They naturally try to get their "finger on the pulse" of their circumstances. Leaders are always monitoring the *place, people, problems* and *possibilities* around them.

Leaders are very much like thermometers, they are always measuring the spiritual, mental, and emotional climate they are in. Good leaders are highly sensitized people who are attuned to their immediate surroundings. They are not like a turtle or a clam that has a hard shell that makes them insensitive to their environment. Humans have their nervous system just beneath their skin – so they are very sensitive to their environment. Christian leaders should be the most sensitive people of all – because to be *Christianized is to be sensitized!* The more sensitive and perceptive we are to our circumstances, the better we can give true leadership.

Principle:
*"To be Christianized is to be sensitized. Successful
leadership comes from sensitive leadership."*

Even though leaders are perceptive to the *external environment* around
them; they are even more concerned about the *internal environment* in the
hearts, minds, attitudes, and moods of the people with them. Wise leaders
are acutely aware that every person they lead will follow them while
carrying certain spiritual, mental and emotional baggage. If leaders are
not perceptive and sensitive to the "unseen baggage" many people are
dragging with them, they will be insensitive and imperceptive leaders.
Effective leaders learn to "look beneath the surface." They are not deceived
by initial appearance. They do not quickly jump to conclusions before
considering all of the evidence and weighing all the facts. They want to
hear both sides of the issue. They seek to have as broad a perspective of
the situation as possible. The wisdom of Proverbs points out: **"The heart
of the discerning acquires knowledge…The first to present his case
seems right, till another comes forward and questions him"** (Prov.
18:15, 17). Wise leaders have learned not to make snap decisions based
upon superficial surface appearances.

In his excellent book, *The Heart of an Executive,* Richard Phillips compares
and contrasts the life and leadership of King Saul to that of the young
man David. Initially Saul always looked better. He struck a good pose.
He had a good political posture. He appeared more kingly than the ruddy
shepherd boy. So Phillips wisely cautions against snap judgments based
solely upon appearance and first time impressions.

> *I have always been fascinated by the expression, "The first impression
> is what really matters." I do not doubt that there is practical truth
> to this statement. But first impressions are necessarily shallow,
> external. The cut of the clothing, the posture and gestures, the
> enthusiasm in the eye – I assure you that Saul can do these better
> than David, at least for thirty minutes. But the corollary to the
> principle of first impressions is this: "You get just what you are
> looking for.[1]*

Like so many of us, the people of Israel judged by outward appearance
– and chose their king accordingly. They were terribly deceived. Before

long, their choice of Saul as king proved to be very costly to them from every perspective! On the outside he looked kingly – but on the inside he had the heart of a tyrant. Even though he was physically tall and had the stature of a "man's man", his spirit was infantile and his emotions were childish. Since Saul never "mastered his moods" – his moods mastered him. His leadership vacillated from one fleshy outburst to another. His people were constantly victimized by his carnality! The life and leadership of King Saul is a poignant and perpetual reminder that surface appearance is not God's perspective. God reminded Samuel as he sought for Saul's successor: **"Man looks at the outward appearance, but the Lord looks at the heart"** (I Sam. 16:7). When it comes to leadership in His Kingdom, God always looks for **"...a man after His own heart"** (I Sam. 13:14).

Most leadership gifts require some degree of public speaking. A good leader must learn to "read his audience." He must be ever discerning of the internal emotional atmosphere in the heart and mind of his listener. A leader is acutely aware that his listeners and followers are generally preoccupied mentally and emotionally with certain recurring *thoughts, memories, feelings* and *emotions.* Most people are *scarred by hurts; pained by memories; crippled by fear; paralyzed by failure.* The Christian leader must help them to consciously recognize – and positively deal with – their mental and emotional baggage. If he is unable to help them change their focus from *fear to faith,* they will not be able to follow him to new goals. He must, therefore, be able to lead them from where they are to where God wants them to be.

If the leader is not perceptive of where his listeners and followers are *spiritually, mentally,* and *emotionally,* then he will not know whether they are "with him" – or whether he has "lost them." If the leader is not sensitive to the people, he will waste time "answering questions no one is asking." He will "scratch where no one is itching!" He will pour out a lot of energy and effort on "non-issues."

Principle:
*"You can't make important decisions
without talking about the real issues."*[2]
(John Kotter, Harvard Business School)

When we express this ability in Biblical terms, it is the spiritual gift of *discernment* (I Cor. 12:10; I Jn. 4:1). It is because of this spiritual gift that the Biblical leader has an advantage over the worldly leader. Through the exercise of this spiritual gift, the Spirit-filled leader is able to be more perceptive into the human spirit – as well as into the spiritual realm of angels and demons. In addition to the *discernment* of the *Spirit of God*, he also has the *dynamic* of the *Word of God* to help him minister to people. Only the Word of God used by the Spirit of God can **"…divide soul and spirit…"** But it does not stop there; it goes on to **"…judge the thoughts and attitudes of the heart"** (Heb. 4:12). No natural leader could ever be that perceptive! That is only the leadership ministry of the *Spirit of God…* through the *Word of God…* by the *man of God…* for the *people of God!*

Principle:
"To increase your leadership potential you must increase your perception of people."

Effective leaders are *lifelong students of people*. The better they are able to discern and "size up" people, the better they will be able to lead. Leaders seek to be *perceptive of people* for the sole purpose of *helping people reach their full potential*. Since leaders are interested in *motivating people* rather than *manipulating people*, their leadership is based upon an unshakable belief that people can be and do more in life. They can live at a higher level and achieve more. Effective leaders *believe in people* – even when people do not believe in themselves. They are able to *call forth the potential in people* that the people did not know that they had. Through the eyes of faith, they are able to *perceive potential* in people – and call it forth. They are able to *activate dormant desire* in people for meaning and fulfillment in life. As they rally the people around a *noble cause*, they help them achieve the greatest longing of the human spirit - *significance* in life.

John Maxwell interestingly categorizes people in four groups. Even though it is always dangerous to summarize the complexity of people by simplistic reductions, there is a lot of truth in what Maxwell writes. When it comes to the leadership challenge of activating people, he summarizes humanity into four types of people:

1. Cop-Outs: People who have no goals and do not commit;
2. Hold-Outs: People who are afraid to commit;
3. Drop-Outs: People who drop out when the going gets tough;
4. All-Outs: People who pay the price to reach the goals.[3]

Effective leaders are always trying to *activate the potential within people.* Leaders are not just interested in *reaching their own potential.* They are interested in *helping others reach their potential.* A leader reaches his potential by helping other people reach their potential. Leaders are especially *perceptive of people potential.*

Principle:
"A leader's potential is reached
by helping others reach their potential."

Leaders also understand that a *person's potential* is reached as he or she loses themselves in a cause greater than themselves. It is a *great cause* that makes people great. Simply put: *"Vision produces valor."* Leaders are not only perceptive of people, they are also perceptive to the opportunities that will call forth the potential within people. Leaders often see *potential* where others see *problems.* They see *opportunity* when others see only *opposition.* They see in people and situations opportunities that others do not see. While others either *can't see* or *won't see,* leaders see what *could be.* Others see things as they *are* – rather than as they *could be.* The leader's spiritual and mental vision of the things that *could be* are greater than his physical vision of the things *as they are.* The Apostle Paul spoke of this principle when he reminded the Corinthian Christians:

> **"God chose the foolish things of the world to shame the wise; God chose the weak things of the world to shame the strong. He chose the lowly things of this world and the despised things – and the *things that are not – to nullify the things that are,* so that no one may boast before Him"** (I Cor. 1:27-29).

It is only Godly leadership that transforms *obstacles* into *opportunity*... *problems* into *potential* – and replaces the *seen* with the *unseen.* One person's *setback* becomes another person's *set-up!* As a result, effective leadership overcomes the *obstacles, objections* and *opposition* around them. A leader always seizes the *opportunity* as a means of reaching his *objective*. A leader's *objective* must be greater than both the *objections* and *opposition* of others – and the *obstacles* that will inevitably come his way. That's why author Alfred Armand Montapert wrote:

> *The majority sees the obstacles; the few see the objectives; history records the successes of the latter, while oblivion is the reward of the former.*[4]

Principle:

"Leadership overcomes obstacles, objections and oppositions in the pursuit of great objectives."

Leaders have learned that there is often a *strategic timing* for taking advantage of opportunity. When "opportunity comes knocking", they quickly open the door. They do not run and hide in the face of opportunity. While others lock and bolt the door out of a fear of failure – a leader boldly "seizes the moment" and takes advantage of the opportunity. As my friend Franklin Graham writes:

> *It has been said that opportunities multiply as they are seized; they die when neglected…If we truly want to go beyond the limits, we will be willing to act decisively when opportunities come.*[5]

In his autobiography, Franklin goes on share how this "opportunity principle" practically works itself out in his own life:

> *With God directing my path, I discover a new element in everyday living. The people I meet and the situations I find myself thrown into become full of new opportunities. God's got me here for a reason, so I sit back and watch His Spirit move. I let God be my appointment secretary. I never imagine that I'm somewhere by accident. Just in case God's behind it, I want to be ready.*[6]

It's that perspective on opportunity – even in the face of great danger – that has caused Franklin to be so greatly used of God around the world, especially in crisis situations. There are several important principles of opportunity in what Franklin writes:

Life is full of opportunities.
We must be decisive when opportunities come.
Opportunities multiply as they are seized.
Opportunities die when they are neglected.

Principle:

"Effective leaders are perceptive of the place they are in, the people they are with, the problems they face, the potential before them."

FURTHER QUOTATIONS ON PERCEPTIVE LEADERSHIP

1. DISCERNMENT:

- *...we immediately begin to rationalize – tell ourselves "rational lies"...[7]*

- *According to Arthur Schlesinger, Jr., leadership is "the capacity to move, inspire, and mobilize masses of people." Former U.S. Supreme Court Justice Arthur Goldberg defines leadership as "great ability and great opportunity greatly employed – an art, not a science and largely intuitive."[8]*

- *...every fact is preceded by a feeling and if we rightly employ our discernment, we can affect the facts by understanding the feelings that precede the facts...[9]*

2. OPPORTUNITY:

- *I've heard it said that wherever there is danger, there lurks opportunity. I'd rather live in the face of fear knowing that God will be with me every step of the way than to shrink back and miss an opportunity to serve Him because of all the what-ifs: What if I get shot? What if they turn their backs? What if they don't listen to me? What if the money runs out?[10]*

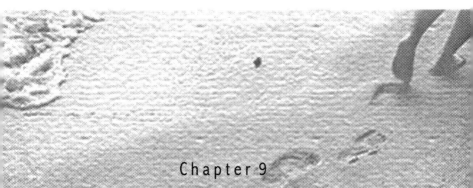

Chapter 9

LEADERS ARE PROBLEM-SOLVERS

"I appeal to you, brothers, in the name of our Lord Jesus Christ, that all of you agree with one another so that there may be no divisions among you and that you may be perfectly united in mind and thought…Some of you have become arrogant, as if I were not coming to you…But I will come to you very soon… and then I will find out not only how these arrogant people are talking, but what power they have…What do you prefer? Shall I come to you with a whip or in love and with a gentle spirit?…Even though I am not physically present, I am with you in spirit. And I have already passed judgment on the one who did this, just as if I were present. When you are assembled in the name of our Lord Jesus and I am with you in spirit and the power of our Lord Jesus is present, hand this man over to Satan, so that the sinful nature may be destroyed and his spirit saved on the day of the Lord" (I Cor. 1:10 to I Cor. 5:5).
"…This will be my third visit to you…I already gave you a warning when I was with you the second time. I now repeat it while absent. On my return I will not spare those who sinned earlier, or any of the others…yet by God's power we will live with Him to serve you…our prayer is for your perfection. This is why I write these things when I am absent that when I come I may not have to be harsh in my use of authority – the authority the Lord gave me for building you up, not for tearing you down"
(II Cor. 13:1-10). (I Cor. 1:10; 4:18-21; 5:3; II Cor. 13:1-10).

The above selected verses from Paul's letter to the church at Corinth clearly show that he was a leader who had an *eye and ear for problems.* In fact, almost every one of his letters was written in part to deal with some problem in one of the churches that he had planted. If he was not personally writing to deal with one or more church problems, he was writing young pastors like Timothy and Titus on how they should deal with various problems that had arisen in churches they were leading. By engaging these young pastors in the problem-solving process, they too were being mentored on how to effectively problem-solve. Paul's focus on problems was not that he was a negative, pessimistic, problem-oriented person. It was just that he was a realist who understood that problems in life are unavoidable – especially since we live in a rebellious fallen world. However, his emphasis was always positive – even when dealing with problems. While Paul never ignored problems, he always spent more time "watering the spiritual flowers" in the church, than he did in "pulling out the weeds of carnality." He was constantly praising and affirming people in the Lord. He always assured them of his constant prayers in their behalf. He chose to believe the best about them and called forth the best within them. So, through his personal presence, through letters, or through emissaries, he was constantly feeding them healthy doses of God's love, mercy and grace – coupled with his own affirmation and praise.

Even though Paul was a very positive person by nature, he was also acutely aware of the fact that the Christian calling is active engagement in lifelong *spiritual warfare.* Satan, as the supreme enemy of the church, was constantly **"...sowing weeds among the wheat"** (Matt. 13:25). When noxious weeds were present – whether through the *flesh* or through *Satan* – Paul did not ignore them. He knew that *spiritual* and *relational weeds* would quickly spread throughout the entire church if they were ignored. Paul clearly understood that through *spiritual immaturity, carnality* or *Satanic deception,* the wheat would be choked out **"...making it unfruitful"** (Matt. 13:22). As a Jew, he well knew the principle that God had taught His people through Moses: **"Make sure there is no *root* among you that produces such *bitter poison*"** (Deut. 29:18). Paul was especially sensitive to the kinds of problems that *compromised the Word... defiled the spirit...broke relationships...*and *spoiled the witness of the Church.* His Apostolic leadership reflected the truth of Hebrews 12:15: **"See to it that no one misses the *grace of God* and that no *bitter root* grows up to cause trouble and *defile many*."** When problems did come, Paul became *spiritually proactive.* He exercised leadership authority. He rolled up his sleeves and quickly set about to root out the "weedy problem" or prune the "thorny issue" – carefully using the sharp edge of the Word of God through the power of the Spirit. Paul understood the leadership principle that says: *Your greatest defense is a strong offense.* Like a wise gardener, Paul regularly fertilized the church soil with the *truth* and *light* of God's

Word and God's Spirit. He constantly nurtured young Christians with the **"water of the Word"** (Eph. 5:26). That balanced combination of *watering* and *weeding* kept the enemy's "seeds and weeds" from *taking root* – and *taking over.*

Principle:
"Your greatest defense is always a strong offense."

It is always easy for each of us to think that our problems are the toughest! We secretly believe that the problems we face are worse than the ones anyone else has ever faced. That's because they are *our problems!* However, *there are no totally new or unique problems.* Satan is just not that creative! He doesn't have to be. The reason is that each new generation of people is susceptible to the same old lies, temptations, and deceptions – resulting in the same old spiritual and relational problems! All Satan does is *re-package* and *re-cycle* the same old problems over and over again – one generation after another. The first thing that we need to do in facing problems is to remind ourselves that there are no totally new or unique ones. Other leaders have also faced some variety of those very same problems.

Principle:
"Effective people are not problem-minded,
they are opportunity-minded. They feed
opportunities and starve problems." [1]
(Peter Drucker)

The church problems that Paul wrote about in the 1st century are basically the same ones we face in the 21st century. His challenges were as varied as the places to which he traveled, and as diverse as the people to whom he ministered. The conflicts and crises he confronted were as daunting as any leader could ever face in any century. In those early churches the problems he faced ran the full gamut of human and demonic expression. They were spiritual, theological, doctrinal, liturgical, personal, marital, moral, cultural, legal, financial, vocational – just to mention a few of the major ones! Unlike some church leaders then and now, Paul never ignored problems. He directly confronted them - *head on.* Rather than ignore them, deny them, or run away from them – he dealt with them *swiftly* and *decisively*. Whenever possible, Paul took the *personal approach* to problem-solving. He would always try go and deal with the issue personally. When he could not *trouble-shoot* personally by going and being there, he would send in one of his young associates, or ministry partners to deal with the issue. As we saw above, this method of trouble-shooting through the mediation of a trusted emissary also taught them the art of *problem-solving*. When it was not possible for either him or them to go, Paul wrote *personal letters* to address the problem. He knew that *to ignore a problem would only make it worse*. The longer it was ignored, the more it would grow – and the more people would become ensnared by it. Like the powerful "black holes" in the galaxies, unsolved problems continue to suck people deeper and deeper into their darkness!

Whatever its nature, Paul clearly understood that a problem not *faced* would only *fester*. He wrote to aggressively and decisively deal with the problem of immorality in the Corinthian Church: **"Don't you know,"** Paul questioned, **"that a little yeast works through the whole batch of dough?"** (I Cor. 5:6). The immature Corinthian Christians wanted to be tolerant of a disobedient sinful brother who was a part of their fellowship – even though he was living in blatant sexual immorality. Like so many churches today, they wanted to "turn a blind eye" to his sin. Because there were so many "alternative lifestyles" in Corinth, they operated by the social policy of "live and let live." The Corinthians boasted about their plurality – and worshipped at the "altar of toleration." Any lifestyle was "socially acceptable" and "politically correct." To be called a "Corinthian" was the same thing as saying that one was a "worldly wise person." Unfortunately, that tolerant attitude had crept into the young church at Corinth. They had already begun to be leavened by the highly pluralistic Corinthian society around them. As a result, it was Paul's most immature and carnal church (I Cor. 3:1)!

The Apostle Paul had to force the Corinthian church to face a problem that they wanted to ignore. He wrote to remind them that the sin that is tolerated in the world around them must never be tolerated in the church! Paul would not let them ignore the *leaven of immorality* working in and through the life of this disobedient brother – who was living in sexual immorality with his father's wife! In tolerating this, Paul says that the church had "out-worlded the world!" The Christians in Corinth had literally become more tolerant than the people of Corinth! He said that the degree of sexual immorality they were tolerating in their midst was **"...of a kind that does not occur even among pagans"** (I Cor. 5:1)! He well knew that *spiritual infidelity* and *sexual infidelity* always walk hand-in-hand in the life of an individual or in a church. *Sexual compromises always follow spiritual compromises.* When a church compromises her *spiritual authority,* she soon compromises *moral authority.* Paul would not ignore either spiritual or sexual infidelity. As a wise leader, he knew that every problem had the potential to produce either *growth and maturity* or *division and disaster,* in the local church. Paul instructed them to exercise *church discipline* with this disobedient brother – even to the extreme degree of *excommunication* if necessary. Even though he could not be present with them personally, he exhorts them to **"...*put out of your fellowship* the man who did this."** Paul carefully gives them the procedure for exercising church discipline to this extreme degree. However, he does not stop there. He goes on to explain to them the reasons why it must be carried out for their sake... for the man's sake...for the sake of the name of Christ.

> **"Even though I am not physically present, I am with you in spirit. And I have already passed judgment on the one who did this, just as if I were present. When you are assembled in the name of our Lord Jesus and I am with you in spirit, and the power of our Lord Jesus is present, hand this man over to Satan, so that the sinful nature may be destroyed and his spirit saved on the day of the Lord Jesus. Your boasting is not good. Don't you know that *a little yeast works through the whole batch of dough?* Get rid of the old yeast that you may be a new batch without yeast – as you really are. For Christ, our Passover lamb, has been sacrificed"** (I Cor. 5:3-8).

The Apostle Paul would go to any degree necessary to deal with a problem in the local church. In this case, he well knew that *immorality* was really an *idolatry* of the flesh. If this sin were left unchecked, it would quickly leaven the whole church there – and effectively destroy the integrity of their witness to the wider Corinthian community. Most of all, it would *profane the Name of the Lord.* But carefully note that the whole purpose of church discipline was to bring *repentance* and *restoration* in the life of the disobedient brother. If he would not repent, they must excommunicate him from Christian worship and fellowship so that the leaven of his immorality would not spread to others. Put outside the spiritual security of the Church, God would use the world and Satan to *discipline him unto death* if necessary "…so his spirit would be saved on the day of the Lord Jesus." As long as this church problem was not dealt with, spiritual life and health could not grow in the church at Corinth.

Principle:
"The measure of success is not whether you have a tough problem, but whether it is the same problem you had last year."[2]
(John Foster Dulles, Former Secretary of State)

Effective leaders must not only be perceptive of the *place* they are in, the *people* they are with, the *potential* that they represent, and the *possibilities* that confront them – they must also be sensitive to the *problems* that inevitably arise in leading people. They must be willing to squarely face those problems – regardless of how difficult or distasteful they may be. Problem-solving cannot be separated from leadership. A leader who cannot – or will not – face and solve problems, will not lead for very long.

Principle:
"A leader should look for what is wrong, not to criticize it but to correct it."[3]
(Fred Smith)

Effective leadership is based upon effective problem-solving. Almost every great leader emerged by confronting and solving some major problem that others either ignored, or failed to solve. As they faced the problem – and found a viable solution – their leadership became evident to others. *People are drawn to someone who is not afraid of problems* and who is able to successfully confront them. *Every problem has within it the potential to produce a leader.* Problems are the building blocks of leadership! They are the raw materials out of which the gifts of leadership are refined. As John Maxwell has observed: *"Every problem introduces you to yourself. It shows you how you think and what you're made of."*[4]

Principle:
"Problems are the building blocks of leadership. Every problem has within it the potential to produce a leader."

Since leadership revolves around people, *people represent problems!* It's that simple. We must never forget that a*s long as there are people, there will be problems.* The more people there are, the more problems there are. *People problems* are the *greatest challenge of leadership*. If a leader wants to *eliminate his problems,* all he has to do is to *eliminate his people!* No followers – no problems! Many followers – many problems! There is no such thing as a totally *abstract problem.* Almost every problem has a major "people element" in it. Most problems become *personified* and *incarnated* in a particular person or group of people. Virtually every problem Paul dealt with was *people-oriented* – like the ones in Corinth. However, the *person is not the problem.* It is the *problem* that is *the problem!* In dealing with a problem, wise leaders must carefully *separate the person from the problem.* They must seek to *defeat the problem* without *destroying the person.* To *win over the problem* at the expense of a *loss of a person,* is never successful problem-solving. That is a *win-lose* scenario. A good leader always works toward a *win-win* solution. He wants to *win over the problem* while at the same time *winning over the person.* But that does not mean *winning OVER him by defeating him;* but rather by *WINNING HIM OVER to your side.*

Every effective leader has learned through personal experience that it takes careful interpersonal surgery to *separate the problem from the person.* The first step in confronting an issue is for the leader to *objectify* the problem. He must first do all he can to remove the *subjective* element from the problem in his own heart and mind. Even though he must *deal with the problem personally,* he must not *take the problem personally.* Many leaders see a problem as a *personal affront* to their leadership. They emotionally interpret the problem as a personal *attack upon their authority.* A leader must begin by first working for a de-catharsis of his own *emotions* that are involved. That's because *passions always intensify problems!* If his passions are inflamed by the problem, then all he will do is lead with his emotions. At that point, the atmosphere becomes "emotionally charged." He will "draw up the battle lines" and begin to "fight *with* his feelings" – rather than "fight *for* the facts." He will have the "search and destroy" mentality of a military general – who must "win at any cost!" *Authority* is abused. *Rank* is pulled. Higher *position* and superior *power* are called into play. Stronger and stronger *defensive postures* are taken. A stalemate occurs. At that point, either the person and problem are both *destroyed* – or they are *driven underground.* A *cold war* sets in with constant outbreaks of guerilla warfare. This kind of in-fighting can quickly destroy an organization or a church. It is just as deadly for *marriage* as it is for *ministry.*

Principle:
"Passions always intensify problems. Therefore,
principle must rule over passion in problem-solving."

In much problem-solving, *emotions reign over reason…passion rules over principle.* We are basically *emotional people* rather than *rational people,* as we saw in an earlier chapter on the *passion of leadership.* We must remember that every person on earth tends to *lead with his heart* rather than *lead with his head.* Nothing confirms this fact more quickly than the issue of *problem-solving!* We first begin to "solve the problem" in the privacy of our thoughts before we seek to deal with it publicly and organizationally. The more we "mull over the problem" in our thoughts, the more our emotions tend to become involved. The problem gets all wrapped up in our feelings. We begin to mentally work out our "plan of attack." We *rehearse it* and *nurse it.* In the process, an "us" versus "them" dichotomy develops. We justify and defend the "rightness" of our position – while attacking the "wrongness" of their position. The problem is increasingly thought of in terms of "right versus wrong," and "win versus lose." When that thinking takes over – everyone is wrong, and everyone loses! We increasingly secure our mental arguments with the passions of the heart. All the while we are seeking the vulnerability of the "other side." When the time of confrontation comes, the issues have already been "blown far out of proportion." Perspectives are lost. Objectivity looses out to subjectivity. Emotions quickly heat up the confrontation and conversation. *Feelings are hurt.* Rather than *attacking the problem,* the *people are attacked!* The *real issues* are seldom discussed and "the baby is thrown out with the dirty wash water!" The person, or people, associated with the problem are destroyed along with the problem. Because *leadership is about people,* we must do everything possible to *salvage the person* while *solving the problem!*

Principle:
"Effective leadership seeks to salvage the person while solving the problem."

When you study the life of the Lord Jesus, you see that the majority of His time was also focused on *people-problem-solving.* He did not have problems with inanimate objects...with nature...or with animals. The physical realm and the world of nature are locked into obedience through *natural law* and *animal instincts.* It is only *man* and his rebellious free will that is the problem! Therefore, Christ's only problem was with people – or with the evil spirits who sometimes inhabit and possess people. Everywhere Christ went He was solving *people problems* – whether they were of the spirit, soul or body. When He was not dealing with the myriad of problems represented by the masses of people who were drawn to Him, He was trying to solve the interpersonal problems between His disciples. Ultimately, His death was to solve the greatest human problem of all – *sin.*

Problem-solving and *conflict resolution* are two of the greatest challenges of leadership. There are many personality types who do not like to face problems. They do not like to deal with conflict. Unfortunately, many leaders fall into this category. I have often heard Christian leaders say: *"I just don't like dealing with conflict."* As a result of that attitude, they either ignore the problem – or run away from it. All the while, it only worsens. If the person at the top will not deal with the problem, someone else around them will have to "face the music" of the problem that the leader refuses to face. In his book, *The Other Side of Leadership,* Eugene Habecker, writes:

> *Confrontation is one of the least glamorous and most difficult facets of leadership. It is, however, one of leadership's most necessary and important responsibilities. Failure to confront produces negative results for both persons and the organization. Only as the art of confrontation is carried out under the divine leadership of the Holy Spirit will the kind of personal and organizational results desired by leaders be accomplished.[5]*

Leaders that last learn how to successfully face problems. They become successful *trouble-shooters.* Rather than *running away* from the problem, they *run toward* the problem. They square off with the problem and face it "nose to nose" – and *the quicker the better.* The problem may be a relatively small one that can be dealt with rather easily if it is confronted quickly so it will not have time to grow and multiply. Or, the problem may be a Goliath-size one like young David faced. In either case, the key is *decisiveness.* In spite of the great odds that were against him in the person of Goliath, **"David *ran quickly* toward the battle line to meet him"** (I Sam. 17:48). Even though King Saul hid in his royal tent, and all of the other seasoned soldiers were cowering in fear before the seemingly unconquerable giant, young David fearlessly *ran toward him.* Because David knew his source of strength in the Lord, he defeated the giant Goliath with a single stone. As the old expression goes: *"The bigger they are, the harder they fall!"* Down came Goliath with a reverberating thud! Then David decapitated Goliath with the giant's own sword! David "cut off the head" of his enemy. This reminds us that problems that have had their heads chopped off no longer pose a threat! As a result of David's victory, great courage and encouragement immediately spread to all of Israel. This story of David reminds us that once a leader, like King Saul, begins to run and hide from problems, his leadership is effectively over. Whoever solves the problem that the supposed leader would not face – becomes the real leader! Even though King Saul continued to hold the *position* of King, David now had the *power* of leadership.

In any situation, look for the person who faces and solves the problems – and you will be looking at the real leader of that group, movement, organization, or church. Problems have to be squarely faced – whether they are large or small. Whoever is the major problem-solver is the *real leader.*

Today our world is becoming more and more complex. The problems are also more complex. Like it or not, our world has become a *global village* wired together through the instantaneous communications of Fax machines, e-mails, the Internet, and cell phones! Crises happen more quickly...problems are more widely known...the people involved are more diverse...the issues are more complex...and the ramifications are more far-reaching. J. Oswald Sanders said this about leadership in our world today:

Our own day presents leaders with difficult problems as never before. If leaders are to survive, they must view the difficult as commonplace, the complex as normal.[6]

Sanders also deals with the seemingly *impossible problems* that every leader faces. He quotes John R. Mott who said that these kinds of "big problems" are the issues that really separate leaders from followers. The bigger the problem, the bigger the leader must be who faces and solves the problem. Mott said: *"I long since ceased to occupy myself with minor things that can be done by others. A true leader rises to face battling circumstances and complex problems."*[7]

Principle:
"You can measure a leader by the problems he tackles. He always looks for ones his own size."[8]
(John Maxwell)

Not only do problems have to be faced and overcome, the *right problem* has to be identified, analyzed, and excised. Many people, including many young leaders, *identify the wrong problem.* They focus on the wrong issues. They put their spiritual emphasis on the wrong theological syllable. They draw the battle lines in the wrong places. They zealously lead their followers into war – but to fight the wrong enemy. They misdirect a lot of energy and effort jousting with windmills. They spill a lot of innocent blood needlessly. Their followers often experience unnecessary "battle fatigue" from *conflicts with little eternal consequences.* At the end of the day, there are a lot of spiritual and emotional fatalities where there should not have been any. That's because the *cause was unworthy of the cost!* The *causalities* were of more value than the *cause!* So many of the battles within the church should never have been fought in the first place, like the Crusades. Too often Christians get focused on the wrong problems. In their spiritual confusion and distorted priorities, they make their brothers and sisters the enemy when they have a common enemy in the devil!

Concerning the importance of identifying the right problem and fighting the right enemy, Fred Smith writes:

Great leaders have known the power of uniting against a common enemy. The enemy must be defined vividly, urgently, and must be current. America was united against Russian communism. Ever since the collapse of the USSR, the United States has been casting about for a new unifying enemy, with limited success. Christian leaders are fortunate in having a common enemy, but too often we direct our shots not in his direction but toward others. Our eternal enemy is Satan.[9]

Effective leadership is based upon wise problem-solving – of the *right problem!* Both secular and Biblical histories reveal that far too many people get side-tracked by dealing with "fruit problems" rather than with "root problems." In other words, they waste a lot of time, energy and effort dealing with the *effect* rather than with the *cause*. There is an inviolate principle in both the natural and spiritual world that says: *"The root determines the fruit."* When you have a *fruit problem* you usually have a *root problem*. The *root* is the *cause*, while the *fruit* is the *effect*. You don't solve the "fruit problem" by just *picking the fruit*. That's superficial problem-solving with few lasting results. You must deal with the *root that is producing the fruit*. Only then will you lastingly solve the problem. The person who can most quickly spot a "fruit and root problem" is an agronomist – not an auto mechanic! In others words, when a leader gets far afield from his natural and spiritual giftedness, his discernment will become less and less trustworthy. John Maxwell has a helpful insight along these lines:

> *If you can see the root issue of a problem, you can solve it. The closer a leader is to his area of gifting, the stronger his intuition and ability to see root causes. If you want to tap into your discernment potential, work in your areas of strength.*[10]

It is only the wisdom of God's Word and the discernment of the Holy Spirit – coupled with a commitment to one's giftedness – that can keep a leader focused on the right problems. As Herman Cain rightly summarized: "To lead is to define the *right problem, ask the right questions, select the right alternative,* and *achieve the desired results.*"[11]

Principle:
"The most important step in solving a problem is making sure you are working on the right problem."[12]
(Herman Cain)

Finally, after a leader has successfully led his people to victory over a problem, he needs to lead them in a *time of celebration*. (A leadership lesson I am still learning!). So often leaders are off to the next battlefront before they have taken time to regroup and celebrate with their people the victory from the last battle. They are ready to take on a new and bigger problem before pausing to celebrate their corporate success over the last one. Leaders often become addicted to the "blood and guts" of battle. Their leadership style is summarized by General Patton who exclaimed: *"War is hell – but I love it!"* These kinds of leaders live off a constant "adrenaline high." They are like adventurers and thrill seekers – always trying to find a *new thrill* with a *higher high!* However, God did not create us with the spiritual, mental, emotional, or physical ability to always be tense and taut. We were not meant to be always "psyched-up up for battle." A muscle cannot perpetually be flexed. The emotions cannot always be high. The adrenaline cannot continuously flow. The shield and armor must be laid aside for a time. The battle bow must be periodically unstrung – or constant tension will destroy its strength. The sword must be sharpened and put back into its sheath for a season. Wounds must be given time to heal. Depleted emotions must be restored. Physical rest must come – or battle fatigue will deplete the ranks.

Problem-solving can be very fatiguing – spiritually, mentally, emotionally, physically – and organizationally. God set the perfect example when **"...He rested from all the work of creating that He had done"** (Gen. 1:3). Just as He set aside one day a week as His **"Sabbath rest"** (Ex. 20:8), He instructed us to keep it as holy unto Him.

We can see Jesus teaching the importance of rest in the lives of the leaders He was mentoring. After He sent the Twelve out to preach, heal the sick, and drive out demons, He took them away for a time of "R & R," or *rest* and *relaxation*. During that intense time of ministry, they had given much of themselves spiritually, emotionally and physically. After their return, Jesus called them to Himself for a time of reporting and celebrating. The Bible records that they "returned with joy" and excitedly reported to Jesus: "Lord, even the demons submit to us in Your name," they exclaimed! That's *real* problem-solving based upon deliverance from the demonic realm! Jesus explained the full significance of their victory:

"I saw Satan fall like lightning from heaven…However, do not rejoice that the spirits submit to you, but *rejoice* that your names are written in heaven."

We read that Jesus rejoiced and celebrated with them:

"Jesus, *full of joy* through the Holy Spirit, said, 'I praise You, Father, Lord of heaven and earth, because You have hidden these things from the wise and learned, and revealed them to little children. Yes, Father, for this was Your good pleasure'…Then He turned to His disciples and said privately, 'Blessed are the eyes that see what you see. For I tell you that many prophets and kings wanted to see what you see but did not see it, and to hear what you hear but did not hear it" (Lk. 10:17-24).

After Jesus had fully entered into their joy, and celebrated their victories with them, He said to them:

"Come with Me by yourselves to a *quiet place* and *get some rest.*" So they went away by themselves in a boat to a *solitary place*" (Mk. 6:31-32).

The Authorized Version translates this verse as follows: "Come ye yourselves apart…and *rest a while…*" Paraphrasing this verse, the prince of preachers, Vance Havner humorously said: *"If we do not come apart and rest awhile – we will soon just come apart!"* There is a lot of truth in that wise observation!

Jesus sent His disciples out to face some incredible "people problems." Some were physical. Some emotional. All were in some way spiritual. But through His shared authority, coupled with the power of His Holy Spirit, all problems were successfully faced…all needs were met…each sickness was healed…and all demons were exorcised. After that intense time of spiritual warfare, Jesus *processed* the *problem-solving* with His disciples. After a time of doing that, He led them in a time of *praise* and *thanksgiving.*

It is highly important for a wise spiritual leader to lead his people in *problem solving*, *processing*, and *praise.* Harvard Business School's John Kotter, wisely points out:

These little wins offer an opportunity to relax for a few minutes and celebrate. Constant tension for long periods of time is not healthy for people. The little celebration following a win can be good for the body and spirit.[13]

May God make each of us leaders good *problem-solvers*. But in the process, we need to also learn to be leaders who help our people *process* the experience – and then *celebrate* with them the victory!

FURTHER QUOTATIONS ABOUT
PROBLEM-SOLVING LEADERS

1. PROBLEMS:

- Anytime we think the problem is "out there," that thought is the problem. *We empower what's "out there" to control us. The change paradigm is "outside-in" — what's out there has to change before we can change. The proactive approach is to change from the inside out.*[14]

- *The problems we face fall in one of three areas:* direct control *(problems involving our own behavior);* indirect control *(problems involving other people's behavior);* or no control *(problems we can do nothing about, such as our past or situational realities).*[15]

- *So often the problem is in the* system, *not in the people. If you put good people in bad systems, you get bad results. You have to water the flowers you want to grow.*[16]

- *If the person is in the wrong job for whatever reason, then removing the barrier means removing the person from the job...I learned from Peter Drucker that if you have a 'people problem,' then fix it immediately. There is obviously a compassionate way to achieve this, but procrastinating on the action — once you are convinced you have identified the person as the barrier to their own success — is not fair to the organization or to the individual.*[17]

- THERE IS NO JOY IN EASY SAILING:

    There is no thrill in easy sailing
      when the skies are clear and blue.
    There is no joy in merely doing
      things which anyone can do.
    But there is some satisfaction
      that is mighty sweet to take;
    When you reach a destination
      that you thought you'd never make![18]

                                        (Spirella)

- *A leader can give up anything – except final responsibility.* [19]

- *Look at the word* responsibility *– "response-ability" – the ability to choose your response. Highly proactive people recognize that responsibility. They do not blame circumstances, conditions or conditioning for their behavior. The behavior is a product of their own conscious choice, based on values, rather than a product of their conditions, based on feeling...* [20]

- *...***"We want a king over us. Then we will be like all the other nations, with a king to lead us and to go out before us and fight our battles."*** *(1 Samuel 8:19-20)...Not wanting to bear their share of responsibility for the future of their children, they sought a king to do all the thinking and planning and fighting for them. They didn't want a leader to ask them what they thought, to inspire sacrifice and commitment in them, or to expect participation and creativity from the ranks. They wanted a magical leader to usher in an age of fantasy, not one of purpose and achievement. And for this, they were prepared to offer themselves and their children upon his altar...* [21]

- *Anytime we think the problem is "out there"* that thought is *the problem.* [22]

- *Decision-making and problem solving go hand in hand. The ability to make good decisions and solve problems effectively is among the most important skills a leader or manager can acquire.* [23]

- *Throughout human history the improper handling of conflicts has destroyed marriages and friendships, dissolved business partnerships and corporations, caused the downfall of great leaders and political empires, and sparked wars.*

  It is clear then, that conflict is a potentially dangerous phenomenon capable of destroying the effectiveness of any organization or leader. Scripture vividly describes the destructive potential of conflict. ***"If you keep on biting and devouring each other, watch out or you will be destroyed by each other"*** *(Gal. 5:15).* [24]

- Conflict creates divisions within the organization. *Unresolved conflict is the cause of every church split, labor strike, and divorce. Jesus said,* ***"Every kingdom divided against itself will be ruined,*** *and every city or household divided against itself will not stand'* (*Matt. 12:25*).[25]

- *We should never procrastinate in dealing with a conflict. As long as conflict exists we are harboring hostility toward others. This violates the Scriptures which tell us,* **"If you are angry, don't sin by nursing your grudge. Don't let the sun go down with you still angry – get over it quickly; for when you are angry you give a mighty foothold to the devil"** *(Eph. 4:26-27 LB).* [26]

- *Always keep in mind that conflict provides an excellent opportunity to serve those involved in the problem. And be committed to resolving the conflict quickly. The longer the conflict drags on, the more difficult it is to develop satisfactory solutions. Also, take the initiative in confronting those involved; don't wait for them to come to you. And finally, keep your emotions under control. Remember, hostility is always present in conflict. The more hostility you display, the more angry and hostile the others involved will become.* [27]

2. CONFRONTATION:

- *Afraid to confront the problem, we convince ourselves that Jerry isn't so bad or that we can maneuver around him. So we move on only to curse ourselves later for not dealing with the issue. In this kind of situation remember the following:* Personnel problems that can be ignored during easy times can cause serious trouble in a tougher, faster-moving, globalizing economy. [28]

- *A change agent is…one with the courage…to face the music today so there may be singing tomorrow. He speaks out against our inertia-driven methodologies and politically-minded priorities. She explains, persuades, and cajoles, unafraid to be challenged in return or to commit herself to the mandates of her own program.*[29]

- *When a difficult situation required his attention, he dipped his pen in tears, not acid.* **"For I wrote to you out of great distress and anguish of heart"** *(2 Corinthians 2:4)…*[30]

- *Discipline is yet another responsibility of the leader, a duty often unwelcome. Any Christian society requires godly and loving discipline* *to maintain divine standards in doctrine, morals, and conduct...*The fundamental ingredient in all discipline is love...[31]

- *Whoever is under a leader's direction should be under his protection...*[32]

3. DECISIVENESS:

- *It is not what others do or even our own mistakes that hurt us the most; it is our response to those things. Chasing after the poisonous snake that bites us will only drive the poison through our entire system. It is far better to take measures immediately to get the poison out...Our response to any mistake affects the quality of the next moment. It is important to immediately admit and correct our mistakes so that they have no power over the next moment and we are empowered again.*[33]

4. CELEBRATION:

- *Short-term performance improvements help transformations...They show people that the sacrifices are paying off, that they are getting stronger...these little wins offer an opportunity to relax for a few minutes and celebrate. Constant tension for long periods of time is not healthy for people. The little celebration following a win can be good for the body and spirit...*[34]

5. REST:

- *As Elijah waited on the Lord, he observed, in order, a mighty wind, an earthquake, a fire, and then a gentle whisper. God was not in any of the first three but He apparently was in the fourth (verses 11-12). And out of the gentle whisper Elijah heard anew the voice of God along with instructions for his continued service. Solitude, holy stillness, in the presence of the Lord. This was critical to the process used by God for Elijah's restoration. For leaders and others it still is...*[35]

- *During a class at Regent College on the Book of Mark, Professor Michael Green was discussing Mark 6:30-32, verses dealing with the disciples' return after having been sent out by Jesus:*

The apostles gathered around Jesus and reported to Him all they had done and taught. Then, because so many people were coming and going that they did not even have a chance to eat, He said to them, 'Come with Me by yourselves to a quiet place and get some rest.' So they went away by themselves in a boat to a solitary place.

Professor Green noted that in these three verses we are given insight on how we can avoid burnout. First, the disciples told Jesus everything, something Jesus still desires of us. Then, we see shared leadership. Not only did Jesus share His load, but He sent them out by twos. And third, when the pace got too hectic, He took them to a solitary place – away from the people – to get some rest.

God desires workers and leaders who are personally refreshed and renewed...[36]

Chapter 10

LEADERS ARE PROMOTERS

"There is no need for me to write to you about this service to the saints. For I know your eagerness to help, and I have been boasting about it to the Macedonians, telling them that since last year you in Achaia were ready to give; and your enthusiasm has stirred most of them to action. But I am sending the brothers in order that our boasting about you in this matter should not prove hollow, but that you may be ready, as I said you would be. For if any Macedonians come with me and find you unprepared, we – not to say anything about you – would be ashamed of having been so confident. So I thought it necessary to urge the brothers to visit you in advance and finish the arrangements for the generous gift you had promised. Then it will be ready as a generous gift, not as one grudgingly given"
(II Cor. 9:1-5).

A good leader must not only exemplify attributes and attitudes like being *purposeful, positive,* and *passionate;* he must also be a good *promoter.* If the leader's purpose is positive, it is worthy of promoting so others can become involved in it. An effective leader understands that people are looking for worthy causes in which to invest their time, talent and treasures. A leader blesses and dignifies other people's lives by involving them in a noble cause. Not to promote a worthy cause among people is to allow them to settle down to a lower and less noble life. It is to rob them of the joy and satisfaction of giving themselves to something that is greater than they. In spite of the innate sinfulness and selfishness of mankind, everyone has a deep inner call of the spirit to *altruism* – an unselfish concern for others. A wise spiritual leader knows that it is only this kind of involvement in the needs of others that brings lasting happiness and contentment in life. Both Jesus and the Apostle Paul were constantly calling people to that kind of other-oriented life-style. They promoted the spiritual and physical needs of other people to the degree that it called their followers out of being consumed with their own needs. Neither Jesus nor Paul ever hesitated to promote legitimate needs – and call others to involvement in those needs.

In the above verses we can clearly see that the Apostle Paul had learned how to *promote* a worthy cause which was very near and dear to his heart – *collecting money for the needy saints in Jerusalem* (Acts 11:29; 24:17; Rom. 15:25-28, 31; I Cor. 16:1, etc). In doing this, Paul sent both *letters* and *people* in advance of his coming to promote his cause. In asking for money, Paul did so positively and unashamedly – because he knew he was asking for a worthy cause. He was not asking money for himself, but for others in need. He expressed to the Corinthian Christians about his **"confidence in them,"** and about their **"eagerness"** to give. When he talked about the size of their gift, he did not speak in small terms. Since the need he was promoting was great he had high expectations for them and communicated that! He wrote to them about their promised "generous gift." Paul knew how to promote a cause by building a positive attitude and high expectation in the mind of the donor.

Without this ability to promote his cause, a leader will not be a good *motivator.* If he does not have a positive mind-set about asking for resources, he will not be able to build that attitude in others who have the ability – and need – to give. If the leader is hesitant, tenuous, and apologetic in promoting his cause, others will not be moved. If he is not *positive* and *passionate* in his *promotion,* then other *people will not be activated* – and *resources will not be allocated.* It is the leader's promotion of a cause that causes both human and financial resources to be galvanized into action. Effective leaders must be able to *positively* and *passionately promote* their *purpose* to others. Effective leaders are almost always very *persuasive people.* It is only because they are fully persuaded in their own hearts that they are able to fully persuade others. Without this *gift of persuasion,* they would not have anyone believing in them…following them…supporting them…giving to them – even sacrificing for them! Effective leaders have an ability to enlist others in their cause. Through effective promotion, they are able to co-opt others into their vision to the degree that their cause is not a "one man show." Leaders are able to *gain* and *sustain* the confidence, loyalty, and affection of those whom they lead.

Principle:
"Before a leader can fully persuade others; he must first be fully persuaded himself."

It is also important to remember that all *promotion* by a leader is for some particular purpose. It is impossible to promote something that is vague...nebulous...ethereal...surreal. There must be some tangible and specific cause. Some *particular purpose to promote.* All leaders then have a *cause celebre*, or a *celebrated cause*, as the French language calls it. It is this *cause* to which they want others to commit. It is the cause that challenges others to some course of action. John Maxwell reminds leaders:

> *As you communicate, never forget that the goal of all communication is* action. *If you dump a bunch of information on people, you're not communicating. Every time you speak to people, give them* something to feel, something to remember, and something to do.[1]

If leaders cannot *articulate* and *communicate* their vision to others, people will not follow! It's that simple. As Paul said: **"...if the trumpet does not sound a *clear call*, who will get ready for battle?"** (I Cor. 14:8). An effective leader must be like a good bugler in the military – he must sound a *clear call.* If his bugle call is not clear, the soldiers will not know whether he has given the sound for *charge* – or *retreat!* There's a BIG difference between the two! A good leader must have his purpose clear in his own mind before he can effectively articulate it and communicate it to others. *Leadership* and *communication* can never be separated from each other. *Effective leadership is based upon effective communication.* Simply put, *"a person who can't communicate – can't lead."* Every leader must always be striving to be a more effective communicator – whether through speaking...through body language...through letters...through phone calls...through e-mails...through the Internet – through any and every communication medium available to him. The whole subject of *communication* is a major study unto itself, which is not the primary theme of this book. There are some helpful quotes at the end of this chapter about the importance of communication in the life of a leader.

Principle:

"Effective leadership is based upon effective communication. A person who can't communicate, can't lead."

There must be a *positive* and *passionate presentation of the purpose* by the leader. The more persuasive it is, the easier it is to promote with others. An effective leader is always aware that it often takes *positive, passionate –* and *persistent – persuasion* to prod and provoke people into action. Sedate and sedentary human inertia is not easily overcome! Many people are like frozen ice cubes that have become crystallized and solidified. Or they are like water contained and confined in a glass. Just like a liquid always runs down to the lowest level, human nature almost always settles down to the lowest level of living! Only when it is "heated up" will it "move up!" It is only when H_2O is heated that it is transformed from a *solid to a liquid.* Then when it is boiled, it will be transformed from a *liquid to a gas.* Only when it is changed into *steam* will it permeate its surroundings. Like frozen ice, or confined water, people naturally stay within their "comfort zones" unless something or someone "heats them up" with a passionate vision! Mustering and motivating mankind is always one of the perennial challenges of leadership. Fred Smith explains and illustrates this motivational issue as follows:

> *Everyone is motivated...Those who are doing nothing are motivated to do nothing. Those who are active are motivated to be active. To motivate people who are motivated to do nothing, we have to overcome the first motivation in order to get them in a forward movement. I was told by a corporate president who manufactured railroad engines that the biggest problem was harnessing enough power to start the train rolling. Aircraft designers have to build enough power into plane engines to break the pull of gravity before they can power the flight itself. As leaders we need to recognize that inertia is a motivation, not simply the lack of it.[2]*

We can see that *everyone is motivated.* However, everyone is not *positively motivated.* Far too many people are *negatively motivated* – to do as little as possible in life! It is the call and challenge of leadership to arouse people out of their apathy and lethargy through the promotion of a great cause.

They must be *provoked into action* by a *clear, compelling, clarion call.* For the purpose to be *compelling,* it must first of all be *clear.* It is often very important and helpful for a leader to reduce his purpose or cause to a clear, succinct *mission statement.* Be well assured: "If the purpose is not *crystal clear* to the leader, it will be *cloudy* and *confusing* to the followers!" As John Maxwell says: *"Educators take something simple and make it complicated. Communicators take something complicated and make it simple."* [3]

Principle:
"Effective leadership is based upon a positive, passionate, persuasive – and persistent – promotion of the purpose."

The vision and goals of the leader must be *precise* and *concise* if they are to be effectively transmitted to others. Secular advertisers have learned the importance of this as demonstrated by their simple, catchy slogans – often set to music – that promote their products. Even young children learn to recognize the product logos and sing the promotional jingles at a very early age. The more clear and concise the purpose or mission statement, the easier it can be transmitted to others.

A good leader must be a *positive promoter* of the vision in his own heart and mind. The more positive the promotion of his purpose, the greater will be the power and persuasion of his leadership.

Principle:
"The more precise and positive the promotion, the more powerful and popular the purpose."

When it comes to *promotion,* balanced Biblical leaders understand this principle: *"Promotion cannot be separated from possessions."* In other words, *it takes possessions to do promotion.* We saw above that the Apostle Paul was never ashamed to ask for funds for a worthy cause. *Effective leaders must become effective generators of resources.* Without resources, leaders cannot accomplish their goals. It takes *goods* to reach *goals.* It requires *resources* to achieve *results.* It is impossible to separate *money* from *ministry.* It takes *possessions* to *promote the purposes of God* and prosperity to meet the needs of the *people of God.*

Principle:
"**Promotion cannot be separated from possessions. Money cannot be separated from ministry. It takes goods to reach goals; resources to achieve results. There must be possessions to promote the purposes of God, and prosperity to meet the needs of the people of God.**"

It is very unfortunate that so many leaders find this whole matter of "raising money" distasteful. That is partly because they have so often seen fund-raising abused by unscrupulous charlatans! However, a leader will never be effective for God until they work through this *negative mental barrier concerning money and materialism.* Nor will they ever meet a lot of real spiritual and physical needs without some resources. It certainly does not take money to meet every human need – because the most basic needs of mankind are spiritual, emotional, and relational by nature. To feed hungry stomachs…clothe naked bodies…house the homeless…heal the sick – there must be resources raised. It takes money to evangelize the lost…send out missionaries…train national pastors…print Bibles… transmit Christian radio and television…build local churches…equip the body of Christ. Effective Christian leaders MUST become *generators of resources.* They must become effective in the *promotion* of the need to the degree that *possessions are produced and provided for the Kingdom of God.* Leaders must be able to inspire God's people to *release resources* and *redeem riches* for the glory of God. They must be able to unashamedly inspire people to become *Kingdom investors!*

Principle:
"**Kingdom leaders inspire Kingdom investors who redeem riches and release resources for the Kingdom of God.**"

Christian leaders have come to understand from the Bible that calling people to invest in God's work is not *taking from them* – but rather *giving to them*. The Bible promotes a *lifestyle of giving* because we serve and follow a *giving God!* We *give to others* because *God first gave to us*. When people become *Kingdom investors*, they are storing up *eternal dividends*. They are investing where God is investing. *To call people to give is one of the greatest favors you can do for them*. No one will ever stand before God in judgment and lament the fact that they *gave too much!* Their only *eternal regret* will be that *they did not give more to the cause of Christ!* They will clearly see that the only thing they did of *eternal significance* was to invest in God's Kingdom. All else will be reduced to *ashes* in the fires of God's judgment (I Cor. 3:10-15). By calling people to invest their lives and resources in a Kingdom cause is to *secure their eternal reward*. You are calling them to *give away what they can never lose!* As the young missionary martyr, Jim Elliot, said: *"He is no fool who gives up what he cannot keep in order to gain what he cannot lose!"*

If people become offended or "turned off" by *legitimate appeals* to meet *legitimate needs* in *legitimate ways*, it only reveals something about them rather than something about the leader! Defensiveness about possessions shows that a person does not have God's perspective on resources and riches. It shows that their orientation is toward self, rather than toward God – and toward others. It also reveals that they have a faulty, earth-bound, temporal view of possessions. That possessive attitude shows that *their possessions have possessed them*. In reality, it *reveals their heart* – because Jesus clearly taught: **"Where your *treasure* is, there will your *heart* be also"** (Matt. 6:21). God calls Christian leaders to help others have a *change of heart* about possessions. To help them become *investors* of resources for His glory and others' good – and turn them from being *inverters* of resources for selfish living! God wants Christian leaders to help people move their *treasure chests from earth to heaven* – by investing in things that are *eternally significant*.

In his excellent book, *Lead On*, John Haggai contrasts these two diverse and divergent views of resources and riches this way:

> *To many people*, giving *means a reduction in the giver's net worth. Such people have a* scarcity mentality. *That is not a proper understanding of giving because giving is investment. The term* investment *carries*

the idea of increasing the investor's net worth. Those who understand this have an abundance mentality. They understand that the more they give away in time, money, or encouragement, the more they will receive back of time, money, or encouragement.[4]

Haggai goes on to make a statement that shocks many people:

> The motivation for giving (or investing), therefore, is self-interest, a motive not only commended by Jesus, but the only motive He ever used in the Scriptures...Investment is the ultimate path to permanent gain. Every command and promise that Jesus made was based on the assumption of self-interest – that obeying the command would benefit the individual. The principle of investment is so powerful because it has built into it the motivation of legitimate self-interest of the individual. 'Give and it will be given to you.' Everyone wins.[5]

Haggai contrasts the *investors* with the *inverters* by saying:

> Too often giving which is seen as reducing the giver's net worth is motivated by charity, sentiment, peer pressure, recognition, and even guilt. Such motivation never *sustains meaningful philanthropy...* there are just two kinds of people who make up the world: the investors and the takers. By their nature the investors practice the principle of investment; the takers are the one who do not see giving as an investment and so try to hoard whatever they have. Ultimately, the investors win and the takers lose.[6]

In his summary of this whole matter of giving, Haggai calls a person's giving level their "IQ," or their *investment quotient*. Whereas a leader may not be able to increase a person's *intelligence quotient*, he can increase their *investment quotient* through the promotion of giving to worthy causes. Haggai concludes by saying:

> The effective leader devotes his life to bringing his group into the joy of giving. He leads by his own example. His life demonstrates to his group the validity of self-interest as the motive to which Christ appealed. The leader will bring honor to God, benefit to the world, blessing to his people, and enrichment to his own life to the degree that he is successful in moving his people to the habit of perennial investment through the motive of self-interest.[7]

Christian leaders are not embarrassed or timid about the *promotion of giving.* Why? Because they understand that *Jesus was not timid about the promotion of giving.* They understand this principle given by Christ:

> **"Give, and it will be given to you.** A good measure, pressed down, shaken together, and running over, will be poured into your lap. For with the measure you use, it will be measured to you"** (Lk. 6:38).

The Apostle Paul understood this same principle, and promoted it among the early churches. He first stated the negative side of the giving equation: **"Whoever *sows sparingly,"*** wrote Paul, **"will also *reap sparingly."*** He concluded the principle with the positive statement: **"And whoever *sows bountifully* will so *reap bountifully"*** (II Cor. 9:6).

This Biblical principle of *"sowing and reaping"* is an *absolutely inviolate life principle!* As such, it relates not only to money – but to every other area of life! It is this *principle of investment* that assures us that *whatever we give will some day – in some way – come back to us.* Whether in this life or the next – whatever we invest for Christ will result in *eternal dividends.* What better way to summarize this discussion than with the little phrase that almost every Christian has seen or heard: *"Only one life t'will soon be passed; only what's done for Christ will last!"*

FURTHER QUOTATIONS ON PROMOTION IN LEADERSHIP

1. PROMOTION:

- *...you only get one chance to make a first impression...*[8]

2. COMMUNICATION:

- *Developing excellent communication skills is absolutely essential to effective leadership. The leader must be able to share knowledge and ideas to transmit a sense of urgency and enthusiasm to others. If a leader can't get a message across clearly and motivate others to act on it, then having a message doesn't even matter.*[9] (Gilbert Amelio, President and CEO of National Semiconductor Corp.)

- *Keep it simple...The time and energy required for effective vision communications are directly related to the clarity and simplicity of the message. Focused, jargon-free information can be disseminated to large groups of people at a fraction of the cost of clumsy, complicated communication. Techno-babble and MBA-speak just get in the way, creating confusion, suspicion and alienation. Communication seems to work best when it is so direct and so simple that it has a sort of elegance. The challenge of simple and direct communication is that it requires great clarity of thought...It is much harder to be clear and concise than over-complicated and wordy.*[10]

- *Even a desirable, focused, and feasible description of the future is useless if it is so complex that communicating it to large numbers of people is impossible. The point here is not to take a good idea and 'dumb it down.' But...communicating even a simple vision to a large number of people can be enormously difficult. Simplicity is essential.*[11]

- *Repeat, repeat, repeat! The most carefully crafted messages rarely sink deeply into the recipient's consciousness after only one pronouncement. Our minds are too cluttered, and any communication has to fight hundreds of other ideas for attention....As a result, effective information transferal almost always relies on repetition...All successful cases of major change seem to include tens of thousands of communications that help employees to grapple with difficult intellectual and emotional issues...collectively, these can add up to a massive amount of useful communication, which is generally what is needed to win over both hearts and minds.*[12]

- *...recent studies conducted by Management Training Systems with numerous organizations – both Christian and secular – indicated that poor communication was their number one leadership and management problem...Communication can be defined as* the process we go through to convey understanding from one person or group to another. *Unless understanding occurs, we have not communicated... Jesus knew the importance of communication and He worked hard to make sure understanding occurred between Him and His disciples. After sharing several parables with them Jesus asked, "**Have you understood all these things?**"(Matt. 13:51) Jesus recognized that unless understanding occurred He was not communicating, regardless of how much preaching or lecturing He did...*[13]

- *...every good leader is a good communicator. He has the ability to convey understanding to others. Good communication develops and maintains unity, commitment, and motivation in achieving a goal. In fact, communication is the lifeblood of an organization; without it the group dies.*[14]

- Communication is the most important skill in life. We spend most of our waking hours communicating. But consider this: You've spent years learning how to read and write, years learning how to speak. But what about listening? What training or education have you had that enables you to listen so that you really, deeply understand another human being from that individual's own frame of reference? Comparatively few people have had any training in listening at all...[15]

3. MOTIVATION:

- *The early Greeks had a magnificent philosophy, which is embodied in three sequentially arranged words:* ethos, pathos, *and* logos. *I suggest these three words contain the essence of seeking first to understand and making effective presentations.* Ethos *is your personal credibility, the faith people have in your integrity and competency. It's the trust that you inspire, your Emotional Bank Account.* Pathos *is the emphatic side – it's the feeling. It means that you are in alignment with the emotional thrust of another person's communication.* Logos *is the logic, the reasoning part of the presentation. Notice the sequence:* ethos, pathos, logos *– your character, and your relationships, and then the logic of your presentation. This represents another major paradigm shift. Most people, in making presentations, go straight to the* logos, *the left-brain logic, of their ideas. They try to convince other people of the validity of that logic without first taking* ethos *and* pathos *into consideration.*[16]

- *"The difference in a good organization and a bad organization is structure. There must be structure. But the difference in a good organization and a great organization is motivation." (Fred Smith)*[17]

- *The key to motivation is motive. It's the* why. *It's the deeper "yes!" burning inside that makes it easier to say "no" to the less important.*[18]

- *... management thinker Peter Drucker...*"You can't motivate people; you can only thwart their motivation because people motivate themselves."*...even though you can't motivate people as a leader, you must identify and remove the barriers to self-motivation...High self-motivation...is not a characteristic that everyone possesses. This is why I consider it a* critical *quality for a leader because without it, and without being able to recognize it in other people, one cannot lead anybody anywhere...*[19]

- *"I have yet to find the man, however exalted his station, who did not do better work and put forth greater effort under a spirit of approval, than under a spirit of criticism." – Charles Schwab, Industrialist.* [20]

- *Without involvement, there is no commitment. Mark it down, asterisk it, circle it, underline it.* No involvement, no commitment. [21]

4. POSSESSIONS & GIVING:

- *"No person was ever honored for what he received. Honor has been the reward for what he gave." (Calvin Coolidge, American President)*[22]

- *Giving is the highest level of living.*[23]

- *Writer John Bunyan affirmed, "You have not lived today until you have done something for someone who can never repay you."*[24]

~~~~~~~~~~~~~~~~~~~~~~~~~~~~~~

Chapter 11

LEADERS ARE PACE-SETTERS

"Jesus...went on ahead, going up to Jerusalem"
(Luke 19:28).

In this succinct verse we can see a summary of this leadership principle in the life of Christ. Jesus was always *ahead of* His disciples. In *taking the lead*, Jesus was not trying to distance Himself from them – He was just *out in front* giving directive leadership. Like a wise shepherd, a good leader must always be out in the front of the flock *leading* – not in the back *driving* the herd.

Effective leaders are like the *lead runner* in a marathon, or the *pace car* in a stock car race, they *set the pace* for others to follow. In the ecclesiastical realm, they are not *pew sitters* – but *pace setters!* As John Piper rightly observes:

> *Spiritual leaders have a holy discontentment with the status quo. Non-leaders have inertia that causes them to settle in and makes them very hard to move off dead center. However, leaders have a hankering to change, to move, to reach out, to grow, and to take a group or an institution to new dimensions of ministry.*[1]

A "divine discontent" is a characteristic of authentic spiritual leaders. They always have an inherent spiritual hunger and thirst. They have a "holy dissatisfaction" in their spirit that urges them onward, outward and upward. John R.W. Stott described this vision-producing *creative dissatisfaction* this way:

> *So what is vision? It is an act of seeing...an imaginative perception of things, combining insight and foresight...it is compounded by a* deep dissatisfaction *with what is and a clear grasp of what could be. It begins with indignation over the status quo, and it grows into the earnest quest for an alternative.*[2]

The same principle of "driving dissatisfaction" is just as true in the secular realm of corporations as it is in the church. Lawrence Miller wrote:

> *Satisfaction and excellence are inherently in conflict. Satisfaction implies acceptance of things as they are.* Dissatisfaction is the source of motivation. *It leads to actions to change that which is the source of discomfort. The achievement of excellence can occur only if the organization promotes a culture of* creative dissatisfaction.[3]

Leaders are the visionary "headlight" – rather than the "tail-light" – of society. They are always *looking ahead* rather than *looking back!* They are like a powerful piercing "spotlight" probing and permeating into the future. The very nature of a *visionary* is that he is always looking into the future – whether into next week...next year...next season... next decade...next millennium! They are not only *looking ahead,* they are also *thinking ahead.* Leaders must first of all be ahead of their people in their *thinking* before they can be ahead of them in their *leading.* When your people *out-think you,* they soon *out-lead you!* A leader must be *ahead in learning* in order to be *ahead in leading.* It has always been true that *learning* and *leading* go together. *The moment a leader ceases to learn, he soon ceases to lead.*

Principle:
"A leader stays ahead by thinking ahead and looking ahead. Learning and leading always go together. Therefore, a leader must continue to learn in order to continue to lead."

Fred Smith wisely points out that *"Leaders stay in front by raising the standard by which they judge themselves and by which they are willing to be judged."*[4] A leader with longevity must always be pushing himself or herself towards higher standards. They must always maintain a "holy discontent" with the status quo. They must always be *raising the standard...adjusting the bar of performance upward...pursuing excellence with more intensity.* Only that attitude will keep them *out front.* Oswald Sanders says that every leader must constantly *"...resist the idea of "leadership from the rear."*[5] Sanders goes on to say:

> *True leadership is always from the top down, never from the bottom up. It was leadership from the rear that led Israel back into the wilderness.*[6]

A leader's desire to stay *out front* is not motivation by ego or some sick need to be number one. It is motivated by the desire to *lead people in the right way.* A good leader wants people to *get to the right destination* – not spend their lives wandering meaninglessly around in the wilderness of carnality! He seeks to be *out front* so that he can *pull the people in the right direction.* One of the greatest leaders and motivators of youth of all times was John R. Mott. He was an early leader of the YMCA and the Student Volunteer Movement for Foreign Missions. He said: *"A leader is a man who knows the road, who can keep ahead, and who pulls others after him."* [7] That's a pretty good summary of effective leadership, whether of young people or adults!

"A leader is a man who knows the road, who can keep ahead, and who pulls others after him."
(John R. Mott)

In setting the pace, a good leader must not get too far out ahead of his followers. If he does, he easily becomes a *martyr* rather than a *leader!* Many visions have been killed and many leaders have been destroyed by running *too far, too fast* ahead of their followers. If a leader gets too "far out", physically, emotionally, spiritually, or methodologically, he will soon self-destruct – and may destroy others in the process! While a leader must always be a *pace-setter*, he must also be sensitive to the *pace he sets.* If he sets too *fast a pace*, his followers will not be able to keep up. If he sets too *slow a pace* some of his followers will either lose interest, or surpass him. As the noted humorist, Will Rogers, wisely said: *"Even if you are on the right tracks, you'll get run over if you just sit there!"*[8] A leader cannot afford to stay in one place too long – he must always be *pressing ahead... pioneering new territory...pushing the perimeters...preaching new principles... promoting new paradigms.* He must be "outside the box" in his thinking and his leading.

Jesus was the perfect example of a wise and sensitive Shepherd Who gave balanced *out-front leadership* to His disciples. When it came time to lead during the most *dark* and *difficult* time in His life, Jesus did not fall back. It was time for Him to go to Jerusalem and die. He knew that this was the culmination of His life. This final visit to Jerusalem was the focal point of His earthly leadership. It had been sovereignly ordained and divinely planned before the creation of the world (Matt. 25:34; II Tim. 1:9; Titus 1:2; Rev. 13:8). This was to be the point where eternity would intersect time. Where sin and salvation would meet. Where human wrath and divine love would collide. And it would all happen on a cross! Just before this final visit, Jesus had been down in the lush green valley where the city of Jericho was located. To go to Jerusalem from there was literally an *uphill climb* – physically, spiritually and emotionally!

Even when He was leading the way to His own death, Jesus was still *out front.* The Bible records that

> **"They were on their way *up* to Jerusalem, with *Jesus leading the way,* and the disciples were *astonished,* while those who followed were *afraid"* (Mark 10:32).**

That kind of bold leadership through the *valley of the shadow of death* caused some of His disciples to be *astonished* – and others of them to be *afraid.* Nevertheless, Jesus continued to lead on – *up* to Mount Zion, and further *upward* to Mount Calvary! That's the boldest leadership the world has even seen!

The noted Prussian thinker, Friedrich Nietzsche, was an eternity away from Christ in terms of where he sought to lead people. However, when it came to the loneliness and difficulty of *leading uphill,* Nietzsche made a wise observation: *"Life always gets harder toward the summit. The cold gets colder, the wind stronger, the burden of responsibilities heavier.*"[9] Understanding this reality, Oswald Sanders wrote:

> *Because the leader must always be ahead of his followers, he lives with loneliness. Though he may be friendly, there are areas of life where he must walk alone.*[10]

Principle:
"Loneliness and leading often walk together in solitude."

A leader, like a shepherd, must be *ahead of the pack...out in front...taking the lead...setting the pace.* But he must not get *too far ahead* or he will lose his followers. People, like sheep, have different paces. Some can move fast, while others move more slowly. While some sheep are natural adventurers who want to go new places, others enjoy the security of the known pastures. Some are avid climbers who have the heart of a mountain goat that wants to press on to the heights (Hab. 3:19), while other sheep prefer the flat lands. The Bible emphasizes two different kinds of sheep that need special leadership, sensitivity, and care.

First, there are some followers – like *young lambs, sick sheep,* or *wounded sheep* – who must move at a much slower pace. At times, because of their immaturity or wounds, they must even be *tenderly carried.* Otherwise they will fall behind and be left behind by the rest of the flock. They will become isolated and vulnerable to the attack of the enemy. They will fall prey to despair...despondency...depression...defeat...death. A wonderful leadership verse that reflects the sensitive heart of God is Isaiah 40:11:

> **"He tends His flock like a shepherd: He gathers the *lambs* in His arms and carries them close to His heart; He *gently leads those that have young.*"**

By contrast, some of the other more healthy and robust sheep are *eager followers, quick learners* and *high flyers.* They will become easily frustrated, bored and unchallenged by too slow a leadership pace. A wise leader must spend some more individual time with these more eager and able followers – just like Jesus did with Peter, James and John (Matt. 17:1). Without that extra time and attention, they will not be kept challenged and growing. Their leadership potential will be *neglected* – or *misdirected*. It is through the extra mentoring with these special followers that *leadership development* takes place. It is by pouring himself into these eager and able younger followers that the leader reproduces himself in the life of others. This is where the *reproduction of leadership* takes place. It is with these "eager beavers" that *leadership potential* is developed in others. This is where the *exponential leadership factor* kicks in. It is with these followers that leadership development moves from *addition* to *multiplication!* A wise leader never neglects these potential leaders for the next generation. It is only through the lives of these young leaders that an older leader outlives himself!

A good leader – like a good shepherd – must learn how to *pace himself* and *pace his followers*. All the while he has an eye and heart for the potential young leaders around him. When he identifies these would-be young leaders, he does not squelch or squash their leadership potential out of insecurity, fear or paranoia. Neither does he "put them in their place." Rather, he begins to nurture them to be "put in *his* place!" He knows that an effective leader – like effective parents – must always work himself *out of a job*. It has always been true that: *"It takes a leader to spot a leader –* and *it takes a leader to build another leader.* As John Maxwell says: *"It takes one to know one, show one, and grow one."* [11]Leaders who are *reproducers of reproducers* are always selectively pouring themselves into the lives of others. Wise leaders want to *build leaders* – not just gain more followers.

Principle:
"Leaders that last beckon leaders, birth leaders and build leaders."

Finally, as we saw in an earlier chapter, to be a pace-setter means that a good leader must often be *prophetic*. To be truly prophetic, one must have clearly heard from the Lord. Like the prophets of old, a good leader will have his *spiritual ears finely tuned to God* – and *his physical ears finely tuned to his followers*. However, a wise spiritual leader does not seek to reinforce his position by going around saying: *"God told me..."* or *"Thus says the Lord!"* Those kinds of pontifications come more from *immaturity* and *insecurity* than from God! If the leader has truly heard from the Lord, it will be more evidenced by his *life* than by his *lips!* There will be a *prophetic lifestyle* that authenticates his calling. A maturing spiritual leader increasingly knows the *voice of God*...through the *Spirit of God*...and the *Word of God* – which never conflict or contradict each other.

Principle:
"To be a good pace-setting leader, you must have your spiritual ears tuned to God and your physical ears tuned to man."

FURTHER QUOTATIONS ON
LEADERS AS PACE-SETTERS

- *"Every place that the sole of your foot shall tread upon, that have I given unto you" (Josh. 1:3). The Lord was saying, "If you want it, step on it." Later, when it came time to cross the Jordan River into the land, it was swollen out of its banks. It presented an insurmountable barrier to them. The Lord spoke again: "As soon as the soles of the feet touch the water, they will part" (Josh. 3:13).*[12]

- *"The only way to drive cattle fast is slowly." (Old Texas saying) Some things just can't be done in a hurry. A good leader knows that and moves with deliberate speed.*[13]

- *"You lose your leadership when you cease to lead" (Henry Cabot, Harvard Professor).*[14]

- *If we are going to advance the cause of Jesus Christ in areas of the world where the gospel has not penetrated, it will take men and women willing to put themselves aside and walk with God regardless of where those footsteps may lead...*[15]

Chapter 12

LEADERS ARE PRECIPITATORS

"Now thanks be to God, Who always leads us in triumphal procession in Christ and through us spreads everywhere the fragrance of the knowledge of Him. For we are to God the aroma of Christ among those who are being saved and those who are perishing. To the one we are the smell of death; to the other, the fragrance of life. And who is equal to such a task? Unlike so many, we do not peddle the word of God for profit. On the contrary, in Christ we speak before God with sincerity, like men sent from God"

(II Cor. 2:14–17).

The word *precipitator* basically means: *"To cause to happen."* Leaders are people who *make things happen*. To do that, they must primarily be *actors* rather than *reactors*. They must live on the *offense* rather than on the *defense*. Leaders are generally far more *proactive* than they are *reactive*. Oswald Sanders rightly noted:

> *When all the facts are in, swift and clear decision is the mark of a true leader. A visionary may see, but a leader must decide…Once sure of the will of God, a spiritual leader springs into action, without regard to consequences. Pursuing the goal, the leader never looks back or calculates escape strategies if plans turn sour.*[1]

In the above verses, it is easy to see that the Apostle Paul was a *precipitator*. Everywhere he went, he always *made things happen!* Like the Lord Jesus, you just could not ignore the presence of the Apostle Paul! The moment he "hit town," people began to take note of him. But the thing that made Paul stand out in a crowd, was not his size or appearance. Tradition suggests to us that Paul was rather short of stature. He himself writes about how some of the Corinthian Christians belittled him because he was not physically impressive. Their criticism was that Paul was *"…'timid'* when face to face, but 'bold' when away!" They further said that **"…in person he is *unimpressive* and his speaking amounts to nothing"** (II Cor. 10:1, 10). Paul even admitted that he had come to them **"…in *weakness* and *fear*, and with much *trembling"*** (I Cor. 2:3). Paul further suggests that he was not that eloquent of a speaker. **"My message and my preaching,"** Paul admits, **"were not with *wise and persuasive words…"*** (I Cor. 2:4).

If it was not Paul's physical appearance or his speaking ability – what was it that made him stand out? What was it that caused people to stop and take notice of him? Why was it that his presence could not be long ignored? What was it that made his life such a spiritual and social catalyst? Why was his presence so divisive that you were either *for him* or *against him?* I think there were two distinguishing marks of his life. First, the *presence of Christ*, and secondly, the *power of the Holy Spirit*. Let's look at those two distinguishing things for a moment – attributes that made Paul such a *personal precipitator:*

The Presence of Christ: Everywhere Paul went, he was marching in a *victory parade* – which is hard to ignore! He exclaimed: **"Thanks be to God, Who always leads us in *triumphal procession* in Christ…"** Paul used a familiar mental image for his readers. It was one of a victorious military general returning from battle – with both his soldiers and captives following along behind his chariot in "triumphal procession." That kind of victory parade marching through town would be impossible to ignore! But it did not stop there. It was not a physical battle that Paul was celebrating. It was a spiritual "triumphal procession" over Satan, sin and death. It was not *his victory* that Paul was celebrating – like some egotistical Roman General. It was *Christ's victory* that Paul celebrated everywhere he went. It was because he was "in Christ" that everywhere he went God used him to **"…spread everywhere the *fragrance* of the *knowledge of Him."*** But not everyone wanted to smell the "fragrance of Christ." They preferred the more familiar *stench of death and decay* that they had grown up with. Paul's provocative presence was the "…smell of death" to those who were perishing, and the "…fragrance of life" to those who were being saved.

Through it all, there was also a *humble integrity* about Paul's life that could not be ignored. He readily admitted that in and of himself, he was **"…not**

equal to such a task" of ministry. In a world marked by the abuse of temporal and religious power, financial corruption, idolatry and sexual immorality – Paul's life stood out. Both his hands and heart were clean. He was a shining example of a man who had found his source of integrity in Christ when the world around him had lost theirs! Paul could honestly, but humbly affirm:

> **"Unlike so many, *we do not peddle the word of God for profit.* On the contrary, in Christ we speak before God with sincerity, *like men sent from God"*** (II Cor. 2:14-17).

The Power of the Holy Spirit: Another thing that distinguished Paul's presence was *spiritual power.* Even though he admitted that his words were not the most eloquent – they were confirmed by the presence and power of God. **"My message and my preaching,"** Paul reminded them, **"were not with wise and persuasive words, but with a *demonstration of the Spirit's power."*** He knew that he could not regenerate a dead human spirit through the eloquence of human speech. He was not asking them to put their faith in *his words,* but in *God's Word* **"...so that their faith might not rest on men's wisdom but on *God's power"*** (I Cor. 2:4). With similar words Paul reminded the Christians in the city of Thessalonica: **"...our Gospel came to you not simply with words, but also with *power,* with the *Holy Spirit* and with *deep conviction"*** (I Thess. 1:5).

Wherever Paul went, the people quickly sensed that he was a **"...man sent from God"** (II Cor. 2:17). That kind of person can never long be ignored! They will always be a *powerful precipitator!*

It was Paul's *purpose* that compelled him to be *proactive.* Simply stated: *"Purpose provokes proactivity."* Leaders always seek to *provoke positive activity* – rather than *perpetuate inactivity.* As we saw at the beginning of this book, it is a leader's *vision* that causes him to be *value-driven* through life. It is the *value of the vision* that makes the difference between a *proactive* and a *reactive* person. It is the higher value of their vision that makes leaders become *agents of change* in their environment. They just cannot settle down with the status quo when they have received a vision of something better! Richard Philip correctly states: *"...the first qualification for the role of change agent is vision."*[2] Phillips also expresses the sense of urgency that makes good leaders *precipitators* rather than *procrastinators:*

A change agent is a visionary and a dreamer, but not a starry-eyed over-optimist…The change agent acts not just out of a conviction that the message is right, but that it is essential, that the very future hangs upon the thread of today's decision.[3]

If there is no over-arching, all-consuming vision, a leader will never become an *agent of change* in his world. On the contrary, rather than change his environment, he will be changed by it. Instead of *reforming* and *transforming* his environment, he will be an *agent of conformity.*

Principle:
"*Leadership feeds on the vision of something great.*"[4]
(Richard Phillips)

Either consciously or unconsciously, the *values of their vision* guide everything a proactive leader does. Their moral and spiritual values become the grid through which they process everything else that comes their way in life. Their values become the touchstone by which everything else is tested. Whether it is opportunities…change…problems…setbacks… disappointments…or defeats – effective leaders remain true to the values of their vision. Richard Phillips concludes:

Visionary leadership is not neutral, nor even objective. It is passionately committed to particular principles and actions that themselves embody the vision.[5]

Stephen Covey emphasizes this same principle about leaders as change agents because of their value-driven orientation:

The ability to subordinate an impulse to a value is the essence of the proactive person. Reactive people are driven by feelings, by circumstances, by conditions, by their environment. Proactive people are driven by values – carefully thought about, selected and internalized values…Proactive people are still influenced by external stimuli, whether physical, social, or psychological. But their response to the stimuli, conscious or unconscious, is a value-based choice or response.[6]

Leaders do not spend much of their lives reacting to the activities of others around them. Rather than being *conformers* – they are *reformers* and *transformers.* History shows that it has always been some leader who responded to a need or crisis – and in the process became the *catalyst for needed change*. Their leadership caused them to become the *precipitator* and *initiator of reformation* in society.

Leaders who are *reformers* rather than *conformers...innovators* rather than *imitators* have learned that *change does not come easily!* It is basic to human nature to *resist change* – to *cling to the status quo*. That tends to be true individually, maritally, or organizationally. Every leader who *leads change* has learned this principle: *Significant change seldom takes place easily*. The *greater the change* – the *greater the resistance to change*. Lasting significant change usually comes more through *gradual evolution*, rather than through *sudden revolution*. In his excellent book, *Leading Change*, Harvard's John Kotter reminds leaders:

> *Real transformation takes time...Never underestimate the magnitude of the forces that reinforce complacency and that help maintain the status quo...Major change takes time, sometimes lots of time.*[7]

Leaders who want to be *significant change agents* – rather than *superficial change agents* – must have a "long haul" mentality. They have to traverse the organizational or ecclesiastical *"canyon of complacency,"* as Kotter calls it. Any hiker knows that no great canyon is crossed quickly or easily. The greater the size of the canyon – the greater the effort and the longer the time required to get through it. Many people become overwhelmed by the enormity of the challenge, and quit before they ever start. But any leader worth his salt and sweat knows that every journey must begin with a *first step* – regardless of how difficult or painful. Leaders that *live* and *last* never try to jump the "canyon of change" with one LARGE single bound! If they do, they will usually "crash and burn!" No, first survey the size and difficulty of the challenge – and then attack it one step at a time. They will first begin to work for the *small short-term changes* that will pave the way for the *larger* and *harder changes*. One becomes the stepping-stones for the other, rather than stumbling blocks – or tombstones!

At the end of the day, every leader fully realizes that there is *risk* involved in every major change. The *greater the change* – the *greater the risk!* The *risk factor* is one of the great divides between leaders and followers. The *risk barrier* is really a *fear barrier* that every leader has to break through early in his life of leadership. If he will not take risks, he cannot lead. It's that simple. There is just no such thing as *leadership without risk*. Virtually every book I have ever read on leadership addresses the issue of *risk* at some point or another. Realizing the importance of the *risk factor* in leadership, I want to share a few helpful insights from a variety of writers:

- *By far the biggest mistake people make when trying to change organizations is to plunge ahead without establishing a high enough sense of urgency in fellow managers and employees... Establishing a sense of urgency is crucial to gaining needed cooperation...If many others don't feel the same sense of urgency, the momentum for change will probably die far short of the finish line...Creating a strong sense of urgency usually demands bold or even* risky *actions that we normally associate with good leadership.*[8]

- *The most striking thing about highly effective leaders is how little they have in common. What one swears by, another warns against. But one trait stands out: the* willingness to risk.[9]

- *Leadership is especially risky because every time you make a decision you run the risk of being wrong, but you also run the* risk of being right!*...At each destination point on my journey, I was always faced with the decision to* take the risk of a new opportunity *or stay comfortable where I was at the time.*[10]

- *I believe that if we have nothing we're willing to die for, we really have nothing worth living for.*[11]

- *The greatest achievements in the history of missions have come from leaders close to God who took* courageous, calculated risks*...More failure comes from an excess of caution than from bold experiments with new ideas.*[12]

PRINCIPLE:
*"The greatest mistake one can make in life is to
be continually fearing you will make one."*[13]
(Elbert Hubbard)

Leaders are *risk takers* – and *great leaders* are *great risk takers!* They don't hover around in the safety zones of life. They agree with poet Robert Louis Stevenson, who referred to the attitude of safety and security as, "... *that dismal fungus."*[14] Fungus spreads on things that are still and sedentary – which is seldom characteristic of real leaders who are usually "on the move!" Real leaders are real "shakers and movers" who are characterized by a *pioneer spirit* that causes them to want to be on the *frontiers* of uncharted territory! They are challenged and energized by being on the "cutting edge" of new thought...new ideas...new paradigms...new programs. Like TV *Star Trekkers,* they are prone to *"boldly go where no one has ever gone before!"* While others find security in their *safety zone* – leaders are challenged by the thrill of the *danger zone!* They understand that life is like a football game. They know that you can't win by staying in the safety of the stands - or by sitting on the comfort of the bench. Neither can you win by always being in the *safety zone.* You only score in the *end zone* – which is always the *danger zone* because it is the stronghold of the opposing team. That's where the goal post is – in "enemy territory." The closer you get to the finish line, the greater the "goal line defense" that the enemy sets up. Spiritual leaders especially understand that the further you penetrate into the enemy's territory – the more fierce the battle! The closer you get to spiritual victory – literally "all hell breaks loose!"

Principle:
*"The frontiers of the kingdom of God were never
advanced by men and women of caution."*[15]
(Archbishop Mowll)

Visionary leaders are never content to be the *chaplains of the status quo.* The people who do that are *managers* instead of *leaders* – and managers are definitely needed in every organization or movement. They follow in the wake of the leader, and apply their much-needed administrative and managerial skills to his vision. Leaders, however, are not *"custodial*

Christians" who are content in passively maintaining the tradition established by others. Rather than being bound by tradition, they are bound by the Spirit and the Word! *Biblical leaders precipitate positive, needed change!*

Principle:
"An accomplishing leader originates and innovates.
The 'maintenance leader' protects the status quo." [16]
(Fred Smith)

Leaders are most often the *precipitators...motivators...*and *innovators* of society. They are willing and eager to try new ideas while others around them are more comfortable with the status quo. All you have to do to destroy a leader is to *take away his ability to try new ideas!* He believes that God is always ready to **"...do a *new thing"*** (Isa. 43:19)...give **"*new wine...*"** (Mtt. 9:17)...cause us to sing a **"...*new song"*** (Ps. 40:3), and speak in **"...*new tongues"*** (Mk. 16:17)! Since God's mercies are **"...*new every morning"*** (Lam. 3:23), most leaders have a *new idea* every day – if not every hour!

Christian leaders are first and foremost committed to *"Biblical change,"* rather than to carnal, fleshly, or worldly change. They know that change based upon the flesh will not last – while change based upon the Spirit will be both *temporally relevant* and *eternally significant.* Leaders want to be God's catalysts to bring about positive Biblical change in the lives of individuals, the church, and the society. Godly leadership is only motivated in precipitating authentic spiritual change that is in step with what God's Spirit is doing in the world to exalt the Lord Jesus so that **"...in everything He might have the *supremacy"*** (Col. 1:18).

Principle:
"Good leaders precipitate Christ-centered change that
has temporal relevance and eternal significance."

That kind of positive Christ-centered change does not take place through some kind of impersonal "spontaneous precipitation" or a "random alignment of lucky circumstances." All *benevolent change* that takes place in individuals or in groups is the result of *strategic prayerful planning* initiated by some key leader – which brings us to our next crucial attribute of leadership – *planning*.

FURTHER QUOTATIONS ON
LEADERS AS PRECIPITATORS

1. CHANGE:

- *...the initiation of change within an organization is the most challenging of all organizational tasks and rarely occurs without strong pressure outside the organization.*[17]

- *A leader must* initiate. *Some leaders are more gifted at conserving gains than starting new ventures, for maintaining order than generating ardor. The true leader must be venturesome as well as visionary. He must be ready to jump start as well as hold speed. Paul constantly took calculated risks, always carefully and with much prayer, but always reaching for what lay beyond.*[18]

- *The leader must either* initiate *plans for progress or recognize the worthy plans of others. He must remain in front, giving guidance and direction to those behind. He does not wait for things to happen, but makes them happen. He is a* self-starter, *always on the lookout for improved methods, eager to test new ideas.*[19] (Sanders, p. 127)

- *Managing change is important. Without competent management, the transformation process can get out of control. But for most organizations, the much bigger challenge is leading change. Only leadership can blast through the many sources of corporate inertia. Only leadership can motivate the actions needed to alter behavior in any significant way.*[20]

- *Visible crises can be enormously helpful in catching people's attention and pushing up urgency levels. Conducting business as usual is very difficult if the building seems to be on fire!*[21]

- *Little by little, preoccupation with method, technique and procedure gains a subtle dominance over the whole process of goal seeking. How it is done becomes more important than whether it is done. Means triumph over ends. Form triumphs over spirit. Method is enthroned. Men become prisoners of their procedures, and organizations that were designed to achieve some goal become obstacles in the path to that goal.*[22]

- *Organizational change requires individual change and growth, first and foremost among our leaders…Change agents lead not on the basis of power or position, but on the force of their arguments. They challenge the status quo…with the very values and principles that define the organization…that is what it means to be a change agent: to plant and to sow new possibilities, and to tend them with passion and conviction.*[23]

- *No one can persuade another to change. Each of us guards a gate of change that can only be opened from the inside. We cannot open the gate of another, either by argument or by emotional appeal.*[24]

- *People can't live with change if there's not a changeless core inside them. The key to the ability to change is a changeless sense of who you are, what you are about and what you value.*[25]

- *Leaders face the danger of contentment with the status quo. After all, if a leader already possesses influence and has achieved a level of respect, why should he keep growing? The answer is simple:* Your growth determines who you are. Who you are determines who you attract. Who you attract determines the success of your organization.[26]

- *Henry Ford reminds us that it isn't the incompetent who destroys an organization. The incompetent never get into a position to destroy it. It is those who have achieved something and want to rest on their achievements…To keep an industry pure, you've got to keep it in perpetual ferment.*[27]

- *"There is nothing more vulnerable than entrenched success. You become a prisoner of what you've done in the past." (George Romney)*[28]

- *So beware of the comfortable rut! Comfort comes as a guest, lingers to become a host, and stays to enslave us. If you are a leader…you must never let up. The longer you stay in a position of leadership the harder this becomes…But in the final analysis the best leaders are people who keep on keeping on. They never stop dreaming, changing, growing, thinking, and leading. They know if they do, they're dead in the water. They know that progress stops when the leader stops. There are at least three areas where leaders need to keep on keeping on:*

- o *They need to keep open to progress;*
- o *They need to keep dreaming of the future;*
- o *They need to keep growing in their abilities.* [29]

- *Change has always been and will always be a part of life... The fact is, the only people who won't change are dead people. And the only people who have no problems with change are in the cemetery. But progress is impossible without it. And those who cannot change their mind will never be able to change anything...Change is inevitable, but progress is not. The best leaders are those who anticipate and initiate change rather than react to it, and thus they guarantee progress.*[30]

- *WALK THE TALK, OR LEAD BY EXAMPLE*
  Often the most powerful way to communicate a new direction is through behavior. When the top five or fifty people all live the change vision, employees will usually grasp it better than if there had been a hundred stories in the in-house newsletter. When they see top management acting out the vision, a whole set of troublesome questions about credibility and game playing tends to evaporate ...[31]

- **THE POWER OF A PARADIGM SHIFT...** *The term* paradigm shift *was introduced by Thomas Kuhn in his highly influential landmark book,* The Structure of Scientific Revolutions. *Kuhn shows how almost every significant breakthrough in the field of scientific endeavor is first a break with tradition, with old ways of thinking, with old paradigms...if we want to make significant, quantum change, we need to work on our basic paradigms. In the words of Thoreau, "For every thousand hacking at the leaves of evil, there is one striking at the root." We can only achieve quantum improvements in our lives as we quit hacking at the leaves of attitude and behavior and get to work on the root, the paradigms from which our attitudes and behaviors flow...Remember that* *your paradigm is* the source from which your attitudes and behaviors flow. *A paradigm is like a pair of glasses; it affects the way you see everything in your life...*[32]

2. RISK:

- *Most organizations begin as risk-takers, they become caretakers, and wind up as undertakers.*[33]

- *All leadership requires moral courage. The essence of moral courage is placing one's self at risk for the greater good.*[34]

- *Throughout history the most common, debilitating human ailment has been cold feet. A leader with cold feet is no leader.*[35]

- *"Before any big moment of decision there are moments of indecision." (Alan Haynes) There is always an element of fear because there is always a chance of failure. It is the risk, the doubt, the uncertainty that can create indecision.*[36]

- *To be a leader you must believe in your cause enough that you are willing to risk – to risk failure, to risk criticism, to risk opposition, to risk termination, to risk financial loss, even to risk your own life if the cause is big enough.*[37]

- *Courage is contagious and so is the lack of it.*[38]

- *What does it take to make the decisions a leader must make? Good decisions? It takes 3 things:*

    o *Wisdom to discern*
    o *Confidence to believe*
    o *Boldness to risk*[39]

- *A life without risks is a life without rewards. Every leader knows that. He knows that the greatest hazard in life is to risk nothing. The person who risks nothing does nothing, has nothing, is nothing.*[40]

- *Unless you are willing to take a risk, you will suffer paralyzing inhibitions, and you will never do what you are capable of doing. Chained by fear you become a slave. You forfeit your freedom for security. We are sometimes afraid of losing money, losing face, losing position, but what about losing opportunities? If we don't make a decision, if we don't act boldly, that's what will happen…If you wait until all possible obstacles are overcome, then you will never do anything.*[41]

- *Peter Drucker said: "Whenever you see a successful business, someone once made a courageous decision."*[42]

- *The time to be absolutely worried is when you are comfortable – absolutely comfortable.*[43]

- *The element of risk. The leader has no way of knowing the actual results of his decision. That means each decision contains an element of risk. Some leaders are reluctant to take risks and as a result have problems making decisions. The good decision-maker learns to calculate risks and make them work for him in the decision-making process.*

  When evaluating alternatives, the leader should consider the risks involved in each potential decision. However, he should not try to eliminate all risk. The best decision is not necessarily the alternative with the least risk. As a general rule, risks decrease as facts and information increase.[44]

~~~~~~~~~~~~~~~~~~~~~~~~~~~~

Chapter 13

LEADERS ARE PLANNERS

*"As the time approached for Him to be taken
up to heaven, Jesus resolutely set out for Jerusalem.
And He sent messengers on ahead...to get things ready for Him..."*
(Luke 9:51-52).

Good leaders must also be *good planners.* To use a term from the secular business world, a leader must always *"do diligence." His planning is based upon diligent preparation.* A leader reads, researches, studies, analyzes, discusses, modifies and refines as a part of his planning process. As he plans, a wise leader seeks to "leave no stone unturned" in his attempt to fully consider all of the issues. Unfortunately people of the world are often better at "doing diligence" than God's people. As Jesus said: **"The people of this world are more *shrewd* in dealing with their own kind than are the people of the light"** (Lk. 16:8). Too many Christian leaders "spiritualize" the planning process. They often gloss over the necessity of "doing diligence" with a veneer of spiritual verbiage, "faith talk" and presumptuous prayer!

We have seen earlier in this book that *Jesus was a planner.* Just because He was the Son of God, Jesus did not cease to plan. Even though He was *God Incarnate,* Jesus did not live His life spontaneously or randomly. Even though He was always open and responsive to what appeared to be the unplanned erratic events on the part of others around Him, Jesus always had a plan that He was following through life. When it came to sending out the *Twelve,* and the *Seventy-Two,* Jesus gave both evangelistic teams very specific plans to follow (Lk. 9:1-6; 10:1-12). They were not sent out to just "wing it" after being entrusted with a message of such eternal consequence. No. Jesus gave them a very specific plan to follow.

When we look at the introductory verses for this chapter, Jesus is preparing for the culmination point of His brief three years of ministry. He is about to go to Jerusalem to die for the sins of the world. Jesus is totally confident in God's redemptive plan that is about to be consummated in Jerusalem. Even though this salvation event had been planned in the council of the Godhead before the creation of the world, Jesus still carefully planned as He approached Jerusalem. He did not take a passive fatalistic attitude toward these divinely ordained plans – even though He was **"…the Lamb that was slain *from the creation of the world"* (Rev. 13:8). As a member of the triune Godhead, Jesus had been a part of the planning of man's salvation from eternity past. But now in the **"fullness of time"** (Gal. 4:4), Jesus still planned as He prepared to enter Jerusalem for His last week of life before His crucifixion. We read that **"Jesus…sent messengers on ahead… *to get things ready for Him."* One of the first things that Jesus made plans for was the celebration of the Passover Feast. He said to Peter and John, **"Go and *make preparation* for us to eat the Passover"** (Lk. 22:8). Jesus made *human plans* within the context of the *divine plans* laid out before the world began. As Bible commentator Sir George Smith wrote: *"It is a great truth that the Almighty and All-merciful is the All-Methodical too."* [1]

If Jesus planned, we must plan. Every mature Christian leader knows that there is never a contradiction between wise planning and a life of faith. The book of James clearly teaches us that: **"Faith without works is dead"** (Ja. 2:17, 26). Also, *works without faith is dead.* To impart life, *faith and works must go together.* The Bible has married *faith and works* in an indissoluble spiritual union. In the well-balanced Christian life, faith and works…planning and preparation…prayer and "doing diligence" must go together. Without these two working together, plans are doomed to failure. "Doing diligence" is part of the *work* side of the life of *faith* for effective Christian leaders.

> *"The best way to predict your future is to create it.*[2]
> **(Stephen Covey)**

Knowing the importance of planning, good leaders do not just live spontaneously...erratically...randomly...or capriciously. Because they have an all-consuming *life purpose,* they have to be *lifelong planners. Good leading* and *good planning* go hand-in-hand. In order to fulfill their vision and reach their goals, leaders know the absolute necessity of good planning. They have *long-term plans* that necessitate *short-term goals.*

> **Principle:**
> **"Good leading and good planning *always go hand-in-hand.*"**

At the beginning of this study we looked at the importance of a leader's defining *life vision.* That spiritual vision is summed up in the words of one of my favorite Bible verses:

> **The noble man makes *noble plans,* and by *noble deeds* he stands"** (Isa. 32:8).

That verse should provoke a *divine pause* in each of our lives. It should cause each of us as leaders to ask ourselves: *"Am I giving my life for noble plans* or for *nominal plans?"* The thing that lifts our plans to the realm of *nobility* is that they are *glorifying to God* and *edifying to man.* Too many people live by plans that have little inherent nobility. They are selfish plans...petty plans...carnal plans...worldly plans...ignoble plans. It is only when *God's plans* become *our plans* that there is *nobility* involved. Only then do plans cease being *nominal* and become *noble.*

> **Principle:**
> *"When integrity fails, the leader falls."*

It is not enough just to have *noble plans* – we must also implement them with *noble deeds.* If the plans are noble, the deeds that are done in their name must also be noble. Noble plans can never be fulfilled by *ignoble deeds.* As Christian leaders, there must always be a consistency between our *theology* and our *methodology.* Our *deeds* must match our *creed...*our *beliefs* must be reflected in our *behavior...*our *walk* must match our *talk.* That's where the security comes from for Christian leadership. When we say one thing *publicly* while acting a different way *privately,* then the *integrity factor* is removed from leadership. That *integrity gap* will always eventually catch up with a leader – and bring him down! You can never separate *leadership integrity* from *leadership insecurity.* Once a leader's *walk* does not match his *talk,* he begins to live and lead in insecurity. He begins to live in the secret fear of being "found out" – exposed. God has created a moral fiber in the universe – which He has inscribed on the conscience of every person. When we violate it, we forfeit His blessing upon our lives. That's why the *secret sin* is so dangerous and deadly in life and leadership (Ps. 19:12; 90:8; II Cor. 4:2). When we try to silence that voice of moral conscience, our life takes a downward turn. We make a deadly detour from the **"...path of righteousness"** (Ps. 23:3). We leave the place of blessing and anointing. Every leader must often remind himself of this principle: **"He who *conceals his sins does not prosper"*** (Prov. 28:13). When our life and leadership lose their integrity, God no longer prospers us. When leadership integrity *fails,* the leader *falls.* It is only **"...by noble deeds he *stands."***

Leadership that lasts is based upon a lifelong commitment to *noble plans.* Whereas a leader's *noble plan* is long-term and will take his entire life to fulfill, he must have shorter-range *noble deeds,* or *goals* that help him fulfill his vision. *Without clear goals, a vision becomes only wishful thinking!* We might think of these goals as the *stepping-stones to the fulfillment of his life's vision.* These goals become so important in the life of a leader that he is often thought of as a *goal-oriented person.* But achieving the goals is not the ultimate purpose of a leader's life. Fulfilling his vision is what he lives for. The short-term and long-term goals are just stepping stones to help him fulfill his life's vision. The goals are the *means to the end* – not an end in themselves. Obviously, the study of goals is a whole focus unto itself – which is not the primary theme of this book. However, let me look with you at a few basic principles concerning goals.

Principle:
"Short and long-term goals are the practical
stepping-stones to the fulfillment of a leader's
life-vision."

Goals are both *short-term* and *long-term.* Once again we can see a good
example of this in the life and ministry of the Lord Jesus. As we have
seen, His life had one consuming purpose and passion – which was to
die for the sins of the world. According to prophecy, that could only
take place in Jerusalem. As He was on His way to Jerusalem to fulfill the
ultimate purpose of His life, He said:

> "...I will drive out demons and heal people today and
> tomorrow and on the third day *I will reach My goal.* In
> any case, I must keep going today and tomorrow and
> the next day – for surely no prophet can die outside
> Jerusalem!" (Lk. 13:32-33).

The ultimate goal that He came to earth to fulfill was "... **to give His life
a ransom for many**" (Mtt. 2:28); "...**to save what was lost**" (Lk. 19:10);
"...**to destroy the works of the devil**" (I Jn. 3:8) – not just to "...**drive
out demons.**" To fulfill His life's purpose, He had to go to Jerusalem and
die. But on the way to the cross, He would "...**preach...teach...heal...
drive out demons**" (Lk. 4:14; 40-44; 5:17; 6:6; 8:1, etc).

Goals   need to be as *simple* as possible. When plans and goals get too
complex and complicated, they are seldom followed – either by the leader
or the follower! There is a humorous **KISS** maxim that says: *"Keep It
Simple Stupid!"* Simplicity is a sign of genius – not complexity. The person
who cannot reduce complicated ideas to their simplest form has not yet
fully understood it himself. The simpler the plan the better the plan,
and the more people who will follow. Conversely, the more complicated
the plan, the fewer the people who will "catch the vision" and follow the
leader. Einstein said: *"Whatever God does, He does in its simplest form."*[3]
That's a profound statement for perhaps the smartest man of the Twentieth
Century! Understanding this principle of simplicity, Fred Smith wisely
reminds leaders:

Be sure the plan is as simple as it can be...Elaborate plans seldom get carried out...Every element of the task should be simplified as much as possible...Leaders need the humility of simplicity, a simplicity developed beyond complexity, not before it.[4]

Goals need to be *written down* and reviewed regularly. Francis Bacon said: *"Writing maketh an exact man."* He correctly understood that writing things down helps a person crystallize his thoughts and be more specific and precise. The human mind finds it very difficult to grasp a vacuum or understand an abstraction. We all think in specific, concrete images – not in ethereal abstractions. As John Haggai says: *"Goals must have the motivational force of a positive mental image if it is to move us and others."*[5]

"Goals must have the motivational force of a positive mental image if it is to move us and move others."
(John Haggai)

Goals give guidance. Without clear goals, our life is set adrift on the ever-changing sea of subjectivism. Without goals to guide our lives, we are always victimized by our mood swings, other people's agenda, the pressing needs around us, changing circumstances – and the *tyranny of the urgent!* All of these things – and more – will take charge of our lives unless we take charge of them. If we do not let our *goals guide us*, other people's lack of goals will take over.

Goals change because conditions change. Goals have to be constantly *reviewed...refined...readjusted.* In the business realm, they often speak of *"SMART Goals."* That means that goals must be:

S = *specific*
M = *measurable*
A = *attainable*
R = *realistic*
T = *tangible*

As we have seen earlier in this study, leaders by nature and calling are *visionaries.* As such, they see through the *eyes of faith* what others often cannot see, or will not see. They are *visionaries* simply because they *envisage* and *envision* their *vision.* As the familiar cliché says: "Every person views life through some kind of *'rose tinted glasses.'*" The tint of those emotional lenses determines how we see all of the rest of life. We may have a negative and pessimistic perspective of life because we view life through the dark and distorted lenses of insecurity...hurt...bitterness... resentment...anger...and depression. Or we may have a more positive and optimistic viewpoint because we see life through the clearer emotional lenses of faith...love...hope...joy...happiness...security...contentment. Leaders, however, constantly *envision life through their vision.* The visionary views all of life through the perspective of his vision – which causes a continuous *revision* of his own life. The *imagination* of his mind is focused and fixed on his vision. A leader's *insight* largely determines his *sight!* What they see through their spiritual eyes is more important and compelling to them than what they see through their natural eyes – even though their vision may at times be blurred as **"...through a glass, darkly"** (I Cor. 13:12; KJV).

Principle:
"A leader's insight largely determines his sight."

Because leaders often see what others do not see, their prayer for their followers is often similar to what Paul prayed for the saints at Ephesus. Just as is the case with every young Christian, some of the Ephesian saints were having problems with their spiritual eyesight:

> **"I pray also that the *eyes of your heart may be enlightened* in order that you may know the hope to which He has called you, the riches of His glorious inheritance in the saints, and His incomparable great power for us who believe"** (Eph. 1:18-19).

It is obvious from this prayer that Paul was somewhat frustrated that these young Christians at Ephesus could not spiritually see what God had made available to them through Christ. He was praying for them that their spiritual eyes would be opened so that they could see for themselves what he could so clearly see for them. God had a wonderful plan for their lives that involved far more than they were seeing or experiencing. Paul wanted them to see the **"hope...riches...power"** that God had provided for them through the life, death, resurrection and ascension of the Lord Jesus. Take special note here that it was *God's plan* for them that Paul wanted them to see – not some plan of his own. That's what authentic spiritual leadership is all about. Remember how we saw earlier that true *servant-leadership* is concerned about helping people accomplish a benevolent goal that is beneficial for *them.* On the other hand, *selfish leadership* tries to get people to accomplish a plan that is good for the leader. When the leader substitutes his plan for God's plan, it is a perversion and prostitution of spiritual leadership!

Spiritual leaders are *wise planners* as opposed to *worldly planners.* Wise planners plan according to God's Word. Worldly planners plan according to the values of Wall Street. The Apostle Paul asked: **"Do I make my plans in a worldly manner so that in the same breath I say, 'Yes, yes' and 'No, no?'"** Paul knew that worldly leadership and worldly planning is often deceitful and contradictory. People give their word and make promises they never intended to keep. They often say one thing and mean another. They sign agreements, contracts and covenants that they quickly break. Paul said that as a spiritual leader he did not live or plan that way. He said that **"…as surely as God is faithful, our message to you is not 'Yes' and 'No'"** (II Cor. 1:17-18). Paul writes to assure the saints at Corinth of the integrity of his words and deeds: *"I say what I mean, and mean what I say! Since I serve and represent a faithful God, you can trust my words and plans."*

To be a truly spiritual leader like Jesus and Paul, one must be a *Biblical planner.* A leader who is a Biblical planner does his planning and preparation with an *open Bible…open heart…open mind.* He depends upon God's Spirit to guide his planning through God's Word. If he has any doubt and confusion, he seeks mature Godly counsel. He humbly believes: **"Plans fail for lack of counsel, but *with many counselors they succeed"*** (Prov. 15:22). Every wise leader will **"Make plans by seeking advice…"** (Prov. 20:18).

A spiritual leader is committed to the clear principle: *"God's Will is God's Word."* If his own plans contradict God's revealed Word in any way, then the leader's plans must be changed, modified or abandoned. To the best of the Christian leader's understanding, his plans must be in perfect accord with the revealed will of God through His Word. Nothing more, nothing less. As the songwriter expressed it: *"To will with Him one perfect will..."* A wise leader is always open and obedient to God making a *revision of his vision.* He always wants his plans to conform to God's plans. Authentic Christian leaders want their earthly plans to be a reflection and incarnation of God's sovereign plans that are eternally settled in heaven – and will therefore one day be firmly established on earth.

Principle:
Spiritual leaders are always Biblical planners who allow God's Spirit and God's Word to refine and make continuous revisions of their vision.

As we saw at the beginning of this study on leadership, a leader's chief concern is to help people fulfill God's plan for their lives – which will always be for *their good* and *God's glory.* It must be a plan that *helps people make progress toward their potential. Leaders must plan from an eternal perspective.* Spiritual leaders are not so much concerned about the short-term *happiness* of their followers – as for their long-range *holiness.* They have learned from their own experience that *happiness is a by-product of holiness.* When people seek happiness, they seldom find it – except in fleeting illusive dosages. But when they seek holiness of heart and life through obedience to God, true happiness abounds! Holiness is the *root,* while happiness is the *fruit.* That kind of spiritual, mental and emotional change totally shifts the axis of one's life from self to God. This radical shift from self to God doesn't happen quickly, easily, or painlessly! This kind of radical *transformational change* of our nature takes time – and often lots of it. When working with people, leaders must plan with the "long haul" in mind. Without this long-range perspective, their plans will be naïve and unrealistic – and they will produce frustration and disappointment when there are no "quick results." In addition, their followers will become disillusioned when there is no immediate "quick fix" for their problems. Both the leader and the follower must not plan as *sprinters* on a brief hundred-yard dash – but as *long-distance runners* who are on a life-long marathon! When both the leader and the follower plan with this view in mind, they will be like the Apostle Paul, and **"...finish the race"** (II Tim. 4:7).

When leaders have this long-range BIG PICTURE in mind, they are not nearly as upset or troubled by the normal failures and temporary set-backs that are always faced in life and leadership. They know that if the Lord does not immediately return, they will always have tomorrow to either continue their work – or start all over again. With this perspective, leaders make decisions more in terms of *tomorrow* rather than *today*. By nature, leaders have to be *forward-looking* and *future-oriented* – rather than *backward-looking* and *past-oriented*. As a result of this future orientation, leaders are not overly preoccupied with either their *past failures* or *present victories*. It has often been said that *most people live in the present, through the past in fearful anticipation of the future*. As a result of being negatively bound to the past, they forfeit both the present and the future. Leaders, on the other hand, *view the past – and live in the present – in anticipation of the future*. They *glance at the past...glimpse the present...*but *gaze into the future*. Mature spiritual leaders eagerly embrace the future through the confidence of the Psalmist when He exclaimed:

> **"Many, O Lord my God, are the wonders You have done.**
> **The things You planned for us no one can recount to You"** (Ps. 40:5).

Even after facing difficulty or defeat, the spiritual leader continues to press on into the future, believing God's promise to His people:

> **"'For I know the *plans* I have for you,' declares the Lord,**
> **'plans to prosper you and not to harm you, *plans to give you* hope and a future'"** (Jer. 29:11).

As a result of this time perspective, leaders do not spend a lot of time dwelling on past problems...grieving over former failures...mulling over minor mistakes...putting out yesterday's fire...or crying over spilt milk. They focus on *today's opportunities* and *tomorrow's potential* – rather than on yesterday's failures or mistakes. *Learning to successfully deal with failures and mistakes is one of the most important lessons for any leader.*

By way of summary, *good leaders are good planners.* The better the planning, the better the possibility of success – and the greater their success, the more others will want to follow them. Successful leaders *have a plan... work their plan...stick to their plan.* Because they believe in good planning and preparation, wise leaders do not just "wing it"..."fly by the seat of

their pants"..."make up as they go along"...or "do whatever feels natural."
Nor do they just mindlessly "let the Spirit lead!" True spiritual leaders
plan...Plan...PLAN!

Biblical leaders understand that true spiritual leadership is *10% inspiration
and 90% perspiration!* The 10% is the "faith factor" while the 90% is the
"work factor." Thomas Edison said: "Genius is one percent inspiration and
ninety-nine perspiration." Much of the *perspiration* of good leadership is
brought about by *careful, prayerful planning.*

Principle:
*"Successful leadership is based upon 10% inspiration
and 90% perspiration."*

Biblical leaders are committed to the fact that *because God plans, they must
plan.* God is a God Who planned all things before the creation of the world
– especially our salvation (Matthew 2:43; Hebrews 4:3; 9:26; Revelation
13:8; 17:8). That's true long-range planning! If God did long-term
planning that resulted in our salvation, leaders should also do long-range
planning that will result in the salvation and sanctification of others. Just
as God stuck to His sovereignly ordained plan of redemption that will
ultimately result in the restoration of all things and consummation of
the ages (I Cor. 15:24-25), Christian leaders must also *prepare a plan...
pray their plan...promote their plan...persist with their plan!* Every authentic
spiritual leader knows that it is only God's blessings that will make his
plans prosper. The wisdom of Proverbs reminds us: **"Commit to the
Lord whatever you do, and your *plans will succeed"*** (Prov. 16:3).

Principle:
**Effective leaders prepare a plan...pray their
plan...*promote their plan...persist with their plan.***

My heart's desire and prayer for you at the end of this crucial chapter on
the importance of planning in the life of the leader is this:

> **"May He give you all the desires of your heart and *make
> all your plans succeed"*** (Ps. 20:4). **Amen!**

FURTHER QUOTATIONS ON
LEADERS AS PLANNERS

1. PLANNING:

A. BIBLICAL WARNINGS AGAINST *WORLDLY PLANS*:

"Woe to the obstinate children, declares the Lord, to those who *carry out plans that are not Mine*...heaping sin upon sin" (Isa. 30:1).

"Do not grant the wicked their desires, O Lord; do not let their *plans* succeed, or they will become proud" (Ps. 140:8).

"Woe to those who go to great depths to *hide their plans from the Lord*, who do their work in darkness and think, 'Who sees us? Who will know?'" (Isa. 29:15).

"The Lord *foils the plans of the nations;* He thwarts the purposes of the peoples" (Ps. 33:10).

"The Lord Almighty planned it, to bring low the pride of all glory and to humble all those who are renowned on the earth" (Isa. 23:9).

B. BIBLICAL EXHORTATION ABOUT THE CERTAINTY OF *GOD'S PLANS*:

"The *plans of the Lord stand firm forever,* the purposes of His heart through all generations" (Ps. 33:11).

"Many are the plans in a man's heart, but *it is the Lord's purpose that prevails*"(Prov. 19:21).

"The Lord Almighty has sworn: 'Surely, *as I have planned, so it will be, and as I have purposed, so it will stand...*' For the Lord Almighty has purposed, and who can thwart Him? His hand is stretched out, and who can turn it back?" (Isa. 14:24, 27).

"What I have said, that will I bring about; *what I have planned, that will I do*"(Isa. 46:11).

- *If you don't plan ahead, you'll get behind.*[6]

- *Planning puts you in charge of your energies and activities. It gives you an organized approach to your work. It helps you move with purpose and determination.*[7]

- *Plan your work, and work your plan.*[8]

- *(Charles Kettering) I plan to spend the rest of my life in the future, so I want to know what it will be. That's why I plan.*[9]

- *By contrast, we read in Scripture, "**Any enterprise is built by wise planning, becomes strong through common sense, and profits wonderfully by keeping abreast of the facts**" (Prov. 24:3-4 LB).*[10]

2. DILIGENCE:

- *If there's no gardener, there's no garden!....Most of us think it would be great if we could just put our gardens – or our lives – on automatic and somehow get the quality-of-life results that comes from careful, consistent nurturing of the things that create it. But life doesn't work that way. We can't just toss out a few seeds, go ahead and do whatever we want to do and then expect to come back to find a beautiful, well-groomed garden ready to drop a bountiful harvest of beans, corn, potatoes, carrots, and peas in our basket. We have to water, cultivate, and weed on a regular basis if we're going to enjoy the harvest. Our lives will bring forth anyway. Things will grow. But the difference between our own active involvement as gardeners and neglect is the difference between a beautiful garden and a weed patch.*[11]

3. GOALS:

- *It's a dream until you write it down. Then it's a goal...all great leaders have been persons of vision who established goals...Goalless-ness is one of the worst diseases of the 20th Century. I have read that 3% of the people in America have written goals. Seven percent know what goals are. And 90% have no goals at all. They just take what comes. Unfortunately, most churches are the same. Their only goal is to meet next Sunday. Beyond that, they aren't going anywhere.*[12]

- *If you don't set your own goals you'll always be accepting other people's goals.*[13]

- *7 Marks of a Good Goal:*
  - *A goal should be challenging*
  - *A goal should be measurable*
  - *A goal should be achievable*
  - *A goal should have a deadline*
  - *A goal should be written down*
  - *A goal should be flexible*
  - *A goal should be shared* [14]

- *The goal should relate to your mission, to your vision, to your great purpose. So if you are going to be a leader, set you some goals and get started accomplishing them.*[15]

- *The bigger and more challenging your goal, the more excited people are apt to become about it.*[16]

- *"When you get in a fox chase, don't stop to hunt mice." (J. B. Gambrell, Texas Baptist leader) A leader must be single minded.*[17]

- *Spiritual goals can be achieved only by spiritual people who use spiritual methods. How our churches and mission agencies would change if leaders were Spirit-filled! The secular mind and heart, however gifted and personally charming, has no place in the leadership of the church...*[18]

- *Goal setting is obviously a powerful process. It's based on the same principle of focus that allows us to concentrate rays of diffused sunlight into a force powerful enough to start a fire. It's the manifestation of creative imagination and independent will.*

It's the practicality of "eating our elephants one bite at a time," of translating vision into achievable, actionable doing. It's a common denominator of successful individuals and organizations.[19]

- ### *The Size of Your Goal Reflects the Size of Your God...*

...Show me a person with small goals and I will show you a person with a small God. The size of our goals reflects the size of our God...

...Our concept of God determines what we ask for and believe God will provide...

...If you want to know how big your God is, look at the size of your goals and what you are asking God to do. We never ask God for more than we think He is capable of providing...

...Paul wasn't a great missionary because he was a great man; he was a great missionary because he had a great God.[20]

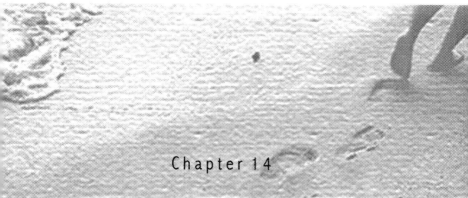

Chapter 14

LEADERS ARE PRAGMATIC

"A nobleman was called away to a distant empire to be crowned king and then return. Before he left, he called together ten servants and gave them ten pounds of silver to invest for him while he was gone"
(Luke 19:12-13; New Living Translation).

Jesus gave the above teaching immediately after the conversion of Zacchaeus, who was a businessman. He was the *"chief tax collector"* in Jericho – what we in America would call the *"head of the IRS."* Because of the corruption of the system of levying taxes in the Roman Empire, tax collectors were especially hated! Zacchaeus was no exception. Many were not pleased that Jesus had visited his home and dined with him. Neither were they excited that he had been converted to the degree that he **"…gave half of his possessions to the poor."** Nor did the people believe his commitment to make a four-fold "tax return" to **"…anyone he had cheated"** (Lk. 19:8). In the face of the people's murmuring and unbelief over the conversion of Zacchaeus, Jesus gave a telling parable. Since money was the issue here, Jesus told a timely parable about *investing money.* The punch line of the parable is verse 13. Let me share it from several translations:

> **"Occupy till I come."** (KJV)
> **"Do business with this until I come back."** (NASV)
> **"Trade with these till I come."** (RSV)

"Buy and sell with these while I go and return."
(Amplified)
"Use this money to trade with until I come back."
(Phillips)
"See what you can earn with this while I am gone."
(TEV)

Regardless of the translation, you quickly get the picture of what the money investor had in mind for his servants. He wanted them to *wisely invest*, and *produce a profit*. The key word in this passage is the word that is variously translated: **"Occupy, do business, trade, buy and sell."** This is the only place in the entire New Testament where this word is found. It is the Greek word *pragmateuomai*. Even if you can't read Greek, it is easy to see the meaning of this word. It rightly sounds like our English word, *"pragmatic."* The Greek root word is *pragma*, which can mean: *"a deed, a work, to busy oneself, to trade, occupy, to be busy, active, practical."*

Jesus is giving a *Parable of Practicality*. He is challenging this newly converted businessman, Zacchaeus, to change his perspective of money. He is to no longer *pervert profit* for his own selfish use – but to *practically invest it for God's glory*. Zacchaeus was to be as *pragmatic* and *practical* as he had always been with money – but for a new purpose! No longer was he to go for the "fast buck" through cheating and corruption. Now he was to be a wise and practical investor of his resources where it would bring the greatest return for God's glory. That's what this *Parable of Practicality* is all about. It is a special call to Christians in the business world to use their natural entrepreneurial abilities for the Kingdom of God. To be *pragmatic* and *practical* in their pursuit of *profits* – for God's glory for the good of others.

Every effective leader – just like every effective businessman – must be *pragmatic* and *practical* in his leadership. A good leader is oriented toward *practical solutions* to people's problems. He or she does not "spiritualize" everything by giving simplistic "pat answers" that will only further complicated life problems. *Pragmatism is based upon realism!* A wise leader must continually face *reality*. He must constantly ask himself the *hard questions* that others don't want to face. He is not interested in whether the organization is just *efficient*. He wants to know if it is *effective*. He knows very well that something may be *efficient in getting results*, but is it *effective* in getting the *right results?* The organization may be *smoothly running* and very *efficient*. But it may be *efficiently running in the wrong direction!* A wise and pragmatic leader often asks himself the question: *"Are the right kind of results taking place?"* Fred Smith has been an advisor to many successful Christian businessmen and church leaders in America and around the world. He makes this observation about the ones who are effective and successful:

> *No matter what the organization is doing, it is well disciplined in getting* defined results. *These leaders are not interested in maintaining a program. If there's no wheat coming out of the thresher, they shut it off. I have been impressed at how quickly they stop non-productive activity.*[1]

That's the mentality of *pragmatism* in business or ministry. If the wheat is not coming out of the thresher, you shut down the activity – regardless of how *efficient* it is. It is only *effective* when it is producing the *defined results*.

While the Biblical leader is committed to seeking spiritual solutions for real life problems, they are *pragmatic* and *practical* in the application of those solutions. They are fully committed to the fact that *spirituality cannot be divorced from practicality* – any more than *faith* can be divorced from *works*. Mature Biblical leadership is based upon the understanding that: *"spirituality is practicality!"*

A good leader does not get caught up in the *theoretical...ethereal...mystical... hypothetical...philosophical...*or a*bstract.* An authentic spiritual leader is always practical and *"down to earth"* in living and leading. The more practical the leadership, the greater the appeal of the leader.

Principle:
*"The more practical the leadership,
the greater the appeal of the leader."*

An effective leader – just like a successful businessman – is always asking himself questions like these:

"Does it work?"
"Is it time effective?"
"Is it cost efficient?"
"Does it produce the desired results?"
"How can it be done better?"
"Are real needs being met by this activity?"

Over and over again the Bible asks pragmatic questions to sinful rebellious people. Through these many questions and "earthy descriptions" of the problem, God wants to show man how impractical and foolish his sinful and selfish way of life is. Consider just a few such practical exhortations:

"Why spend money on what is not bread, and your labor on what does not satisfy?" (Isa. 55:2).

"My people have...dug their own cisterns, broken cisterns that cannot hold water" (Jer. 2:13).

"Can the Ethiopian change his skin or the leopard its spots? Neither can you do good who are accustomed to doing evil" (Jer. 13:23).

"Give careful thought to your ways. You have planted much, but have harvested little. You eat, but never have enough. You drink, but never have your fill. You put on clothes, but are not warm. You earn wages, only to put them in a purse with holes in it" (Hag. 1:5-6).

The whole Book of Ecclesiastes is a pragmatic personal study to show that all of life's pursuits without God are ultimately nothing more than **"vanity and striving after the wind"** (Ecc. 2:11, KVJ). There is a lot of church activity...mission activity...para-church activity that is little more than *religious vanity* and *striving after the prevailing winds of society* – rather than being billowed by the winds of the Spirit! In order for individuals and groups to face and deal with these tradition-bound mentalities and failed methods, some real pragmatic questions have to be asked.

Many Church leaders are afraid to ask themselves some hard questions about their *religiosity* and *church-anity.* Their spirit of creativity in ministry has been *suppressed by denominational bias...bound by religious tradition...* and *stifled by ecclesiastical bureaucracy.* Much of their church activity is what one critic called *"the incarnation of irrelevant grandeur!"* This critic and skeptic further described the church where he grew up with these chilling words: *"We were faultily faultless, icily regular, and splendidly dull!"* What a devastating, but accurate, description of so much of traditional church-anity! That kind of *"incarnation of irrelevant grandeur"* is perpetuated when church leaders lose touch with the *Incarnate Christ* - Who was constantly in touch with the needs of the people around Him. His life was intensely *practical.*

In contrast to the very *practical* life and leadership of the Lord Jesus, most of the Judaism of His day had become rigid, tradition-bound and lifeless. Jesus was constantly in conflict with the religious leaders – the Scribes and Pharisees – who refused to ask themselves the hard *pragmatic* questions about the religion they were perpetuating. Jesus heaped *Seven Woes* upon these **"..teachers of the law and the Pharisees"** who sat in the seat of Moses and pontificated *religious irrelevancy* upon the people of God! Jesus called them **"hypocrites...blind guides...blind fools...snakes... brood of vipers!"** Not very complimentary titles – especially for the very religious people who had been privileged to receive the **"...adoption as sons...the divine glory, the covenants...the law, the temple worship... the promises...the patriarchs, and...the Christ"** (Rom. 9:4-5). Some of the most severe words of judgment and condemnation that ever came out of the mouth of Jesus were directed to these very blessed and privileged Jewish religious leaders! What He accused them of could equally be said of much of traditional denominationalism in the Western World today.

> **"Woe to you...you *hypocrites!* You shut the kingdom of heaven in men's faces. You yourselves do not enter, nor will you let those enter who are trying to...You travel over land and sea to win a single convert, and when he becomes one, you make him twice as much a son of hell as you are...You blind guides! You strain out a gnat but swallow a camel...You clean the outside of the cup and dish, but inside they are full of greed and self-indulgence...Woe to you, teachers of the law and Pharisees, you hypocrites! You are like whitewashed**

tombs, which look beautiful on the outside but on the inside are full of dead men's bones and everything unclean. In the same way, on the outside you appear to people as righteous but on the inside you are full of hypocrisy and wickedness...You snakes! You brood of vipers! How will you escape being condemned to hell?" (Matt. 23:11-33).

A good Biblical leader does not become *"tradition bound"* – regardless of how "sacred" that tradition may be to himself or to others. He must never be afraid to try new ideas...new approaches...new methods. He understands the important practical difference between a *sacred message* and a *non-sacred method*. If something is no longer effective and efficient, an innovative and practical leader will set it aside for a new approach that is more productive. He also must be *pastorally practical* in bringing his people along in their understanding and appreciation of why that change is necessary, timely and healthy.

Principle:

"Personal leadership pragmatism must be translated into practical collective ownership for positive change to take place."

Everyone who has taken the time to study it knows that the Bible is the most *practical* and *pragmatic* book in human history. It really "tells it like it is!" Its message always goes to the *heart of the problem* – which is always the *heart of man*. Its approach is first and foremost *pragmatic* – because it deals with the *root of the problem*, rather than the *fruit of the problem*. It is also *practical* in its solutions because it helps man deal with the *fruit* – or *consequences* of his sin and disobedience – through repentance, restitution and restoration.

The Bible is both *pragmatic in its diagnosis*, and *practical in its prognosis!* It confronts man with the *real problem* and offers him a *realistic solution*. Because of this resource, *Christian leaders should be giving the most practical and pragmatic leadership in society!* Remember: *"Spirituality is practicality."* The more authentically spiritual a leader is, the more practical his leadership will be. If a person is not intensely *practical,* he is not innately *spiritual!* To *grow in spirituality* is to *grow in practicality.* In other words, true spirituality means to *be like the Lord Jesus* Who was *the world's most practical Person!*

Principle:

"Since the Bible is pragmatic in its diagnosis, and practical in its prognosis, Christian leaders are to be the most pragmatic and practical people in society."

FURTHER QUOTATIONS ON
PRAGMATIC LEADERS

- *Many times we rationalize a questionable method as practical because 'it works.' But is 'working' the real test of spiritual endeavors?...Working isn't the perfect test, for Moses struck the rock twice and* it worked. *That is, water came out – but he was kept from the Promised Land. Our nonscriptural human methods might work, but do they keep us from entering the "Promised Land" of peace and joy?*[2]

- *Having the world's best idea will do you no good unless you act on it. People who want milk shouldn't sit on a stool in the middle of a field in hopes that a cow will back up to them.*[3]

- *Availability has been defined as "being willing to start where you are, use what you have, and do the best you can."*[4]

- *Truly adaptive firms with adaptive cultures are awesome competitive machines. They produce superb products and services faster and better. They run circles around bloated bureaucracies...*[5]

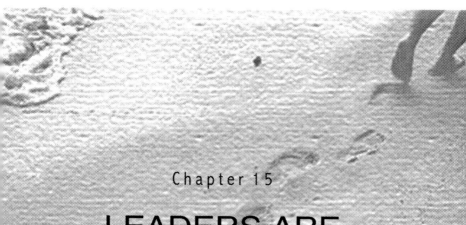

Chapter 15

LEADERS ARE PUNCTUAL

"Therefore be careful how you walk, not as unwise men, but as wise, making the most of your time…"
(Ephesians 5:15-16).

"Time efficiency is leadership efficiency." *Management of time* and *management of people* always go together. If you cannot manage one, you cannot manage the other. Leaders are always *time-conscious people* – which means that they are *"on time people."* As a result of that philosophy, they do not *waste their own time* nor do they *waste other people's time.* Leaders live with a growing awareness, which increases and intensifies with time, that *TIME is their most precious gift!* Leaders understand that time is their single greatest resource. It is far more valuable than gold or silver – or any other material possession! Unlike money, *time cannot be saved up.* There is no bank account for time. Unlike other resources, time cannot be stored-up…stocked-piled…reserved…or contained. It can only be used. Once time is used, it cannot be re-used or un-used. *Time is a non-renewable resource.* Once it is spent, it is gone forever. For each and every person, *death marks the end of time.*

All effective leaders understand the nature and importance of time – those increments of our lives that are measured by our watches and by our calendars. Because time is *linear,* it is described by words like *past, present* and *future.* As a result, *time marches relentlessly onward!* It will not stand still or turn back for anyone. By nature, time is always *one-way.* There are no quick detours from the present to the future – just as there are no turn-arounds back to the past. All that time allows us is this *present moment.* Time does not permit any of us the luxury of re-runs. There are no "time machines" that allow us a reversal to the past, or a fast-forward to the future, except in the movies! We can only go back to the past in our minds through *memory* – or move into the future through our *fantasy.* Even though there is a great element of *mystery about time,* there are some important *principles of time* that we can and need to understand – and then live and lead by.

Like all of creation, *time was created by God.* It is not self-existent, or eternal. Neither is time cyclical or repetitive, as believed in Eastern mysticism. Since time was created by an omnipotent God, *there was a time when time did not exist.* But God – Who exists outside of time – spoke into the void of timeless, empty space – and *time began.* That was the *alpha point* of time. Since He created time **"...in the beginning"** (Gen. 1:1) – one day He will bring it to an end. As the Eternal **"I Am,"** (Ex. 3:14: Jn. 8:58), God is sovereign over time, and totally unaffected by its progression. Until then, Jesus Christ is the *Eternal Word* (Jn. 1:1), Who is Sovereign Lord over all time. He alone is the **"*Alpha* and *Omega*...the *Beginning* and *End*...the *First* and *Last*"** (Rev. 1:8; 21:6; 22:13). Everything else in creation has had a *beginning,* and will have an *ending.*

The Bible describes this kind of created time by the word *chronos,* from which we obviously get the English word *chronology.* In the Bible, *chronos* generally means the "space of time" or the "duration of time" – whether that time is *short* or *long* (Mtt. 2:7; Lk. 4:5; 8:27; 20:9, etc). It is by this kind of time that we mark the passing of our lives – in increments of seconds...minutes...hours...days...weeks...month...years...decades... centuries...millennia. It is the events that have happened in *chronological time* that historians record in their annals. Futurologists, on the other hand, try and predict things to come. The tick of the clock measures the passing of one's life. Like the beating of one's heart, the ticking of the clock is not infinite! All of us have a *finite* number of heartbeats – and a *finite* number of ticks of the clock!

Effective leaders know they cannot "beat the clock"…turn back the time…reverse the flow of the sand in the hour glass…or turn back the shadow on the sun dial! *Time relentlessly marches on!* Wise leaders can and do learn to become good *managers* of the time that they have. It is *chronos time* that is the focus of attention in *Time Management Seminars* that are so popular in the business world today.

As important as *chronos* time is, there is another kind of time that is even more important. The Bible calls this time *kairos*. It is a "divine moment." Wise and effective leaders – and especially *spiritual leaders* – understand the difference between these two kinds of time. Let's take a moment to examine the difference between them.

Kairos is a "God moment" that sovereignly intervenes in time. This is a *chronos* moment when *kairos* invades human history with divine intent. *Salvation* was one of those *kairos* events planned by God in *eternity past* "**…before the beginning of time**" (II Tim. 1:9; Titus 1:2). As a result, "**When the *time* had fully come, God sent His Son, born of a woman…**" (Gal. 4:4). It was the *kairos* moment of Christ's birth that divided *chronos* into *B.C.* and *A.D.* Since His Incarnation, human history in most of the Western world has been reckoned in terms of *Before Christ*, and Anno Domini, *or "in the year of the Lord."*

Kairos time is a *sovereignly significant moment when eternity invades and interrupts time.* It is a *kairos moment* when God intervenes in human events in a special way – which we later refer to as the *miraculous*. *Chronos* becomes *sanctified* and *significant* when touched and transformed by *kairos*. A *kairos moment* has to do with God fulfilling…completing…consummating in time, a preordained plan and purpose of His own. Watches and calendars are not very effective in predicting or telling this kind of time. Our foreknowledge of *kairos* comes only through divine revelation. *Kairos* is the *God-kind-of-time* known only to Him. It is only the *Spirit* and the *Word* that can sensitize and attune our hearts and minds to this kind of *kairos* time!

All of time is important to God – whether it is *chronos* or *kairos*. However, it is *kairos* that especially has *eternal significance*. It is a manifestation of *eternity*, and is measured against the backdrop of *eternity* – which is *timeless*. This is the realm that God alone dwells within. While we are encapsulated in time, God dwells in *eternity* and is untouched by time (Ps. 90:2; 93:2). God is *immutable* or *changeless* throughout the ages (Mal. 3:3; Ja. 1:17). Only of God can it be said:

> **"You, O Lord, sit enthroned *forever*, Your renown endures through all generations...*Your years go on through all generations*. In the beginning You laid the foundations of the earth, and the heavens are the work of Your hands. They will perish, *but You remain;* they will all wear out like a garment. Like clothing You will change them... But *You remain the same, and Your years will never end*"** (Ps. 102:12, 24-27; Isa. 51:6).

It is because of His *omnipotence over time* that God can be *omnipresent in time!* When He supernaturally manifests Himself within the *chronos* of the *cosmos*, it is a *kairos moment!* Jesus was the only person Who has ever lived Whose *chronos time* was perfectly synchronized with God's *kairos time!* Jesus often spoke of this kind of *kairos* time when He said:

> **"My *time* has not yet come"** (Jn. 2:4);
> **"My appointed *time* is near"** (Matt. 26:18);
> **"Father, the *time* has come"** (Jn. 17:1).

Ultimately, it was **"...at the *right time* that Christ died for the ungodly"** (Rom. 5:6; Eph. 1:10). Since that divine saving moment, we all live in the "Age of Grace" – or God's **"...*acceptable time* of salvation"** (II Cor. 6:2). Both *chronos* and *kairos* find their focus and fulfillment in Jesus Christ! In all of our *chronos time*, Christ is to **"...have first place in everything"** (Col. 1:17-18). That only takes place when our *chronos time* is managed by God's *kairos time!*

We understand *chronos* by asking questions like: *"What time is it? Am I early or late? Am I out of time?"* By contrast, *kairos* asks a different question: *"What is time for? What am I living for? Am I ready? Is this the right time?"* Whereas *chronos* is concerned about the *quantity* of time, *kairos* is more concerned about the *quality* of time. We imply this when we ask a question like: *"Did you have a good time?"* The emphasis is not upon the *quantity* of time spent – but rather upon the *quality* of the time invested. Was it meaningful...rewarding...fulfilling...significant?

Principle:

Chronos is concerned about
the *quantity* of time and asks:
"What time is it?" **Kairos** is concerned
about the *quality* of time and asks:
"What is time for?"

Chronos time tends to be characterized by *doing*, while *kairos* time tends to be more concerned with *being*. Without the revelation of *kairos*, we just go through life expending our *chronos* – or just "putting in our time." It is only a sense of *kairos* that gives meaning and purpose to whatever *chronos* we may be entrusted with by God. Without a sense of the *kairos* of God, we will be reduced to living our lives by the *tyranny of the clock*. We may be very busy in *going* and *doing* – but we may be "hurrying big for little reasons!"

It is only a sense of *kairos* that enables us to live by God's *compass* rather than by man's *calendar*. It is only *kairos* that gives us *direction* in life and gets us in sync with God's timing. It is *kairos* that helps us balance our *doing* by our *being*. It is *chronos* that asks the question: *"Am I doing things right?"* But it is *kairos* that asks: *"Am I doing the right things?"* The whole area of *Time Management* is concerned with the best use of *chronos*. However, it is *Spiritual Time Management* that is concerned with *kairos*: *"Am I doing the right things? Am I living my life in step with God? Does my life have a divine cutting edge to it? Is there eternal significance in what I am doing? Is my purpose, God's purpose? Is my will, His will? Is my time, His time? Has my chronos been invaded and transformed by kairos?"*

Principle:
Chronos asks: *"Am I doing things right?"*
Kairos asks: *"Am I doing the right things?"*

A good leader is acutely aware of the *natural time*, or *chronos*, by which we all live our lives – measured by the ticks of a clock...the numbers on our calendar...or pages in our Day-Timer. He understands that this kind of *human time* is very crucial because it marks out the days of his life and leadership on earth. He is even more aware of *spiritual time*, or *kairos*, and what the Bible calls the **"...times and seasons"** (Acts 1:7). This is *eschatological time* that we only know through *prophecy*. It is only through *Biblical revelation* that we can receive from God an eternal glimpse into His timetable for the universe. It is God's *eternal epoch* that is being played out on the pages of our human calendars until the **"...end of the age"** (Mtt. 24:3). According to the Bible, this is the final time of the *consummation of human history* as we understand it – which is a date known only to God. It was this *eschatological time* that Jesus was referring to when He chided the religious leaders of His day: **"How is it that you don't know how to interpret this present time?"** (Lk. 12:56). Despite the fact that they were very religious – and even had God's Word among them – they were still living in total ignorance of what God was doing at that strategic time in history. The very God Who had created time was right in their midst – but their eschatological clocks were wrong! Therefore, they missed out on the grace God was providing in the **"...fullness of time"** (Gal. 4:4; Eph. 1:10). Tragically, there are still many such religious leaders living today who are completely out of touch and out of step with what God is doing! It is because of the revelation of this eternal perspective on time, that wise Christian leaders are *time conscious people.* They do not want to waste time because they fully understand that *all time has eternal consequences!*

Principle: *"Leaders understand that all time has eternal consequences."*

Christians in general, and leaders in particular, seek to live with a consciousness of *natural time,* or *chronos,* and *spiritual time,* or *kairos.* Through the revelation of the Word, and the inspiration of the Spirit, they seek to discern God's perspective on their time – and then live their lives accordingly. It is only as they live in *time,* from the vantage point of *eternity,* that they can synchronize their lives with what God is doing in the world. As they view the time frame that they live in through the lenses of God's revelation, they are able to discern and interpret the **"...times and seasons."** Only then will their leadership be *timely... strategic... prophetic.*

> *"Even the right decision is the*
> *wrong decision if it is made too late."* [1]
> **(Lee Iacocca, Industrialist)**

At that point they will be like the men of Issachar. The Bible says it was a defining time of national crisis in the life of Israel. It was a time when visionary leadership was desperately needed! We read that **"...the men of Issachar...***understood the times* **and** *knew what Israel should do"* (I Chron. 12:32). It was only when they correctly discerned the seriousness of the hour in which they were living that they could take the proper action and do what **"...Israel should do."**

We can also see in this verse about the **"men of Issachar"** another important principle of leadership: *"A keen sense of timing is often what distinguishes a person and causes him to emerge as a leader."* A common question about leadership is this: *"Do the times make the man, or does the man make the times?"* I think it is *both.* Even though there is a certain mystery in time that we do not always fully understand, we know that history often pauses for a moment at a certain strategic intersection. At that *kairos moment,* certain significant events emerge that provoke a conflict and crisis. This creates a social or political turmoil that makes it a strategic time in the history of that nation. It becomes one of those *defining moments* in life – and often a *turning point* in history. While those events are merging and converging, most people are unaware of their significance. It is often at that moment that a discerning person arises from the masses to *take the challenge* – and in the process ends up *taking charge.* He emerges as a leader who has correctly discerned the *kairos moment* – and seized it, for better or worse. It becomes a *distinguishing moment* for him, and often a *defining moment* in history. This is true in military campaigns...social conflicts... political events...athletic games...or spiritual movements. It is both the *"times that make the leader,* and *the leader that makes the time!"* Strategic leaders therefore need a *good sense of timing.*

> *"The most important ability of a leader is timing."* [2]
> **(Fred Smith)**

As a result of this growing understanding of the *eternal significance of time*, leaders are always very *time-conscious* and *on-time people*. Leaders make it a practice to always be on time. Being tardy or late is a rare exception for a leader, rather than the norm. Usually a good leader is not just "on time", he or she is early! One of my own favorite phrases is: "If you are on time, you're late – but if you are early, you are on time!"

Biblical leaders operate on "God's time", not on "African time"..."Asian time"..."American time"..."Indian time"...or "Haitian time." They believe that all time is God's time – so they take the stewardship of time very seriously.

Principle:
"Leaders understand that all time has eternal consequences. Therefore, they never waste their time, or the time of others."

Leaders understand that constantly being late is a sign of *insensitivity* and *selfishness*. The person who is perpetually late is thinking only of himself – if he is thinking at all! His perpetual tardiness is a measurable example of his complete insensitivity of other people's time and schedule. Constantly being late is a form of *stealing*. It is robbing other people of the time that you have wasted by being late – and by keeping them waiting. *Time theft* is a great relational sin! Tragically, it is rampant in the body of Christ!

Principle:
"Always being late is a sign of selfishness and insensitivity."

Wasting time is more than just *theft* – it is *murder!* In America, young people have an expression that they sometimes use when they are just "hanging out" with nothing to do. They call it *"killing time."* I am so thankful that my parents taught me the importance of wisely using time when I was growing up. They taught me this principle by precept and example: *"Killing time is not murder – it is suicide!"* They helped me understand while I was young that when I wasted time, I was squandering

234

my most precious gift – one that I could never regain once I had lost it. Wasting time is a *slow suicide!* It is nothing short of *killing yourself*, second by second...minute by minute...hour by hour...day by day! Once you "kill time" – regardless of how much or how little – it is forever gone. It is *dead time* that can never to be resurrected. Leaders are committed to doing everything in their power to be *punctual* so they do not waste their time, or other people's time. They increasingly discipline themselves to use their time *purposefully* and *productively*.

"The greatest time wasted
is the time getting started."
(Dawson Trotman, Founder of Navigators)

As we saw by the Bible verse that introduced this chapter, the Apostle Paul was a *time conscious person.* He was a *man on a mission* – a *divine mission.* On the Damascus Road, his *chronos time* was invaded by the *kairos* of Christ to the degree that his priorities were forever changed! From that moment on, Paul was a *sanctified man* who was set apart exclusively for the *kairos* of God! He had a **"heavenly vision"** (Acts 26:19) that gave him *earthly significance!* It was the *kairos* of Christ that gave him a *holy passion* for living and leading! He even went so far as to say that the use of time was one of the distinguishing marks between a *wise man* and a *foolish man.* As such, he preached and practiced the principle of **"...redeeming the time"** (Eph. 5:16; KJV). Various translations render these words of Paul this way:

> **"Be very careful, then, how you live – not as unwise, but as wise, *making the most of every opportunity*, because the days are evil." (NIV)**

> **"So be careful how you live, not as fools but as those who are wise. *Make the most of every opportunity* for doing good in these evil days." (New Living Translation)**

> **"Pay close attention to how you live. Don't live like ignorant men, but like wise men. *Make good use of every opportunity you get*, because these are bad days." (TEV).**

> **"Live life, then, with a due sense of responsibility, not as men who do not know the meaning and purpose of life but as those who do. *Make the best use of your time*, despite all the difficulties of these days."** (Phillips).

There is one theme that rings out loud and clear in all of these various translations of Paul's words: *Use your time wisely!* The word Paul used here for **"redeeming the time,"** or **"make the most of every opportunity,"** is another word straight out of the business world of his day. It was the verb *exagorazo.* The root of this verb is the noun, *agora,* which means *"marketplace."* This was a *commercial term.* It was a very common *business phrase* that everyone in Paul's day fully understood. When someone was going to the *marketplace* to shop, they went to the *agora.* I have personally been to the ruins of the ancient *agora* in Ephesus, Corinth, and Greece. This was the "business district" where all of the shops and kiosks were set up by the merchants and sellers of goods. The ones who were successful were the ones who **"...redeemed the time,"** who **"...made the most of every opportunity."**

This principle of the *economy of time* is a concept that every successful businessman clearly understands. He knows that he will not stay in business very long unless he learns to *"redeem the time."* He well knows that, if he does not *"buy up every opportunity"*, his competitors will! He must be very time-conscious in running his business if he is going to be viable and profitable. Successful businessmen are at their companies early – and often stay late. While some of their employees just "punch the clock" and "put in their time" – the owner always buys up every opportunity to make a sale. He puts forth the *extra effort* and *extra time* that it takes to get the job done. The owner wants to seize every opportunity to do business. He does not want to lose a single customer or sale. He knows if he is going to stay in business and grow, he must stay ahead of the competition and the best way to do that is to use time more wisely than others. The businessman who wastes time destroys his business! Likewise, the Christian leader who wastes time kills his ministry!

No businessman ever becomes successful by lounging around in bed all morning while his competitors are "up early" with the sign on their door beckoning: *"Open For Business!"* He does not become profitable unless he seizes every business opportunity possible. When "opportunity does not come knocking at his door", he goes out and "knocks on its door!"

With very similar words to the ones in Ephesians 5:16, Paul exhorted the Christians at Colosse: **"Walk in wisdom...** *making the most of the* ***time"*** (Col. 4:5). This matter of *time consciousness* was not just something Paul wanted the Christians living in Ephesus to be concerned about. He wanted all of his fellow Christians in every church he planted to learn the *stewardship of time.* He not only taught it, Paul *lived it.* That's why he could remind them of his tireless toil *"...**night** and **day** with tears"* (Acts 20:31).

"The leader must aim himself or herself
to seize the vital chance for action, for
there only may be one golden chance."[3]
(Richard Phillips)

Like the Apostle Paul, every wise leader is a person who **"redeems the time."** Since he is in business for the King of kings, he zealously goes about his ministry with the passion of a businessman who loves his work! As a Kingdom businessman, he **"buys up every opportunity"** to turn a spiritual profit for His heavenly Investor! He eagerly gets out into the *marketplace of life* and does business for the Kingdom of God. He does so with a sense of *urgency* because he remembers the words of the Lord Jesus, when He said: **"As long as it is day, we must do the work of Him Who sent Me. Night is coming, when no one can work"** (Jn. 9:4-5).

"If we progress in the economy of time, we
are learning to live. If we fail here, we fail
everywhere. Time lost can never be retrieved.
Time cannot be hoarded, only spent well."
(Oswald Sanders)

I believe that the Holy Spirit is trying to say to many Christian leaders today what He said to those early Ephesian Christians: **"...Wake up, O sleeper, rise from the dead...** *making the most of every opportunity* **because the days are evil."**

Oswald Sanders wrote this about Paul's use of time – which is a timely model for every effective leader:

> *We are not responsible for our endowments or natural abilities, but we are responsible for the strategic use of time. When Paul urged the Ephesians to 'redeem the time,' he was treating time like a purchase. We exchange time in the market of life for certain occupations and activities that may be worthy or not, productive or not...Herein lies the importance of a carefully planned life: 'If we progress in the economy of time, we are learning to live. If we fail here, we fail everywhere.' Time lost can never be retrieved. Time cannot be hoarded, only spent well.*[4]

That's an incredible quote! It represents so much wisdom and insight into the most basic aspect of living – the *stewardship of time*. As Sanders wisely points out, when we fail in the use of time, we fail everywhere else! When we begin to discipline our time – *master our moments* – then we are on the road to leadership success!

The Apostle Paul was obviously a man who understood *kairos*, or time from God's perspective. He *spoke prophetically* and *lived strategically*. That's why he accomplished so much in his lifetime. It was because he knew that he was living in the **"...last days"** of redemptive history (II Tim. 3:1), that he wanted to wisely use whatever *chronos* time God gave him. He sought to *maximize every moment* for the Kingdom of God! You can hear his sense of urgency when he reminded the Church at Corinth: **"...the time is short!"** (I Cor. 7:29).

Principle:

"Since the times make the leader, and the leader makes the times, strategic leaders need a good sense of timing, so they will know when to seize the moment."

In everything we do, we make a "time purchase." *Time is the currency with which we pay for life.* We exchange a certain portion of time for everything we do. Each payment of time can never be repeated – it is a one-time purchase that allows no exchanges. We should approach each day with the following awareness:

"This is the beginning of a new day. God has given me this day to use as I will. I can waste it or use it for good. But what I do today is important because I am exchanging a day of my life for it. When tomorrow comes, this day will be gone forever, leaving in its place something that I have traded for it. I want it to be gain and not loss; good and not evil; success and not failure; in order that I shall not regret the price I have paid for it." (Author unknown).

As we have already seen, Jesus lived and ministered with an acute understanding of the importance of time. This was reflected in His statement to the disciples: **"As long as it is day, we must do the work of Him Who sent Me. Night is coming, when no one can work."** (John 9:4). No leader knows how long his "day of ministry" will be. For Jesus, it was just three short years. But His life and ministry reveal the principle that it is not so much *how long* we live, as *how well* we live. There are many people who live very long lives – but accomplish very little. They just "put in their time." There are others whose lives are much shorter – but their influence and impact is far reaching. One of the things that make the difference is the *wise use of time.*

Principle:
"The best use of one's life is to spend it for something that will outlast it. Life's value is not its duration but its donation – not how long we live, but how fully and how well."[5]
(William James, philosopher)

Beware of the *sin of procrastination!* It is one of the greatest "time robbers" in life! If you allow this thief to enter your life, he will steal you blind! He will rob you of a life of strategic time investment! This folly of *time and task deferment* known as *procrastination,* seduces us to puts off until tomorrow what should be done *today.* This mentality is based upon the false assumption that tomorrow, or sometime later, we will have the same opportunity...the door will still be open...we will "feel like it"...the time will be better for us than it is now. At that fuzzy future time we hope will come, we will then be able to *begin the project...initiate the change... make the improvement...finish the job.* None of us is promised tomorrow – so we must *seize today!* Many people *procrastinate their lives away!* They are always waiting for that ethereal nebulous *"perfect time!"* They are living their lives waiting for that hoped-for "right alignment of the stars"… "opportunity of a lifetime"…"BIG BREAK" – when they will "hit the jackpot"…and "win life's lottery!" Success in life doesn't accidentally or capriciously come with the BIG BREAK. It comes through *discipline* and *obedience*. It is *faithfulness in the little things* that brings success: *one minute at a time…one hour at a time…one day at a time…one week at a time…one month at a time…one year at a time!* Many wise and successful leaders have learned this principle: *"Success is a long obedience in the same direction."* It does not come through *procrastination* – but through *punctuality*. That means being on time…in your place…doing the job…faithful in the small things…striving for quality…always giving your best. That's where success comes from!

Principle:

"Success is a long obedience in the same direction. It does not come through procrastination –but through punctuality."

Oswald Sanders writes this about the *sin of procrastination* which defrauds millions of people of significance and success in life:

> *Procrastination, the thief of time, is one of the devil's most potent weapons for defrauding us of eternal heritage. The habit of 'putting off' is fatal to spiritual leadership. Its power resides in our natural reluctance to come to grips with important decisions. Making decisions, and acting on them, always requires moral energy. But the passing of time never makes action easier; quite the opposite. Most decisions are more difficult a day later, and you may also lose an advantage by such delay.[6]*

Sanders also writes that it is the motto: *"Do it now,"* that has led so many people to worldly success – as well as to spiritual success. He advises that one of the best ways to practically avoid procrastination is to *"…set deadlines, and never miss or postpone even one."* [7]

> *"Our problem is not too little time, but*
> *making better use of the time we have. Each*
> *of us has as much time as anyone else."*[8]
> **(Oswald Sanders)**

One of the best ways to win over procrastination is to *prioritize* your time. Learn some basic principles of *time management* – and reprioritize your life around them. Priorities will help you move logically and sequentially from goal to goal. Priorities will help you *do the right things* – not just *do things right.* Then and only then will you avoid living your life in irrelevant circles – which does not make you a "Big Wheel!" The Bible calls this the lifestyle of a *fool* who is *on a meaningless circuitous journey to eternal anonymity!*

The principle is still true that says: *"The shortest distance between two points is a straight line."* Effective leaders like *straight lines* to the obvious – rather than *circuitous lines* around the solution! Good leaders usually do not like "holding patterns" or "treading water." They want to "cut to the chase" and get to the *bottom line...goal line...finish line* as quickly as possible. The only way to do that is by *prioritizing your life* and then allotting your time accordingly. Once you get "first things first," it is much easier to prioritize the rest of your life. Here are the basic Biblical priorities for you to build your life around:

>Time with your Savior (Christ);
>Time with the Scripture (Word);
>Time with your Spouse (Mate);
>Time with your Sires (Children);
>Time with your Sheep (People).

Once you prioritize your life around these Biblical values, and commit yourself by God's help to be *punctual in your time allotment* to them, you will be qualified to lead others. In order to be able to lead others, you must first of all be led yourself. The person who cannot *lead himself* through self-discipline and wise time-management, will not be able to *lead others.* If you can't manage your own time, you certainly cannot manage other people's time – which is what leadership is all about.

Principle:
*"If you can't manage time, you can't manage people. If
you can't lead yourself, then you can't lead others."*

I want to close this chapter with a little anonymous poem that really captures and summarizes the importance of time in the life of every person. I first read it in Herman Cain's book, *Leadership is Common Sense.* I have written it in the back of my Bible as a constant reminder of God's *kairos moments.* It reminds us that *eternity* is calibrated into every moment of time. The poem is simply entitled *"God's Minute."*

> *I've only just a minute,*
> *Only sixty seconds in it.*
> *Forced upon me, can't refuse it,*
> *Didn't seek it, didn't choose it,*
> *But it's up to me to use it.*
> *I must suffer if I lose it,*
> *Give an account if I abuse it.*
> *Just a tiny little minute,*
> *But eternity is in it.*[9]

FURTHER QUOTATIONS ON
LEADERS AND TIME

1. TIME:

- *David Livingstone, at age ten, worked in a cotton mill in Dumbarton fourteen hours a day. Surely he had excuses for not studying, for not redeeming the little leisure left to him. But he learned Latin and could read Horace and Virgil at age sixteen. At age twenty-seven, he had finished a program in both medicine and theology. Similar examples are so numerous that we have little ground today to plead insufficient time for achieving something worthwhile in life.*[10]

- *Our emotions have a lot to do with our timing. If we are too anxious, we may fire someone too early. If we are afraid, we wait too long. My experience is that many more miss proper timing by being late than by being early. Fear of making a mistake is the culprit.*[11]

- *To do important tasks, two things are necessary: a plan and not quite enough time.*[12]

- *Never complain about a lack of time until you are equaling or exceeding the great people of history. They all had the same amount of time.*[13]

- *The way we employ the surplus hours after provision has been made for work, meals, and sleep will determine if we develop into mediocre or powerful people. Leisure is a glorious opportunity and a subtle danger. Each moment of the day is a gift from God that deserves care, for by any measure our time is short and the work is great. Minutes and hours wisely used translate into an abundant life.*[14]

- *John Wesley and F.B. Meyer, men who influenced the world for Christ, divided their days into five-minute periods, then tried to make each one count.*[15]

- *Each of us has the time to do the whole will of God for our lives. J.H. Jowett said: 'It is never the supremely busy men who have no time. So compact and systematic is the regulation of their day that whenever you make a demand on them, they seem to find additional corners to offer for unselfish service. I confess as a minister, that the men to whom I most hopefully look for additional service are the busiest men.' Our problem is not too little time, but making better use of the time we have. Each of us has as much time as anyone else. The president of the United States has the same twenty-four hours as well. Others may surpass our abilities, influence, or money, but no one has more time.*[16]

- *When we talk about "the passion of vision," we're talking about a deep, sustained energy that comes from a comprehensive, principle-based, need-based, endowment-based seeing that goes beyond chronos and even kairos. It deals with an* aeon *concept of time, from the Greek* aion, *meaning an age, a lifetime or more. It taps into the deep core of who we are and what we are about. It's fueled by the realization of the unique contribution we have the capacity to make — the legacy we can leave. It clarifies purpose, gives direction, and empowers us to perform beyond our resources...We call it 'passion' because this vision can become a motivating force so powerful it, in effect, becomes the DNA of our lives. It's so ingrained and integrated into every aspect of our being that it becomes the compelling impetus behind every decision we make. It's the fire within — the explosion of inner synergy that happens when critical mass is reached in integration of the four fundamental needs. It's the energy that makes life an adventure — the deep burning "yes!" that empowers us to say "no" — peacefully and confidently — to the less important things in our lives...The power of transcendent vision is greater than the power of the scripting deep inside the human personality and it subordinates it, submerges it, until the whole personality is reorganized in the accomplishment of that vision. The passion of* shared *vision empowers people to transcend the petty, negative interactions that consume so much time and effort and deplete quality of life.*[17]

2. PROCRASTINATION:

- *The man God uses is a* man of action. *He doesn't make excuses or wait for better weather or a more* appropriate time.

He is a man who sees what needs to be done and then does it — in spite of the fact that he might be helping his own worst enemy.[18]

Chapter 16

LEADERS ARE PERSISTENT

"Finally my brothers, be steadfast, immovable, always abounding in the work of the Lord, knowing that your toil is not in vain in the Lord" (I Cor. 15:58; NASV).

Persistency is another distinguishing characteristic of *leaders that last.* By nature and temperament, most leaders are *persistent people.* Their lives are characterized by *steadfastness.* They are not easily swayed from their goal – but are *persistent* and *persevering.* It is not enough for a leader to have a *purpose,* and know his life *priorities.* He must have *persistence* in order to achieve them. It is often the *power of persistence* that helps leaders achieve their goal. *Persistence* causes them to "go the distance" – like a long-distance runner.

Good leaders are people who are *consistently persistent* and *persistently consistent.* One of a leader's greatest *abilities* is his *stick-ability* – or the ability to "*stick with it*" until the desired goal is reached. Walt Disney said: *"The only talent is perseverance."* Good leaders not only have "*starting power*", they also have "*staying power!*" Why? Because they have learned that life is a long series of *obstacles* that are often *opportunities* in disguise. This tenacious persistence is an important leadership quality that attracts other people. People are drawn to a leader who is consistent... persistent...predictable.

Principle:
"One of a leader's greatest *abilities* is his *stick-ability*. He is *consistently persistent* and *persistently consistent*."

The late Bob Pierce, founder of *World Vision,* said this: "The one thing that distinguishes the organization that wins is *staying power.*" Successful organizations have *staying power* because they have a CEO with *staying power.* If the leader is not *consistently persistent* and *persistently consistent,* people will not be attracted to his leadership. A leader must first of all model what he wants to call forth in his followers. If he wants his followers to persist with him toward the accomplishment of his vision, he must first of all model a life of *consistency* and *persistency* in that pursuit. There must be a dogged persistence at the top – in order for there to be an overflow of persistency to the other members of the organization. *Persistence is persuasive* – seeing it in action gives others "staying power."

"*The one thing that distinguishes the organization that wins is* staying power."
(Bob Pierce)

Because leaders are persistent and have *staying power,* they do not easily or quickly give up. By nature they are not quitters. They do not allow negative attitudes to linger long in their own minds – nor do they tolerate that attitude in their closest associates. Defeatist words like *can't...quit... give up...it won't work...throw in the towel* are not in their dictionary or vocabulary! *Difficulties, obstacles, problems* and *failures* do not stop true leaders. These things may set them back or slow them down – but they will not stop true leaders for good. Leaders who go the distance understand that "blood, sweat and tears" are the down payment for success. They are not looking for someone to carry their load – someone on whom they can dump their responsibilities. Leaders are willing to "pay the price" in order to reach their goal. Oswald Sanders says this about the persistence that is needed in Christian leadership:

The spirit of the welfare state does not produce leaders. If a Christian is not willing to rise early and work late, to expend greater effort in diligent study and faithful work, that person will not change a generation. Fatigue is the price of leadership. Mediocrity is the result of never getting tired. [1]

"Fatigue is the price of leadership."
(Oswald Sanders)

One of the reasons more people do not rise to the challenges of leadership is that they want to live in a "welfare state." They are not willing to put forth all of the added effort that is necessary to succeed at something great. They do not want to sweat. They do not want to move out of their *comfort zone* into the unknown – or into the *danger zone*. They want someone else to take all of the risks. They prefer the security of the barracks to the heat of the frontlines. They do not want to experience "battle fatigue." They want someone else to do all of the work and fighting for them. Leaders understand that there are no "free tickets…free lunches….free rides…free successes. "They understand the difference between *welfare* and *workfare.* They are willing to "pay their own way" rather than look to others to "pick up the tab." Leaders that last soon learn to quit looking for the "quick fix" or "easy way out." When things get tough – they get tougher! When they "hit the wall", they dig deep inside themselves for those inner reserves that bring forth that "second wind" so they can go the distance.

Early on in their lives, leaders that last square-off with the giant of *failure.* Not only do leaders have to learn to deal with *fatigue* – they also have to learn to deal with *failure.* By meeting this menacing giant head-on – *face-to-face* – they learn to cut him down to size. Gradually they learn by experience not to be intimidated by his threats of destruction. Maturing leaders soon learn that one of their greatest preparations for life in general, and leadership in particular, is learning to successfully deal with *failure.* It has been said that the major difference between *average people* and *achieving people* is their *response to failure.* One of the greatest freedoms a Christian leader has is the *freedom to fail.* He understands that his relationship with God, as well as his value as a person, is not based upon achievements or success. Because he knows that he is *loved unconditionally*, he is freed from the *success syndrome* that tells him that his worth is determined by his *successfulness* rather than his *faithfulness*. The person who has never learned to deal with failure will never have the opportunity to deal with success. *Failure is one of the routes to success!* Learning to face and overcome our failure builds persistence into our lives. *Failure never destroys anyone!* Never has, never will. It is just not that powerful!

Principle:
**"The difference between *average people* and
achieving people is their attitude toward failure."**

It is not our failures that hurt or destroy us. It is our *response to failure* that is the determining factor. Someone rightly said: "Being defeated is a temporary condition. Giving up is what makes it permanent!" No person is a failure who gets up one more time than he falls down! It is only when they *give up where they fall* that they become a *failure*. It is when a person "rolls over and emotionally dies" where he has failed and fallen – that he becomes a failure. *Failing* and *falling* is not failure – only quitting is. *Persistent leaders always get up one more time than they fall down!* Their "getting up" and "starting again" always exceeds by *one* the number of times they fall!

Principle:
*"The person who has never learned to deal with
failure will never have the opportunity to deal with
success."*

As Fred Smith wisely points out, mistakes in ministry are very similar to mistakes with money. We often deal with our financial mistakes in one way – and our leadership failures in another.

> *In finances we learn to take a loss as soon as possible – cut the loss, don't throw good money after bad; only obsessive gamblers do that. By the same logic, leaders must name and claim mistakes as soon as possible. Minimize the loss, and start remedial actions immediately... Intelligent leaders profit from their mistakes by not repeating them...*

Failures must be recognized as soon as possible. It is better to bury a corpse than to perfume it! [2]

Every great leader has had MANY failures in their leadership journey. In fact, many have had far more failures than they have had successes. They have learned to quickly "cut their losses" and move on. They do not try to ignore or rationalize their mistakes and failures. Nor do they try to blame others for their own failures. Instead, they humbly "name and claim their failures" ASAP. Rather than deceptively trying to cover-up their failures – or "perfuming the corpse" of their mistakes – they immediately go proactive. They take whatever remedial action necessary to correct things. They bury their failures – rather than allow their failures to bury them.

It is a leader's *persistence* that will not allow them to quit in the face of failure. Leaders have learned that some of their greatest lessons came through failure. They often refer to the "school of success" as the "school of hard-knocks!" It was those series of "hard knocks" through falling and failure that broke them so that God could really use them. Note these wise insights about failure...

- "The man God chooses to use, He must first hurt him very deeply" (A.W. Tozer).

- "Breakthrough happened around me when break-up happened within me" (Pastor Jack Hayford).

- "Those who fail in the task of leadership are among its best teachers; for in their glaring mistakes and distorted values we at least see what we must avoid, with a clarity often harder to discern in those more successful." [3]

God redemptively uses the failures and fallings in our lives to break us of our *"self-sins": self-centeredness, self-importance, self-will, self-rule, self-sufficiency, and self-satisfaction.* This is one of the ways that God turns our *blunders* into *blessings.* It is when a leader becomes vulnerable about his failures with his followers that he is most helpful to them. A leader's vulnerability about failure becomes the "highway of hope" and the "bridge of blessing" on which others can walk away from their own mistakes and defeats. People are often more encouraged by our failures than by our successes. Leaders must learn to be *vulnerable...transparent...open...honest.* If a leader will let down the drawbridge protecting his aloofness in the ivory "tower of power", then others will become more open and vulnerable about their mistakes and fear of failure. While we may *impress people with our successes,* we *encourage them with our failures.* Only secure leaders will talk about their failures. Insecure leaders only want to talk about their successes. A leader may temporarily *impress* people by his successes, but he will lastingly *impact* people by the lessons from his failures – lessons that have broken and matured him into a wiser person.

"Many of life's failures are people
who did not realize how close they
were to success when they gave up." [+]
(Thomas Edison)

Through persistence and practice, successful leaders have learned the art of *failing and falling forward!* They seldom ever fall backward – because their emotional engine does not have a reverse gear! When they do fall – as every leader does – they generally *fall forward toward their goal!* Remember the story of the children of Israel who wandered in the wilderness for forty years? Their problem was that most of them continued to fail and fall toward *Egypt* – rather than toward the *Promised Land.* The *nature of their failure* and the *direction of their falling* revealed where their hearts really were. Their affections were more back in Egypt than they were in the Promised Land. There were several among them however, like Joshua and Caleb, who had a very different spirit. Their hearts and affections were no longer in Egypt, but in the Promised Land. Whenever they failed and fell, they *fell forward* – toward the Promised Land! Their spirits and bodies were pointing toward the **"...land flowing with milk and honey"** (Ex. 3:8) – not toward the **"...flesh pots of Egypt"** (Ex. 16:3; KJV)!

Principle:
"Persistent leaders fail frequently – but they always
fall forward."

I repeat again the words of the Apostle Paul with which we began this chapter: **"Therefore, my beloved brethren, be *steadfast, immovable,***

always abounding in the work of the Lord, knowing that your labor is not in vain in the Lord." (I Cor. 15:58; KJV). Paul wrote those words of exhortation to the saints in Corinth because they were not being *persistent* in their pursuit of Christ, nor *consistent* in their spiritual walk. They were constantly being swayed and influenced by the prosperity, paganism, and perversion that was rampant in Corinth. Rather than "**...abounding in the work,**" they were "**abounding in the world!**" He had to lovingly exhort them to *steadfastness...stick-ability...immovability... generosity...good works.*

Leaders that last are *persistent in their purpose.* They have "staying power" that sustains them to the end. They have a *stubborn stick-ability* that will not allow them to "cut and run" when things get difficult. They are characterized by a "hang-in-there" attitude rather than a "hang-loose" attitude. Effective leaders *persist* until they reach their goals – regardless of *how long...how hard...*or *how great the sacrifice.* Mature leaders understand that there is always *resistance* and *opposition* to the needed change they are trying to bring. John Kotter, of Harvard Business School, notes that, "Resistance is always waiting to reassert itself."[5] That's why persistence and perseverance in leadership are so necessary. He further writes:

> *Irrational and political resistance to change never fully dissipates... I'm confident of one cardinal rule: 'Whenever you let up before the job is done, critical momentum can be lost and regression may follow.'...Once regression begins, rebuilding momentum can be a daunting task...progress can slip quickly.*[6]

In time, a leader's *persistence produces prosperity.* If a leader is *persistent enough for long enough*, it will result in greater and greater degrees of *prosperity* in his life and leadership. By *prosperity*, I am not talking about money and material wealth. I am speaking of the greater *prosperity of relationships* that come from a *wealth of humility, integrity, character, trust, influence and respect.* When this kind of internal spiritual, mental, emotional and relational prosperity grows, there will be more and more external *success* in his leadership. *Faithfulness ultimately produces successfulness.*

Finally, the more prosperity...success...achievement...victory a leader experiences, the more *momentum* he develops in his life and leadership. As John Maxwell often says: "*Momentum is a leader's best friend!*"[7] Since *momentum* is a great friend and ally to a leader, let's take a moment to briefly look at this crucial leadership phenomena.

Leadership is like pushing a heavy car up a hill. In the early stages, inertia, immobility, and friction work against your attempts to "get things rolling." There is a lot of "dead weight" that is just "sitting there." A lot of resources and potential are just standing still – not interested in going anywhere! *Inertia* has overcome *initiative!* In order to "get things moving," there will have to be a lot of initial effort. A leader understands that it is impossible to get things off "dead center" effortlessly. There is going to have to be some sweating involved! Inertia is never overcome easily. For a period of time it is very hard work – and slow going. Often the progress seems to be measured only by sweaty inches and bloody centimeters! At times, all forward motion is stopped. There are times in leadership when all you can do is to stand still…tread water…kick things out of gear… idle in neutral. Every leader faces times when he has to stay in a "holding pattern" – like an airplane circling waiting to land. Sometimes even gains and growth are lost. During these times of "standing still" or "uphill battles," there is a lot of *groaning* with little *glory!* With persistence, the crest of the leadership hill is finally crossed – and then the *law of momentum* gradually takes over. More and more speed is picked up to the degree that it takes less and less time to cover distances. Gravity begins to work for you rather than against you. The wind is now at your back rather than in your face! The currents of life are flowing in your favor – rather than an undercurrent of opposition. Just as it is far easier to steer a moving vehicle than one standing still, it is easier to give direction to a life and leadership that has built up momentum. There are even times that you can relax more and just "coast down the hill!"

There is also a danger here. *Momentum can get out of control!* If *momentum is not managed*, it can become dangerous and destructive – just like a coasting vehicle down a curvy mountainous road! More and more speed is picked up until the "growth curves" become dangerous and leadership-threatening! During these times of quick growth, many leaders have "crashed and burned!" They could not – or would not – *manage their momentum!*

History and contemporary events warn us through the example of many leaders that were destroyed because *too much momentum was built up too quickly.* In time, the leader lost control – and was overtaken and crushed under the weight of his own success! It can easily become the problem of "too much too soon!" Too much success…achievement…advancement… notoriety…recognition…prosperity…money …power – too quickly can become deadly! Scores of lives and leaders have been destroyed because of *too much success too quickly.* Time proved that *they did not have the spiritual and emotional maturity to manage their momentum!* As a result of being in the "fast lane," they began to play "fast and loose" with the rules. They began to compromise…take short-cuts…rationalize…justify their excesses. One of the first places that momentum-out-of-control begins to manifest itself is through *money* and *morals.* In the conversations of their mind they rationalize: *"I deserve it…I have worked hard…I have sacrificed… This is what I have worked for…These are just the 'perks and privileges' of my position."* Often their marriage becomes the staging area for their excesses and extravagances. Soon their momentum takes a detour and heads in the wrong direction. It is only a matter of time until they self-destruct! This pattern of momentum-out-of-control is seen in both secular and sacred leaders. That's why the Bible warns us not to put young and immature Christians into positions of leadership too quickly. Listen to these wise words concerning the appointment of church leaders:

> **"He must not be a recent convert, or he may become *conceited* and fall under the same judgment as the devil"** (I Tim. 3:6).

Christian leaders need to remind themselves that it was the sin of pride that led to Lucifer's downfall (Isa. 14:11-15; Ezek. 28:12-17). Most of us are not very well prepared emotionally or spiritually to face either *failure* or *success!* We tend to settle down into *middle class mediocrity* – avoiding the dangers of success and failure. Either of these experiences can lead to the other. Failure can become the school that trains us for success; and success can be that experience that leads to failure. If a genuine spirit of humility accompanies our success, it will only bring glory to God. If our success results in haughtiness and pride, it will lead to our downfall and destruction! The success that comes from sustained momentum can either cause a leader to stand tall in pride and arrogance or bend low in humility and praise to God! Our Creator has given us a good example of leadership humility in nature: *"The limb that bears the most fruit bends the lowest to the ground!"* When God prospers a leader with a lot of successfulness and fruitfulness, He wants him to bow low before Him in humility and thanksgiving. He wants the leader to pass on the fruit of that success to his followers!

Momentum truly is one of the greatest friends of a leader. For it to be a leader's friend and ally, it must be *mature* and *managed momentum.* All leadership momentum must be managed by the maturity that only comes through the Spirit and the Word – and is monitored through accountability. Only then will *momentum* be one of a leader's best friends – rather than one of his worst enemies!

Let me close this chapter about leadership *persistence* and *perseverance* with a personal illustration. It concerns the writing of this book. You see, I have been trying to write this book now for well over two years. It first began to emerge as a teaching outline from Leadership Seminars I have taught in various countries for over a dozen years. As a result, I have had many National pastors requesting that I expand and amplify my teaching notes into a syllabus or book that they could have for further reading and study. I have been trying to complete the writing of this book to meet that need. At the same time, I have been writing and re-writing several other books and teaching guides that I had committed to write. All the while, there are my many other regular duties and responsibilities that I carry as the CEO of NDI: office work…staff meetings…board meetings…fund-raising…counseling sessions…video tapings for TV… telephone calls…piles of correspondence…faxes…emails, etc. Also, there is my regular traveling and speaking schedule locally, nationally and internationally – which is more than full time in itself! On top of all of this, I am a husband to Patt…father to my four children…father-in-law to my sons and daughters-in-law – and now grandfather to my ten grandchildren! Each of these relationships desire and deserve time with me!

"And besides everything else," as the Apostle Paul wrote, **"I face daily the pressure of my concern for all the churches"** (II Cor. 11:28)! That's because God has sovereignly linked us with strategic National partners and projects around the world. Many of them look to us for spiritual encouragement and financial support. I humbly confess to you that I find it very difficult to balance all of these relationships and responsibilities in the home and in the ministry that God has entrusted to me!

What am I saying? Simply this. It has taken a lot of *persistence* and *perseverance* for me to carve out the extra time needed to complete the writing of this book. Anyone who has ever done any writing knows that it is *hard work!* Writing is *10% inspiration* and *90% perspiration!* Therefore, I have had to be…

- *Persistent* over the many interruptions, distractions, and changes of schedule that have constantly pulled me away from this writing;

- *Persistent* over "writer's block" and a sense of "staleness" that comes from often having to lay aside a writing project for weeks at a time;

- *Persistent* in reading over twenty recommended books on Leadership as a part of my research for this manuscript;

- *Persistent* in writing on my laptop computer during the long hours of overseas flying when it would have been easier to just sit back and relax and watch the movies or sleep;

- *Persistent* to go to bed late and get up early – to find the extra meditation and writing time I have needed;

- *Persistent* in delegating and empowering my NDI staff to handle many other responsibilities of the ministry – so I could focus on writing;

- *Persistent* over my natural desires to "kick back and take it easy," and do more relaxing and enjoyable things, rather than read and write;

- *Persistent* over my concerns about whether a publisher will be interested in the book after all of my effort;

- *Persistent* over my innate insecurities that whisper: *"After all of the work, who will want to read the book anyway?"*

What is it that *provokes the persistence* needed to complete the writing of this book – or the completion of any worthy task? It is the *vision*…the *purpose*...the *call*...the *burden*...the *divine mandate!* As I have worked for hours at my computer, I have had the vivid vision of beloved National partners in my mind's eye. In addition, I see in my mind my two sons and two sons-in-law whom I want to encourage in leadership. I also see our NDI alumni – many of whom have become outstanding leaders in various fields of endeavor in both the church and society. You see, I am not writing this book for some nameless and faceless audience "somewhere out there!" It is my love for these specific key leaders that motivates me to persevere! It is my belief in what God is doing in and through their lives that fills my heart with the intense **"...joy of the Lord"** – which becomes my strength to press on and persevere (Ps. 118:24). It is my desire to encourage, equip, and empower these National brethren in their ministries that intensifies my sense of persistence! It is because of my calling to strengthen Christ's church by strengthening church leaders that I can persevere! It is because of what I know God will do in and through their lives and leadership that the writing of this book has become a heavenly mandate. It is the excitement of knowing how these leadership principles will be multiplied a thousand-fold through these strategic National leaders that keeps me going. It is for them that I will **"...stand firm"** – or rather *"sit firm"* – at my desk until the job is complete! That's why I will **"Let nothing move me."** It is because of them that I will **"...give myself fully to the work of the Lord, because I know that my labor in the Lord is not in vain!"** (Paraphrase of I Cor. 15:58). Besides, even if no one else reads this book – I have greatly benefited by writing it! Submitting these principles to writing has sharpened my own understanding of leadership. That in itself has been worth the effort! I will be a more effective leader because I have persevered in the process!

That's the source of *persistence* for me in this specific project. What is the source of persistence for you? That's a question every would-be leader must answer. When you clearly know your *purpose,* you will *persist to the end!*

FURTHER QUOTATIONS ON
LEADERSHIP AND PERSISTENCE

1. PERSISTENT:

- *Determination: "You may have to fight a battle more than once to win it." (Margaret Thatcher)*[8]

- *Leaders are determined people. They "huff and puff until they blow the house down." Leaders don't give up because they know the difference between the impossible and the possible often lies in determination.*[9]

- *"Nothing great is done without great men," Charles de Gaulle wrote, "and these are great because they willed it." The successful leader has a strong will and he is not easily deterred.*[10]

- *A successful leader doesn't give up; he doesn't give in; he doesn't give away. He doesn't give in to failure. He doesn't give up to opposition. He doesn't give way to despair.*[11]

- *To be successful a leader must persist. He takes the cold water people throw on his ideas and sells it as ice cubes.*[12]

- *Thomas Burton wrote: "The longer I live the more deeply I am convinced that what makes the difference between one man and another, the great and the insignificant, is energy, that invincible determination, a purpose once formed, nothing can take away. This energetic quality will do anything that is meant by God to be done in the world, and no talent, no training, no opportunity, no circumstances will make any man a man without it.*[13]

- *I wish for you a restlessness...Victor Frankl, the noted psychiatrist, put it forcefully when he said, "The 'is' must never catch up with the 'ought.' Leaders must keep studying, learning, growing."*[14]

- *George Bernard Shaw described more than one person who*

had stopped growing and progressing when he said: *"He died at 30, but was buried at 60."*[15]

- *Executive leadership at the highest levels is not about peak performance for today, but developing and integrating all the functions and systems for sustained performance.*[16]

2. FAILURE:

- *"Success is never final, and failure is never fatal. It is courage that counts." (Winston Churchill)*[17]

- *The list of leaders who failed and had to try again…is endless. A young man's lifelong dream was to attend West Point. He was turned down twice, but applied a third time and was accepted. His name was Douglas MacArthur. Henry Ford went bankrupt in his first year in the automobile business, and two years later his second company failed. His third one has done rather well! Twenty-three publishers rejected a children's book written by an author who called himself Dr. Seuss. The 24th publisher published it, and the result was sales of 6 million copies…Michael Jordan TV ad: "I have missed more than 9,000 shots in my career. I have lost almost 300 games. Twenty-six times I have been trusted to take the game winning shot – and missed. I've failed over and over and over again – and that's why I succeed."…*

History books are full of stories of gifted persons whose talents were overlooked by a procession of people until someone believed in them. Einstein was four years old before he could even speak, much less read. Isaac Newton did poorly in grade school. A newspaper editor fired Walt Disney because he had "no good ideas." Leo Tolstoy flunked out of college and Werner von Braun failed ninth grade algebra. Joseph Hadyn gave up ever making a musician out of Ludwig van Beethoven, who seemed a slow and plodding young man, with no apparent talent, except a belief in music. Even Winston Churchill showed little promise as a boy. At Harrow, the boy's school he attended, he was far and away the worst pupil. In four and a half years, he never rose above the bottom of the school. "That lad couldn't have gone through Harrow," a contemporary remembered. "He must have gone under it." When he was 15 years old, Winston's father worried about him. All he could see was that the boy was untalented, that there was no prospect of his going on to Oxford, that he was not even good enough to be a lawyer. There is a lesson in such stories; different people develop at different rates.[18]

- "It's not the critic who counts, not the man who points out how the strong man stumbles or where the doer of deeds could have done them better. The credit belongs to the man who is actually in the arena; whose face is marred by the dust and sweat and blood; who strives valiantly; who errs and comes up short again and again; who knows the great enthusiasms, the great devotions, and spends himself in a worthy cause; who at the worst, if he fails, at least fails while daring greatly so that his place shall never be with those cold and timid souls who know neither defeat nor victory." (Theodore Roosevelt)[19]

- Francois La Rochefoucauld said, "Almost all our faults are more pardonable than the methods we think up to hide them."[20]

- In a high-trust culture, honest mistakes are taken for what they are – an opportunity to learn...People are not truly self-governing unless they are free to fail.[21]

- Failure can be one of life's best teachers if people are given an opportunity to correct their mistakes and succeed. On the other hand, if handled improperly by the leader, failure can completely destroy an individual's self-image, motivation, and productivity. Failure can turn a courageous, insightful person into a fearful and defeated one.[22]

3. SELF-SINS:

- All Christians are called to develop God-given talents, to make the most of their lives, to develop to the fullest their God-given powers and capacities. But Jesus taught that ambition that centers on the self is wrong...[23]

- PRIDE: *When a person rises in position, as happens to leaders in the church, the tendency to pride also increases. If not checked, the attitude will disqualify the person from further advancement in the kingdom of God, for **"the Lord detests all the proud of heart"** (Proverbs 16:5). These are strong and searching words! Nothing aggravates God more than conceit, the sin that aims at setting the self upon a throne, making of God a secondary figure. That very sin changed the anointed cherub into the foul fiend of hell...*[24]

4. MOMENTUM:

- *ONLY A LEADER CAN CREATE MOMENTUM: It takes a leader to create momentum. Followers catch it. And managers are able to continue it once it has begun. But* creating *it requires someone who can motivate others, not who needs to be motivated. "If you can't* make *some heat, get out of the kitchen."*

  TRUTHS ABOUT MOMENTUM: Momentum really is a leader's best friend...when you have momentum on your side, the future looks bright, obstacles appear small, and trouble seems temporary.

  MOMENTUM MAKES LEADERS LOOK BETTER THAN THEY ARE: .Momentum changes people's perspective of leaders.

  MOMENTUM HELPS FOLLOWERS PERFORM BETTER THAN THEY ARE: When leadership is strong and there is momentum in an organization, people are motivated and inspired to perform at higher levels. They become effective beyond their hopes and expectations.

  MOMENTUM IS EASIER TO STEER THAN TO START.

  MOMENTUM IS THE MOST POWERFUL CHANGE AGENT: With enough momentum, nearly any kind of change is possible. If your desire is to do great things with your organization, never overlook the power of momentum. It truly is the leader's best friend.[25]

- *...if many others don't feel the same sense of urgency, the momentum for change will probably die far short of the finish line...*[26]

- *...great success creates a momentum that demands more and more managers to keep the growing enterprise under control while requiring little if any leadership...*[27]

- *...Whenever you let up before the job is done, critical momentum can be lost and regression may follow...Once regression begins rebuilding momentum can be a daunting task...*[28]

5. SUCCESS:

- *...success has been a journey and not a destination...*[29]

- *...my own motivation has come from a deep desire to exceed expectations and make a difference. In doing so, life has been fun and I have experienced the true 'secret to success' – happiness. If you are happy doing what you are doing you will be successful...*[30]

- *...success is not measured by a single event, nor is it something which can be achieved in the "twinkling of an eye." I also learned that success is determined more by what's inside of you than what's around you...*[31]

- *Success is about having the motivation to want to succeed, the entrepreneurial tenacity to navigate through its treacherous detours, and the focus to keep your eye toward the next destination. Success is about removing barriers that you encounter and withstanding those that you may not even know are there, asking the right questions along the way, selecting the right alternatives, and then making it happen with exceptional value-added determination...*[32]

- *...the reality is that we are responsible – response-able – for our choices. And while some of these choices may seem small and* *insignificant at the time, like tiny mountain rivulets that come together to create a mighty river, these decisions join together to move us with increasing force toward our final destiny. Over time, our choices become habits of the heart.*[33]

- *There is something else, however, that has ruined more good men and women than failure and trial ever have. It is success, the dangling opportunity for security and advancement. For so many of us, this is the crucible where the fire burns hottest, and it is when faced with the prospect of personal triumph that our character is most tried and tested…*[34]

- *Success has a disorienting effect on most of us. Having struggled so long in the upward climb and worn ourselves out, we arrive at our long dreamed-of position at the top only to stop doing the things that got us there in the first place. Having so long denied ourselves, having sacrificed present pleasure in pursuit of future gain, once there it is difficult not to drop everything in order to smell the roses…*[35]

- *Most people like to win, to be on a winning team, or to be a part of a winning effort. The desire to win inspires people, and a leader who projects a winning attitude or winning ways attracts people who want to win. No one that I know wakes up in the morning hoping their day will be a failure…*[36]

- THINKING

    If you think you are beaten, you are.
    If you think you dare not, you don't.
    If you'd like to win but you think you can't,
    It's almost a cinch you won't.

    If you think you'll lose, you're lost,
    For out of the world we find
    Success begins with a fellow's will –
    It's all in the state of mind.

    If you think you're outclassed, you are;
    You've got to think high to rise;

You've got to be sure of yourself before
You can ever win a prize.

Life's battle doesn't always go
To stronger or faster men;
But sooner or later the man who wins,
Is the one who thinks he can.

Walter D. Wintle...[37]

- *...nothing inspires an organization like a victory...*[38]

- *I believe in myself because I do not believe in those small, thornless, motionless, spineless, parasitic creatures called, "yeah, buts."*[39]

- *Winners are the right people, with the right stuff, in the right game, with the right coach...*[40]

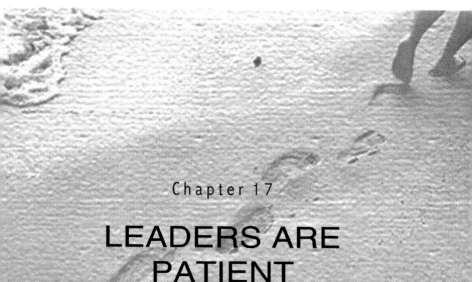

Chapter 17

LEADERS ARE PATIENT

"We urge you, brothers, warn those who are idle,
encourage the timid, help the weak,
be patient with everyone"
(I Thess. 5:14).

Oswald Sanders said: "Spiritual leaders need a healthy endowment of patience."[1] He's absolutely right – as every maturing leader well knows from his own experience! As leaders develop in *persistence*, they must also simultaneously grow in *patience*. Persistence without patience causes a leader to either *run ahead of* – or *run over* – his followers! They become *bulldozers* rather than *trailblazers*. A wise leader also seeks to nurture the virtue of *patience* in his life.

Principle:
"Persistence without patience causes leaders to run
over people."

In I Corinthians 15:58 that I quoted in the previous chapter, Paul exhorted us to be both *"steadfast"* and *"immovable."* Those attributes require *patience* – and often lots of it! Seldom is God's time our time.

As Franklin Graham wrote: "To live beyond the limits is to be on God's timetable. Often that means we must be *patient.*"[2] Every honest Christian leader knows that there is a lot of...waiting...prayer...fasting...setbacks... interruptions...disappointments...detours...postponements in serving the Lord. Leadership maturity and fulfillment of vision do not happen overnight. *"Leadership is developed daily, not in a day."*[3] It takes both *perseverance* and *patience* to become an effective leader. It doesn't happen in a moment...a day...a week...a month...or a year! *Learning leadership is a patient lifelong pursuit.* It is not the passion of a few moments!

"Leadership is developed daily, not in a day."
(John Maxwell)

When it comes to God's timing, leaders must learn lessons from nature about the patience that is required for the maturation process. It does not take much time or patience to grow mushrooms – they flourish almost overnight! But it takes lots of time to grow giant redwoods or strong oak trees that last for centuries! In leadership-development, God has the long-haul in mind. He is not interested in "overnight successes." As we saw in our last chapter, "too much too soon" can become intoxicating to immature leaders. Thomas Paine rightly observed: *"That which we obtain too easily, we esteem too lightly. It is dearness only which gives everything its value. Heaven knows how to put a proper price on its goods."*[4] God is far more interested in doing a *deep work* in us – rather than a *quick work.* He desires to develop "oak tree leaders" who will last, not "mushroom leaders" who are here today and gone tomorrow! God wants *time-tested leaders.* The Bible records that God put all of His great leaders through a season of *testing in the wilderness.*

"That which we obtain too
easily, we esteem too lightly."
(Thomas Paine)

Whether you study the life of Abraham, Moses, Joshua, David, Elijah, John the Baptist, the Apostle Paul – even Christ, they were all *time tested* and *tempered in the wilderness.* It was in the barrenness of the desert that their motives were refined and their character was developed. It was there in the desert that they developed the patience required to persevere under difficult circumstances. It was in the wilderness that they learned to "take the heat" that always goes along with leadership. Men and women who have gotten their education in the *"University of the Wilderness"* have the authenticating look of time-tested, weather-beaten leaders! When you have a *"Desert Degree"* you are really ready to face life. These kinds of leaders do not have the staged-orchestrated-fresh-off-the-shelf-window-dressed-air-brushed-blown-dry look of manicured and pampered people. They do not look like some of the popular "TV preachers" and "video visionaries" who have known only the artificial spotlights and studio lights of professionalism – rather than the searing sunlight of wilderness testing! No! *Desert leaders* have that lean-look that lets you know that they have *"...**walked through the valley of the shadow of death.**"* As a result, **"they are not afraid"** of the tough times (Ps. 23:4)! They have already *faced-off* and *faced-down* their greatest fears in the desert.

It is only patience and perseverance that will sustain a leader during those times of testing and waiting in the wilderness. It is in the *desert of difficulty* that the leader learns how to face and overcome anonymity, loneliness, hardship, suffering, setback, disappointment, discouragement, defeat, despair – even death. It is in the wilderness of testing that many leaders *give up*. But it is also there that many leaders *grow up!* Paul said: **"Let us not become *weary* in doing good..."** (Gal. 6:9). It is easy to become *weary in the wilderness*. It is hard to keep doing the right things... good things...positive things...creative things...godly things – in the wilderness. Again, it takes *perseverance* and *patience,* as any desert shepherd will testify! It is hard to lead sheep – or people – in the wilderness. Just ask Moses!

It is tough enough to have to go through the wilderness *alone*. It is even tougher to have to *lead other people through that experience!* Almost every ministry, organization or business has to *corporately* and *collectively* go through times of testing in the wilderness! It was their sojourn in the wilderness that brought out the very worst in the children of Israel. It was the severity and hardship of the wilderness that manifested their clinging to the past...their paganism and idolatry...their immorality...their rebellion against authority...their inclination to return to their "old life" and "old way of doing things." The wilderness always causes the sin, selfishness, negativity and fear in people's lives to surface and manifest itself. Leadership in the wilderness has had to learn to deal with things like discontentment, dissatisfaction, murmuring, complaining, negativity, quitting, giving up, going back.

In the wilderness a leader very quickly comes to the *end of his rope...end of his resources...end of his energy...end of his perseverance...end of his patience* – the *end of the line*. It is usually then and there that a leader begins to come to the *end of himself* – which is the real purpose of wilderness training from God's perspective! It is in the wilderness that the *flesh* reaches the *end of its limits*. At that point, God usually has His greatest opportunity to manifest Himself. It was through such a time of severe testing that Paul heard God say: **"My grace is sufficient for you, for *My power is made perfect in weakness.*"** As a result of learning that lesson Paul cried out:

> **"Therefore I will boast all the more gladly about my *weaknesses*, so that Christ's power may rest on me. That is why, for Christ's sake, I delight in *weaknesses*, in *insults*, in *hardships*, in *persecutions*, in *difficulties*. For *when I am weak, then I am strong*"**(II Cor. 12:9-10).

Previous to this time, Paul had earnestly beseeched God to remove his painful and debilitating **"...thorn in the flesh"** (II Cor. 12:8). But in His infinite mercy and wisdom, God knew that He could teach Paul something *with the thorn* – which Paul would never learn *without the thorn*. Through the thorn, Paul realized that...

- His *insufficiency* was an opportunity for God's *all sufficiency.*
- His *impotence* was an opportunity for God's *power.*
- His *weakness* was the opportunity for God's *strength.*
- His *impatience* was an opportunity for God's *forbearance.*
- His *ignorance* was the opportunity for God's *wisdom.*
- His *intolerance* was the opportunity for God's *love.*
- His *end* was God's *beginning!*

The wilderness brings out both the worst – and the best – in people. Which again is the reason God puts people through a time of *wilderness wandering*. That's why Moses reminded the people:

> **"Remember how the Lord your God led you all the way in the *desert* these forty years, to *humble you* and to *test***

you in order to know what was in your heart, **whether or not you would keep His commands**" (Deut. 8:2).

While it brought out the worst in the majority of the children of Israel, it also brought out the best in a minority like Joshua and Caleb who had a "**...different spirit.**" As a result, God said that they followed Him "**...with a whole heart.**" God brought them into the Promised Land, and made them the next generation of leaders for His people (Num. 14:24).

The wilderness is a time for *heart-testing*. Physicians today often put people through a rigorous "stress test" in order to check-out the condition of their patient's heart. It is one of the quickest ways to find out whether the heart is healthy or sick. Our Divine Physician does the same thing. He puts us through the severe testing of the wilderness to prove the condition of our spiritual heart. But God is omniscient, and knows everything about our physical and spiritual condition. Unlike a human physician, God does not put us through a "wilderness stress test" so that He will find out the true condition of our hearts. He already perfectly knows that and has given His divine diagnosis in the Bible:

- "The *heart is deceitful above all things* and *beyond cure*...I the Lord *search the heart* and *examine the mind*, to reward a man according to his conduct, according to what his deeds deserve" (Jer. 17:9-10).

- "The hearts of men...are *full of evil* and there is *madness in their hearts* while they live" (Ecc. 9:3).

- "From within, *out of man's hearts*, come evil thoughts, sexual immorality, theft, murder, adultery, greed, malice, deceit, lewdness, envy, slander, arrogance and folly. All these evils come from *inside* and make a man unclean" (Mk. 7:21-23).

This *heart sickness* is not just a condition of pagans. It is the condition of all people – even religious people! I remind you that the children of Israel were "God's chosen people." Yet the wilderness proved that their hearts were still very sick and weak. They were still "going through the motions" of religiosity – but it was only *half-hearted devotion.* Their worship was sporadic and superficial. They had left Egypt geographically – but not affectionately! Egypt was still very much in their hearts! Concerning this kind of half-hearted devotion, God says:

- "This people's *heart has become calloused*; they hardly hear with their ears, and they have closed their eyes. Otherwise they might see with their eyes, hear with their ears, *understand with their heart* and turn and I would heal them" (Matt. 13:15).

- "These people honor Me with their lips, but their *hearts are far from Me.* They worship Me in vain" (Matt. 15:8-9).

- "They are a people whose *hearts go astray...* They shall never enter My rest" (Ps. 95:10-11).

As Paul said, these kind of people have the **"...form of godliness, but lack its power"** (II Tim. 3:5).

In a time of severe testing in the wilderness, Moses learned things about himself...about his people...about God, which he would never have learned otherwise. So did the Apostle Paul. Their lives and leadership were more mature because of it. Every spiritual leader learns the same thing through their personal time of testing in the wilderness. It is there that they really begin to find out the true condition of their heart. Hopefully then they will allow God to begin to do the necessary *heart surgery* – or *heart transplant,* that will result in more health and vitality in their life and leadership! Otherwise they too might spend forty years – a lifetime – learning hard lessons about the condition of their hearts! God exhorts every one of His children: **"Today, if you hear His voice, *do not harden your hearts"*** (Heb. 4:3-7)!

It is the wilderness that *tests our hearts* – and the *hearts of our followers.* It is the wilderness that demonstrates God's infinite patience with us. It is in the wilderness that we learn to have patience with other people. Oswald Sanders wisely pointed out the obvious when he wrote: *"Patience meets its most difficult test in personal relationships."*[5] He goes on to point out two examples:

> Paul lost his patience dealing with John Mark. Hudson Taylor once confessed: 'My greatest temptation is to lose my temper over the slackness and inefficiency so disappointing in those on whom I depend.'[6]

Moses lost his patience in leadership, and angrily **"struck the rock"** rather than speaking to it by faith as God had instructed him so that it would bring forth water (Num. 20:2-12). Paul lost his patience with the immaturity and instability of young John Mark. It is in the crucible of human relationships that a leader's heart is tried – and *patience is purified.* In the final analysis, Paul learned that *patience* – like all other lasting virtues - is one of the fruit of the Holy Spirit (Gal. 5:22). It was not something that he could have through *natural endowment* – but only by *supernatural enduement!* It usually takes *time* – and often *tribulation* – to produce *patience* in our lives (Rom. 5:3; KJV). One of the greatest places to have both mature in your life is in the *university of the wilderness!* That's where leaders that last are built. God reminds us:

- "I will turn My hand against you; I will thoroughly *purge away your dross* and *remove all your impurities"*(Isa. 1:25).

- "See, I have *refined you...*I have *tested you in the furnace of affliction.* For My own sake, for My own sake I do this" (Isa. 48:10-11).

- "I will *refine* them like silver and *test* them like gold" (Zech. 13:9).

- "He will be like a *refiner's fire* or a *launderer's soap.* He will sit as a *refiner* and *purifier of silver;* He will *purify* the Levites and *refine* them like gold and silver. Then the Lord will have men who will bring offerings in righteousness..." (Mal. 3:2-4).

- "In this you greatly rejoice, though now for a little while you may have had to suffer grief in all kinds of *trials.* These have come so that your faith – of greater worth than gold, which perishes even though *refined by fire* – may be proved genuine and may result in praise, glory and honor when Jesus Christ is revealed" (I Pet. 1:6-7).

God is vitally interested in working *patience* in the life and leadership of the people that He uses. Patience is *"leadership gold and silver"* that can only be purged of self and purified of the flesh in the

wilderness furnace of testing! As you read
through the New Testament, you hear
many exhortations to *patience.* A very helpful
study on patience can be found in the
following verses:

- "For in this hope we were saved. But hope that is seen is no
  hope at all. Who hopes for what he already has? But if we
  hope for what we do not yet have, we wait for it *patiently*"
  (Romans 8:24-25).

- "Love is *patient,* love is kind. It does not envy, it does not
  boast, it is not proud" (I Corinthians 13:4).

- "If we are distressed, it is for your comfort and salvation; if
  we are comforted, it is for your comfort, which produces in
  you *patient* endurance of the same sufferings we suffer" (II
  Corinthians 1:6).

- "...being strengthened with all power according to His
  glorious might so that you may have great endurance and
  patience... Therefore, as God's chosen people, holy and dearly
  loved, clothe yourselves with compassion, kindness, humility,
  gentleness and *patience*" (Colossians 1:11; 3:12).

- "And we urge you, brothers, warn those who are idle,
  encourage the timid, help the weak, be *patient* with
  everyone" (1 Thessalonians 5:14).

- "But for that very reason I was shown mercy so that in me, the
  worst of sinners, Christ Jesus might display His unlimited
  patience as an example for those who would believe on Him
  and receive eternal life" (I Timothy 1:16).

- "You, however, know all about my teaching, my way of life, my
  purpose, faith, *patience,* love, endurance...Preach the Word;
  be prepared in season and out of season; correct, rebuke and
  encourage – with great *patience* and careful instruction" (II
  Timothy 3:10; 4:2).

- **"And so after waiting *patiently*, Abraham received what was promised"** (Hebrews 6:15).

- **"Brothers, as an example of *patience* in the face of suffering, take the prophets who spoke in the name of the Lord"** (James 5:10).

- **"Bear in mind that our Lord's *patience* means salvation, just as our dear brother Paul also wrote you with the wisdom that God gave him"** (II Peter 3:15).

- **"I, John, your brother and companion in the suffering and kingdom and *patient* endurance that are ours in Jesus, was on the island of Patmos because of the word of God and the testimony of Jesus...Since you have kept my command to endure *patiently*, I will also keep you from the hour of trial that is going to come upon the whole world to test those who live on the earth"** (Revelation 1:9; 3:10).

No leader will last in the long run without a *balance of persistence and patience!* One of the key components of patience is *self-control*. When a person loses their self-control, they soon become *impatient* and *irritable* – and often *impulsive* and *irrational*. *Self-control* through *Spirit-control* is a very essential quality for *sustained leadership*. *Spirit-control* takes place through *mind-control* or *thought-control*. Almost all victories or defeat first happen in the mind. Every leader must be able to control his *thought-life* by continuing to **"...renew his mind"** through God's Word (Rom. 12:1-2). In order to fulfill his vision, every leader needs to have a *sustained leadership* – rather than a short-lived leadership. Very often it is this attribute of *self-control* that makes the difference between a *sustained leadership* that goes the distance and one that is cut short by carnality. Usually, it is a *lack of self-control* in some area that fosters impatient, irrational, impulsive, and irritable behavior in the life of a leader. His life and leadership become erratic and presumptuous in ways that ultimately disappoint and disillusion his followers – and often destroy his leadership.

Principle:
"Sustained leadership is the result of self-control, which comes from Spirit-control through mind-control."

It is important to remember that a loss of self-control usually happens in an area of *strength* rather than an area of *weakness*. In the areas where a leader recognizes his natural weakness, he tends to stay alert and "be on guard." In the area where he is usually strong, he feels more confident and secure. He relaxes and "lets down his guard" – and finally loses self-control in that area. Let's look at a couple of very familiar Biblical examples of this.

Samson's Strength: It was Samson's physical strength that finally became his weakness. At first he used his God-given strength for the good of God's people. After many great physical exploits and victories, he began to relax. He became more and more confident – even cocky! He lost his humility and dependency upon God. He knew that he could tease and tempt fate – and always win in the end. His physical strength and agility became a game that he used to toy and trifle with. With each victory over the Philistines, he became more and more *self-confident* – and less and less *self-controlled*. What he thought he had mastery over ultimately mastered him. His strength was turned to weakness – and finally destroyed him. He not only lost his leadership, he lost his life.

Solomon's Wisdom: The same thing that happened to the strongest man in the world also happened to the wisest man in the world. Solomon had prayed to God for wisdom, and received it to a fuller degree than any of his peers. In fact, he was wiser than anyone before or after him. He was given God's wisdom for every area of life – and became the foremost teacher of wisdom in his world. For much of his life he humbly lived by the wisdom that God communicated to him, and through him. Gradually, he began to make a common leadership mistake. He succumbed to the subtle deception of equating *information* with *application*. It wasn't that Solomon did not know what to do – it was *he did not do what he knew!* He ceased to practice what he preached – and the wise man became a great fool! After a forty-year reign, Solomon died in infamy, leaving a foolish son behind who divided and destroyed the Kingdom.

It is in the area of *self-control* that so many leaders have fallen – and often in the "sunset years" of their life. It was a lack of self-control in some crucial area of their lives that caused them to become prideful and unaccountable. They made foolish decisions that caused them to lose integrity. They ended up defaming the Lord...destroying their reputations...and losing their ministries.

Let me share a timely and insightful quotation by John Haggai about this matter of *self-control:*

> *An attitude of self-control develops strong character and strong character can be defined as the power to* stand alone. *Holiness never counts its companions; it never intimates that its validity is in proportion to the number of its admirers.*[7]

It takes *patience* and *self-control* to humbly stand alone – which every leader has to do at times. To allow God the time to stamp His *character* on our nature; to strive for personal *holiness* above personal *happiness;* to wait on the fullness of God's time for the fulfillment of a vision – all require *patience.* Every leader must be careful about substituting *patient* for *presumptuous.* It will require a lot of patience to learn to be *Spirit-controlled* and *self-controlled* rather than *flesh-controlled* or *follower-controlled.*

Both the Old Testament and New Testament remind us of the importance of self-control. Proverbs 16:32 says:

> **"He who is slow to anger is better than the mighty, and he who *rules his spirit*, than he who captures a city."**

A man can only **"...rule his spirit"** by first allowing *God to rule him.* Only then will the Holy Spirit be able to mature and manifest His fruit in a leader's life. The Bible assures us that **"...the fruit of the Spirit is... self-control"** (Gal. 5:22). Only as this fruit of *self-control* matures in his life will a leader have the *patience* necessary for a *sustained leadership* that will take him across the finish line with his integrity and character intact!

FURTHER QUOTATIONS ON
LEADERSHIP AND PATIENCE

1. TRIALS & TESTING:

- *Spiritual maturity is indispensable to good leadership. A novice or new convert should not be pushed into leadership. A plant needs time to take root and come to maturity, and the process cannot be hurried. The seen must take root downward before it can bear fruit upward. J. A. Bengle says that novices usually have "an abundance of {vegetation}" and are "not yet pruned by the cross." In I Timothy 3:10, referring to qualifications for deacon, Paul urges, "They must first be tested."[8]*

- *Fenelon writes, "God never makes you suffer unnecessarily. He intends for your suffering to heal and purify you. The hand of God hurts you as little as it can. The yoke that God gives is easy to bear if you accept it without struggling to escape."[9]*

- *No work of God will be left destitute until its purposes are achieved..[10]*

Chapter 18

LEADERS ARE PARTNERS

"I thank my God every time I remember you...because of your partnership in the Gospel from the first day until now..."
(Phil. 1:3-5)

Effective leaders are not rugged *individualists* or *isolationists* – but rather "team players." A *team* can be defined this way: *"Two or more people moving along a path of interaction toward a common goal."*[1] For a leader to be a *team-builder* – he or she must be *people-oriented* rather than *program-oriented.* Programs do not follow leaders – only people do. When a leader does not have a *people priority,* he will develop a *program priority.* People will become a *means to the end* – rather than an *end in themselves.* The leader will ultimately *use people* as *pawns* to accomplish his plans and programs. Once his plans or purposes have been achieved, he will discard the people and continue to "go it alone." This attitude reveals that he was not really interested in the people all along – but only in his own plans.

Good leaders – especially good Biblical leaders – will have a *people priority.* Because they want to *raise up leaders* and *mentor people into maturity,* they will seek to build *covenant relationships* rather than *functional relationships.* They will see their followers as real *partners* and not just *pawns.* Rather than "go it alone," Biblical leaders want to take as many partners as possible along with them to the goal. They know that *the more people who share in the victory – the greater that victory!* There is a well-known leadership maxim that says: *"It's lonely at the top."* If that is true, it is because the leader did not take anyone with him! The role of Biblical servant leadership is to *take as many partners as possible to the top with you!* That way it will never be *"lonely at the top"* – but rather *"lively at the top!"* While reading the August 2005 airline magazine, *Silkroad,* I came across this quote by Wil Rose: "Success is not counted by how high you have climbed but by how many people you brought with you." Always be eager to include others in your climb.

Principle:
"It's only lonely at the top for the leaders who do not take others to the summit with them!"

In most churches and organizations, there are far too many *uninvolved people.* They just occupy the pew...fill up space...sit around the parameters...spectate from a safe distance. Leadership consultant Bobb Biehl has concluded about the American church: *"Our pews are filled with 'relationally disconnected people.'"*[2] They have a *relational vacuum* in their lives that is seeking to be filled by something meaningful. Richard Phillips describes these people as the ones who *"...can be found loitering in the margins."*[3]

Millions of people are *marginalized...on the sidelines...on the outside-looking-in...uninvolved...watching life go by.* Oftentimes it is their own fault...their own lack of motivation...their crippling insecurities...their disabling sense of inadequacy...their simple lack of experience. At other times it is because of the faulty leadership style of the person at the top. Many leaders are "control freaks" who have to have their hands in every part of the organizational pie! They will not give up any power or responsibility to others. Like a *prima donna* on a basketball team, this kind of leader has to "call all the shots" – and "make all the shots!" He is both the *coach* and *star player!* One of the greatest challenges for many leaders is to learn to "let go"..."take their hands off"..."give up control"..."step onto the sidelines." They must discipline themselves to *engage, energize, enable* these on-lookers...by-standers...pew-sitters. Unless a leader becomes a catalyst for them, most of these people will go through life as *spectators* rather than as *participators*. Often *spectators* degenerate into *agitators* and *aggravators!*

In his excellent book, *Management: A Biblical Approach*, Myron Rush points out: *"People form relationships because they have needs that can only be met by others."*[4] It is some "unmet need" that motivates one individual towards another individual. It is the primary motivator for building relationships – whether *healthy* or *unhealthy*. Every person was created with a *relational vacuum* that cannot be lastingly filled by *things*. God created us as *relational beings*. In the final analysis, *relationships are the only things that are eternal*. Only relationships will outlive this life. We were created to have an *eternal relationship with God*, and *temporal relationships with others. Our relationship with others is no better than our relationship with God*. We build relationships by meeting the needs of others. Again I quote Myron Rush: "Meeting the needs of others is the key to developing and maintaining good working relationships…Just as met needs strengthen relationships, unmet needs erode them. You won't find people on their way to a divorce court because a spouse is meeting too many of their needs."[5]

Principle: *"We build relationships by meeting the needs of others."*

We build strong ministries just like we build strong marriages – by *building strong relationships! Relational skills* are the single most important quality for effective leadership! As we saw in our earlier chapter on the leader as a "people-focused" individual, *no other skills and abilities can long compensate for poor relational skills.* Effective leaders are always honing and refining their ability to *build and sustain relationships.* Meaningful and lasting relationships are built through *meeting needs* in the lives of others. Authentic leadership is "other-focused" rather than "self-focused." *Leadership is not about having my needs met* – it is about *meeting the needs of others.* The *more needs met,* the *greater the leadership!*

One of the most effective ways to meet the needs of others is by building a *partnership* with them. A leader adds significance to the lives of others by incorporating them in a worthy cause…by making them a part of his leadership team. This means *delegation of responsibility* and *power-sharing*

– which many leaders are unwilling or unable to do. Let's look at a famous Biblical example.

Principle:

"Relational skills are a leader's greatest asset. Nothing can compensate for poor relational skills. But the better his relational skills, the more needs he is able to meet. And the more needs he can meet, the greater his leadership in the eyes of God and man."

Early in his leadership of the children of Israel, Moses tried to make all of the decisions. Either he was not willing or able to share leadership. He thought he had to hold all of the reins of leadership tightly in his hands in order to be an effective leader. He felt he had to make all of the decisions – whether big or small. His father-in-law, Jethro, came to visit him in the wilderness. There he observed Moses trying to "make all of the decisions" and "settle all the disputes" for over a million people! Because he alone had received the vision from God and the Ten Commandments on Mt. Sinai, he felt that he had to make all of the decisions. We read this account:

> "Moses took his seat to serve as *judge for the people*, and they stood around him from *morning* till *evening*. When his father-in-law saw all that Moses was doing for the people, he said, 'What is this you are doing for the people? Why do you *alone* sit as judge, while *all these people stand around you from morning till evening?*'
>
> Moses answered him: 'Because the people come to me to seek God's will. Whenever they have a dispute, it is brought to me, and I decide between the parties and inform them of God's decrees and laws.'
>
> Moses father-in-law replied, *'What you are doing is not good. You and these people who come to you will only wear yourselves out. The work is too heavy for you; you cannot handle*

it alone. Listen now to me and I will give you some advice, and may God be with you. You must be the people's representative before God and bring their disputes to Him. *Teach them* the decrees and laws, and *show them* the way to live and the duties they are to perform. But select *capable men* from all the people – men who *fear God, trustworthy men who hate dishonest gain – appoint them as officials* over thousands, hundreds, fifties and tens. Have them *serve as judges* for the people at all times, but have them bring every difficult case to you; the simple cases they can decide themselves. *That will make your load lighter, because they will share it with you.* If you do this and God so commands, *you will be able to stand the strain, and all these people will go home satisfied.'*

Moses listened to his father-in-law and did everything he said. He chose capable men from all Israel and made them leaders of the people... They served as judges for the people at all times. The difficult cases they brought to Moses, but the simple ones they decided themselves" (Ex. 18:13-26).

It took some wise council from the "outside" for Moses to learn the principle of *shared leadership.* If he would not have received and heeded the advice from his father-in-law, he would still be in the wilderness! He would still be sitting on the "judge's seat" trying to make all of the decisions! The people would still be chanting: *"Here comes the judge!"* They would have died and rotted **"...waiting in line from morning till evening"** to get their turn to talk to *"king Moses!"* Before this time, his leadership model had been that of Pharaoh – who held all of the power and made all of the decisions! Through the wise council of Jethro, Moses made a strategic leadership shift to *shared leadership.* At that point he made the paradigm shift from exclusive *ownership* to authentic *partnership.* Often every young leader needs a "Jethro" to come into their life to guide them in making this leadership shift.

Later on, there was similar leadership crisis in Moses' life. The people were complaining about the monotony of their daily rations of *manna.* They wanted *meat* instead. Similar kinds of dissatisfaction are not unusual in churches and organizations today. People are not happy with their provisions. They want something different. Like many spiritual leaders, Moses cried out to God under the pressure of the expectations of the people:

> "Why have you brought this trouble on your servant? What have I done to displease You that You put the burden of all these people on me? Did I conceive all these people? Did I give them birth? Why do You tell me to carry them in my arms, as a nurse carries an infant, to the land You promised on oath to their forefathers? Where can I get meat for all these people?...*I cannot carry all these people by myself; the burden is too heavy for me.* If this is how You are going to treat me, *put me to death right now...*"

Moses became burdened-down and frustrated with his leadership responsibilities and the expectations of the people. They again looked to him to *meet all of their needs – and wants.* At that point, Moses sunk into suicidal depression! This is the "burn-out point" for many leaders! But how did God respond? Note His very practical leadership instructions to Moses:

> "Bring *seventy* of Israel's elders who are known to you as *leaders* and *officials* among the people. Have them come to the Tent of Meeting, that they may stand there with you. I will come down and speak with you there, and *I will take of the Spirit that is on you and put the Spirit on them. They will help you carry the burden of the people so that you will not have to carry it alone*...Then the Lord came down...and He took of the Spirit was on him and put the Spirit on the seventy elders. When the Spirit rested on them, *they prophesied...*"(Num. 11:11-25).

There were two men, Eldad and Medad, who were not present at that leadership meeting. They stayed in their tents. We are not told why – they just did not attend the meeting. However, the sovereign "...**Spirit also rested on them, and they prophesied in the camp.**" At that point, a young man ran and told Moses what happened. He reported what appeared to be a "leadership training violation!" Even Joshua exhorted Moses to "...**stop them.**" But Moses had learned the importance of *shared leadership* – and wisely answered:

"Are you jealous for my sake? *I wish that all the Lord's people were prophets* and that the Lord would put His Spirit on them!" (vs. 29).

One of the quickest ways to tell if a leader has really developed a *partnership spirit* is when he manifests a *lack of jealousy* over God's sovereign blessing of another person's life and leadership! In essence Moses said: *"I wish every one of the Israelites were leaders! I wish God would pour out His Spirit of leadership equally on every one! I wish that His Spirit would anoint each of them just as He has me! I wish they were all prophets! I wish that every one of them would become leaders!"* Moses had matured to the degree that he no longer wanted to have exclusive ownership of all of the privileges and powers of leadership. He gladly wanted to share it with as many others as possible! That's true *partnership leadership!*

We can also see this team spirit...delegation of responsibility...shared leadership in the life of Nehemiah. As he faced the daunting task of rebuilding the broken walls of Jerusalem, he knew he could not do it alone. Like Moses, he became a *partner leader.* He said...

"I put in charge of Jerusalem my brother Hanani along with Hananiah the commander of the citadel because he was a *man of integrity* and feared God more than most men do" (Neh. 7:2).

Nehemiah not only *delegated authority* and *shared leadership* – he did so by picking the right men for the job! *Partnership leadership* is crucial – but it must be with the *right men* who have the *right talents* with the *right attitude.* Otherwise, no amount of training can compensate for poor selectivity. As the leadership maxim says: *"You can't do in training what you should have done in selectivity."*

This paradigm of *shared leadership* is a concept that many immature and insecure Christian leaders today have not made! They still want to retain all of the power...make all of the decisions...call all of the shots. They especially resent it when God blesses and anoints someone else in ministry above them!

Partner-leadership is a definite Old Testament principle – as demonstrated through dynamic leaders like Moses and Nehemiah. Both demonstrated strategic leadership at crucial times in their nation's history. The principle of *shared leadership* is equally clear in the New Testament. We see it incarnated in the life of Christ, and demonstrated through the Apostle Paul. Both were *team players*. Because they had a "people priority," they were oriented toward inclusive *partnership* rather than exclusive *ownership*. They took the time to really involve and incorporate their ministry partners in their purpose. They seldom traveled alone...walked alone... ate alone...slept alone...prayed alone...preached along...healed alone – or went to prison alone! Whenever and wherever possible, they had some of their ministry partners along with them. Note briefly several quick examples:

Jesus' Commissioning of the Twelve: Rather than hold all of His divine power in His own hands, Jesus shared His authority with His disciples:

> "He called His twelve disciples to Him and *gave them authority* to drive out evil spirits and to heal every disease and sickness" (Matt. 10:1).

Jesus' Commissioning of the Seventy-Two: Here again we see Christ widening the scope of His empowerment of others:

> "After this the Lord appointed seventy-two others and sent them out two by two ahead of Him to every town and place where He was about to go. He told them...*I have given you authority* to trample on snakes and scorpions and to overcome all the power of the enemy..." (Lk. 10:1,19).

Paul's empowering and encouraging of Timothy:

> "I remind you to fan into flame the gift of God, which is in you through the laying on of my hands. For God did not give us a spirit of timidity, but a spirit of power, of love and of self-discipline...What you heard from me, keep as the pattern of sound teaching...*Guard the good deposit that was entrusted to you* – guard it with the help of the Holy Spirit Who lives in us...You then, my son, be strong in the grace that is in Christ Jesus. *And the things you have heard me say in the presence of many witnesses entrust to faithful men who will also be qualified to teach others*" (II Tim. 1:6-7, 13-14; 2:1-2).

Both Jesus and the Apostle Paul always had people around them that they were training. They brought them into *partnership* with them in the work of God's Kingdom. Jesus called and commissioned the twelve and the seventy-two – and transmitted His power and authority to them. Paul always had a little "traveling Bible School" of men and women he was discipling and mentoring everywhere he went. He names many of them in his various Epistles. Romans 16 has the longest list – some twenty-six people he refers to as his beloved friends and ministry partners. And at least seven or more of them were *women*.

When you study the book of Acts, you see this same emphasis upon *partnership*. One of the defining words of that book is **"together... fellowship."** It comes from the Greek word, *koinonia* which means *"communion, fellowship, sharing in common."* Rather than living in isolation and individualism, the early believers were constantly *together.* The leaders – the Twelve – were right in the midst of them practicing *partner leadership*. We can see this leadership principle being demonstrated in Acts 6. There we read the very straightforward account of one of the very first "leadership crises" in the 1st century church. Look at it briefly with me.

Just like in the case of Moses and the people, this crisis revolved around *meeting the needs of people*. Once again it was another *bread crisis!* In accordance with God's admonition to care for widows and orphans (Deut. 14:29; 16:11; 14:19-21; Ja. 1:27, etc), the early church had a "food kitchen" to care for these needy people among their fellowship. The Jews of the Diaspora, who were living in Jerusalem, felt that their widows were not getting proper care. They felt that the widows of the Jerusalem Jews were being given preferential treatment – and getting a disproportionate allotment of food. So they **"...complained against the Hebraic Jews because their widows were being overlooked in the *daily distribution of food.* "**

In typical "church committee" fashion, they took the problem to the leadership – in this case, the twelve Apostles. They in essence said to the Apostles: *"This is your problem as our church leaders – you solve it!"* Wisely, they followed the example of Moses and the *seventy elders*. They gathered all of the disciples together and said:

"It would not be right for us to neglect the ministry of the word of God in order to wait on tables. Brothers, chose seven men from among you who are known to be full of the Spirit and wisdom. We will turn this responsibility over to them and will give our attention to prayer and the ministry of the word. This proposal pleased the whole group. They chose Stephen, Philip, Procorus, Nicanor, Timon, Parmenas, and Nicholas. They presented these men to the apostles, who prayed and laid their hands on them."

It is important to note what the Bible says happened as a result of this *shared leadership:*

"So the word of God spread. The number of disciples in Jerusalem *increased rapidly,* and a large number of priests became obedient to the faith" (Acts 6:1-7).

It is easy to see how this *shared leadership* resulted in new explosive growth in the early church! Once again we see that the principle of *partner leadership* results in growth by *multiplication –* rather than growth by *addition.*

We can also see that this was the pattern of leadership that Paul gave to the churches he planted. He reminded them that God gave certain leaders to His church – *not to do all the work,* but rather to *train others to do all the work.*

"It was He who gave some to be *apostles,* some to be *prophets,* some to be *evangelists,* and some to be *pastors* and *teachers,* TO PREPARE, TO EQUIP GOD'S PEOPLE FOR WORKS OF SERVICE, so that the body of Christ may be *built up…"* (Eph. 4:11-12).

God's leadership plan for His church has never changed. It is still the role of the leaders to *"…equip the saints to do the work of ministry"* (NASV). When that happens, the body of Christ grows and is "built up."

The above examples from Moses…the *seventy elders…*Christ…the Apostles… the seventy-two…the Apostle Paul…the seven deacons…the early church – all conclusively demonstrate that *leadership partnership* is the authentic Biblical model! It is only through this method of empowerment that a leader can multiply his influence – and leverage his leadership. By effectively involving others in their area of giftedness, he frees himself to focus his time and attention to his own area of giftedness. This increases the fruitfulness and fulfillment of *both* the leader and his co-workers. This is what effective leadership is all about, as Oswald Sanders points out:

> *One facet of leadership is the ability to recognize the special abilities and limitations of others, combined with the capacity to fit each one into the job where he or she will do best.* To succeed in getting things done through others is the highest type of leadership.[6]

For a leader to *"succeed in getting things done through others"*, he must be genuinely committed to *partnership*. As we have seen, authentic partnership is based upon *delegation* and *empowerment*. *A partner who has not truly been empowered is nothing more than a impotent pawn!*

"No man will make a great leader
who wants to do it all himself or
get all the credit for doing it." [7]
(Andrew Carnegie, Industrialist)

Perhaps it is defining the obvious, but it might be helpful to define *delegation*. We saw it demonstrated in the lives and leadership of Moses, Nehemiah, Christ, the Apostles, and Paul – but what exactly is *delegation?* Myron Rush gives some helpful insight:

> *Delegation consists of* transferring authority, responsibility, and accountability from one person or group to another. *In most cases, it involves moving authority from a higher level in an organization to a lower one. Delegation is the process by which* decentralization of organizational power occurs. *Decentralization involves the* dispersion of authority and responsibility from the top downward *through the organization, allowing more people to become involved in the decision-making process.*[8]

Many leaders find it very difficult to *delegate responsibility* – and then "take their hands off." They give power – only to take it back again. Unfortunately, this pattern of limited empowerment is often characteristic of the church. In his book, *The Other Side of Leadership*, Eugene Habecker wrote: *"It is my observation that many Christian organizations do not do a good job in the area of dispersed leadership."*[9] Perhaps that is why more does not get done!

Organizational studies have proven over and over again that the more people are involved in the process, the greater sense of *ownership* they have about it. If the person at the top "owns" all of the leadership, his people will feel very detached from his vision. They may at times ignore strategic opportunities for organizational growth. They may also "turn a blind eye" to organizational problems that may result in disaster. Organizational experts Daniel Katz and Robert Kahn have concluded:

> *People have greater feelings of commitment to decisions in which they have a part...and the wide distribution of the leadership function is likely to improve the quality of decisions...Few indeed are the organizational disasters that occurred unforeseen by someone.*[10]

Wise leadership always seeks to involve as many people as possible in the goal-setting and decision-making process. The wider the sense of ownership in the goal, the better chance there is of reaching that goal. It is the difference between individual *leadership spirit* and *team spirit*.

> *The team goal or mission is the key to developing and maintaining a productive team. The leader or manager interested in developing a productive team should involve the team members in developing or refining the team goal. Such participation gives the team ownership of the goal and motivates commitment to its accomplishment. A team will work much harder to achieve a goal it helped design than one developed solely outside the team.*[11]

Since *delegation* and *empowerment* are such crucial components of partnership leadership, let's look at a few other insightful quotes:

- *The degree to which a leader is able to delegate work is a measure of his success. A one-person office can never grow larger than the load one person can carry. Failing to delegate, the leader is caught in a morass of secondary detail; it overburdens him and diverts his attention from primary tasks. People under him do not achieve their own potential. In some cases, insisting on doing a job oneself is a result of simple conceit.*[12]

- *Effective delegating to others is perhaps the single most powerful high-leverage activity there is. Transferring responsibility to other skilled and trained people enables you to give your energies to other high-leverage activities. Delegation means growth, both for individuals and for organizations.*[13]

- *As I've gotten older, I've found the less I do the more I enjoy it because I'm more selective, more thorough, more conscious of what I'm trying to do. I've learned that activity is not the mark of accomplishment. The more I can delegate tasks that are not uniquely mine, the more attention I can pay to those that are...I retain to myself the things that only I can do and delegate the rest.*[14]

In the final analysis, *delegation of responsibility* and the *empowerment of others* is *synergistic leadership* – rather than *selfish leadership*. The word *synergy* simply means: *"To work together."* It means to *cooperate... combine efforts...correlate action.* Through an under-standing of *synergy*, a leader recognizes that "the whole is greater than the individual parts." That by *pulling together* more can be accomplished. That the group is smarter...stronger...more creative than any single member – including the leader. The whole concept of "team building" is based upon *synergy*. It is a recognition that *every member of the team is important in order to achieve victory.* In an organization – like in sports – no one individual can play every position. It takes a number of players to make a winning team. *Synergy* is essential for a good marriage...a good ministry...a good business...a good organization...a good government. *Synergistic leadership* capitalizes on the strengths of one's partners to compensate for your own weaknesses. A *wise* and *winning leader* is always a *team player* who seeks to optimize the talents and experience of every person around him. Noted author Stephen Covey writes this about *synergy:*

> *When properly understood, synergy is the highest activity in life... It catalyzes, unifies, and unleashes the greatest powers within people...The essence of synergy is to value differences – to respect them, to build on strengths, to compensate for weaknesses...Valuing*

the differences is the essence of synergy – the mental, the emotional, the psychological differences between people. And the key to valuing those differences is to realize that all people see the world, not as it is, but as they are… The person who is truly effective has the humility and reverence to recognize his own perceptual limitations and to appreciate the rich resources available through interaction with the hearts and minds of other human beings. That person values the differences because those differences add to his knowledge, to his understanding of reality. When we're left to our own experiences, we constantly suffer from a shortage of data…Synergy works; it's a correct principle…It is effectiveness in an interdependent reality – it is teamwork, team building, the development of unity and creativity with other human beings.[16]

"I would rather put a thousand men to work
than do the work of a thousand men."[15]
(D.L. Moody)

Leadership in general, and Biblical leadership in particular, is a *journey of togetherness*. It is a *partnership* where the leader *shares responsibility with his followers*. Whether it is with *seventy elders* in the case of Moses, or *seven deacons* in the early church – *authentic spiritual leadership is always based upon partnership*.

Principle:
"Leaders are team players who have a people priority.
They practice inclusive partnership rather than
exclusive ownership."

We must always remember this spiritual and emotional principle: *"It takes a secure servant-leader to incorporate others in his vision."* Selfish and worldly leaders do not want to "take people to the top" with them. They want exclusive ownership of both the *vision* and the *victory*. They want to hold tightly to both the *power* and *prosperity* of their *position*. Biblical leaders, on the other hand, want to share their leadership trip with as many people as possible. They have learned that *there is power in empowering others*. An authentic leader knows that by *enlarging others, he enlarges himself* — that by *adding value to others, he increases his own value as a leader.* A wise leader will not only seek to *raise up good followers,* he will especially seek to *raise up good leaders.* It bears repeating: "Leaders that only raise up followers grow their ministry or organization by *addition;* while leaders who raise up leaders grow their ministry or organization by *multiplication.*" The goal of leadership and discipleship is to *reproduce reproducers!* Leadership development is based upon *encouraging, equipping, enabling,* and *empowering* others to be all that God created and recreated them to be.

Principle:
"Leadership that only raises up followers grows by *addition;* while leadership that raises up other leaders grows by *multiplication.*"

A leader is not interested in surrounding himself with people who are not interested in *going* and *growing.* They know that leadership is a journey that requires *motivation, movement* and *momentum.* Leaders will not surround themselves with *inert* or *inactive* people! A wise leader knows that *his potential will often be determined by the people who are closest to him.* That's what John Maxwell calls the Principle of the Inner Circle: "*Those closest to you determine the level of your success.*" Maxwell also humorously says: "*You can't soar with the eagles if you run with turkeys!*" Neither can you develop as a leader if you have the senses of a *vulture* — always seeking out the dead and decaying! You will always be sniffing out the weaknesses and sicknesses in others...circling over the carcass of their mistakes... picking apart their wrong decisions...feeding off of their faults... dining off of their failures! A leader who has nothing but a "nose for the negative" is a sick leader! He will go through life attacking ... criticizing...tearing down others so he will look good by comparison. Eagle leaders rise high above this kind of pettiness! They emphasize the positive rather than the negative. They discipline themselves to speak well of others — especially other good leaders.

A leader who wants to grow and develop carefully and prayerfully picks the partners who will be in his "inner circle." He seeks to surround himself or herself with people who are smarter...more mature...more experienced…more capable…more talented than they are! They do not surround themselves with "yes men" or "compliant women" who will never challenge their thinking. They understand that they become strong by surrounding themselves with *strong people*. Conversely, they weaken their leadership potential by surrounding themselves with *weak people!* A good athlete knows that he only improves his game by playing with others who are better than he is. You only take your game up to a new level by competing with someone who is a better player. As a leader becomes better at the "game of leadership", he wants to make others better also. A good leader is always *growing* – and is helping *grow others* in the process.

"Identify good talented people and put them in positions they enjoy doing."[17]
(Herman Cain)

We see this principle of the "inner circle" in Christ's ministry through His relationship with "Peter, James and John."

Principle:
"The people closest to you largely determine the level of your success."

At this point, leadership is like mountain climbing: *The higher the ascent, the fewer the climbers.* The higher the mountain, the greater the *dedication* and *skill* required. Mt. Everest is not for novice climbers! The more dangerous and daring the climb, the higher the *trust level* must be between the climbers! Often each one's survival is dependent upon the other. A mistake by one can become fatal to the others. Whether in *marriage* or in *ministry* – TRUST *is the foundation of a lasting relationship and partnership!* *Trust* is based upon *trustworthiness. When the trust is destroyed, the basis for the partnership is destroyed.* When there is a major *violation of trust*, it can seldom – if ever – be fully restored. It can be *forgiven* – but not *forgotten!* Leadership may be *retained* – but trust and respect will probably never be fully *regained.* No person ever lives long enough to fully redeem and restore his trust level once it has been significantly broken. They will go to their grave with a dark cloud of *distrust* lingering over them!

For a ministry or an organization to grow, the *leader must constantly grow*. For the leader to grow and the ministry to grow - the *partners must grow*. For those relationships to grow, the trust level between the leader and the followers must also constantly grow. Every leader must remember that *he cannot build a ministry larger than himself*. If a ministry outgrows the leader, then his leadership is over. Either his ministry will plateau until he catches up and moves back out in front; or the group will look for a new leader who can take them to another level of growth. Followers generally do not outgrow their leader.

Once again we see the importance of *leadership growth*. A *growing leader* is a *going leader*. However, *when he stops growing, he stops going!* He loses momentum. He is no longer "on the move." He plateaus. When the leader stops *growing* and *going*, the same thing happens to the followers. *For his followers to grow, the leader must grow first*. Oftentimes, the leader not only has to *grow first* – he also has to *grow fast!* Leadership by its very nature means being at least one step ahead of the group. If the leader is not "out front" then he is not leading, he's just taking a walk! To keep his followers growing, the leader must first of all *live on the growing edge*. Effective leaders are *lifelong learners*. True learners have an insatiable curiosity... an inquiring mind...a longing to know...a desire to understand...a drive to figure things out. Learners ask questions...listen to different opinions...write down answers...store up information. True learners and leaders like to associate with people who are smarter...wiser...more educated...more experienced...more exposed than themselves. They like to associate with those who are higher achievers and more successful than they are so they can learn from them. They are not afraid to be s-t-r-e-t-c-h-e-d by associating with people who are different from them – who think differently...believe differently...act differently...do it differently. Leaders who are growing are not afraid to move out of their little world...their surroundings...their comfort zone...their group...their church...their denomination...their organization their methodology...their theology...their experiences...their paradigm. All of this is a part of their growth process. It helps keep a leader on a *positive learning curve*. As a result, *good leaders do not develop in a day – they develop daily!*

Because good leaders are always *visionaries* who focus on the "BIG Picture," they need people around them who will focus on the "little details!" Wise leaders surround themselves with good *managers* – detail people who have an eye for those small things that the leader often overlooks as he focuses on the "Big Picture"! There is an important principle that says: *"The devil is in the details!"* The devil will often sabotage a leader's vision by destroying him through overlooked or mismanaged details. As King Solomon wisely pointed out, it is the **"…little foxes that *spoil* the vineyard"** (Song. 2:15). Down through history, many a leader's *visionary vineyard* was destroyed because he ignored or overlooked some important details! At the time, those details may have seemed small and insignificant. Over time those "foxy little details" wreaked havoc – and "spoiled their leadership vineyard!" Ignored details can be like unseen termites that eat away at the foundation of a person's leadership. Little details continuously ignored will ultimately mount up and create an avalanche of destruction!

Because the subject of *management* is so critical to leadership, I want to pause and look at a few principles about this supportive partnership role. Since many books and business journals have been written on this subject alone – it needs at least a full chapter by me! However, I will only share a few principles concerning the roles and relationships of *leadership* and *management-ship* (There are more helpful quotes and insights at the end of this chapter).

- *Management deals most with the* status quo, *while leadership deals mostly with* change.[18]

- *Management works within the paradigm. Leadership creates new paradigms. Management works within the system. Leadership works on the system Fundamental to putting first things first in our lives is leadership before management: 'Am I doing the right things?' before 'Am I doing things right?"*[19]

- *While management is* problem-oriented, *leadership is* opportunity-oriented…*While management works* in *the system, leadership works* on *the system.*[20]

- *Management is doing things right; leadership is doing the right things.*[21]

- *Managers focus on making sure that things 'get done right' while leaders focus on making sure that the 'right things get done'.*[22]

- *Effective management is* putting first things first. *While leadership decides what 'first things' are, it is management that puts them first, day-by-day, moment-by-moment; management is carrying it out.*[23]

- *Management is bottom line focus: 'How can I best accomplish certain things?' Leadership deals with the top line: 'What are the things I want to accomplish?'....Management is efficiency in climbing the ladder of success; leadership determines whether the ladder is leaning against the right wall...Efficient management without effective leadership is...'like straightening deck chairs on the Titanic.' No management success can compensate for failure in leadership.*[24]

Perhaps the most famous leadership guru in the business world today is Peter Drucker. He continuously advises more Fortune 500 companies, and international businesses than perhaps any other person. He exalts the lofty role that good management has played in the Western world by writing:

> *In less than 150 years, management has transformed the social and economic fabric of the world's developed countries. It has created a global economy and set new rules for countries that would participate in that economy as equals.*[25]

What I believe Drucker is saying is this: It has been the combination of leadership *and* management that has caused the developed countries of the world to rise economically to where they are today. The Western world – primarily Europe and North America – has been blessed with many visionary entrepreneurs and business tycoons who have led the industrial revolution. Their people enjoy the highest standard of living known in history. These visionary leaders were also surrounded by a host of good managers who were indispensable in this technological, economic and social revolution. Most of the underdeveloped countries today lack *both* visionary leadership and competent management. They are not able to participate in the new global economy as equals. They are still largely dependent and a drag on the global economy. Their regimes and "governments" are characterized by incompetence, egoism, cronyism, tribalism, caste systems, bureaucracy, bribery, red-tape, blame-shifting, scape-goating, irresponsibility. Their national treasuries are treated like personal bank accounts. Their economies are in shambles, and their people are living in grinding poverty. There are many countries in our global community who are literally dying for a lack of good leaders – and ones who will surround themselves by good managers! As a result, the gap continues to widen in the world between the *haves* and *have-nots*. Now the so-called "digital divide" is widening this gap even further – leaving more and more millions of people on the outside looking in.

From the above quotes, it is easy to see that there is an important difference between *leaders* and *managers*. Both are necessary in any ministry or movement. One is not more important than the other. It is not a matter of *either/or* – but rather *both/and*. Neither is it a matter of one being *better* than the other. The issue is *difference – difference in gifts…talents…calling… perspective …focus*. Effective leaders clearly understand the difference between themselves and managers. They well know that they need good managers surrounding them to enable them to reach their goals and fulfill their vision. While the leader determines the *direction* of an organization – the managers take care of the *details*. There is a cute little poem that describes how important little details can be. It tells how the destiny of a whole nation was changed because of the lack of one small *horseshoe nail*:

> *For lack of a nail the shoe was lost;*
> *For lack of a shoe the horse was lost;*
> *For lack of a horse the rider was lost;*
> *For lack of a rider the battle was lost;*
> *For lack of the battle the war was lost;*
> *For lack of the war the nation was lost!*

A poor job by some blacksmith changed the entire destiny of a nation! A wise leader must either "have an eye for details" or surround himself with partners who have that perspective! Leaders often need to have the input and council of people who are *administrators, bookkeepers, lawyers, accountants, comptrollers*, etc. These are people who have both a natural inclination and professional training that orients them to be "detail-oriented people" – whether in legal matters…money matters …

organizational matters…administrative matters. Every good leader needs the safeguards of those kinds of people – especially as his organization or ministry grows. Leaders understand that growth by its very nature requires *power-sharing* and the *delegation of responsibility*. Leaders must not only *delegate responsibility*, they must *empower their ministry partners to fulfill those responsibilities*. Only insecure leaders will not share power, authority and responsibility with others around them.

Many of these kinds of "detail people" are hard for a leader to work closely with because they are sometimes perceived to be "negative" and "pessimistic." The leader sees them as the ones who always "bring up problems!" They are seen as "nitpickers!" The leader begins to view them as his *enemies* rather than his *enablers*. In his mind, he writes them off as "negative people" who are just out to "kill his vision." Most leaders will not work closely with people whom they perceive as negative, pessimistic, problem-oriented, "gloom and doom people!" Good leaders need partners around them who have a realistic eye for problems. If the partnership is going to work and have longevity, leaders must find a healthy balance of *"positive partners"* and *"problem partners."*

The most effective leaders are always *partner-leaders!* They are not just interested in reaching their goal by themselves. They do not want to cross the finish line alone. When they take their organization or ministry up to the next level of growth, they want to take as many people with them as possible. *Victories that are experienced alone are seldom satisfying or fulfilling.* They are lonely and hollow. Leaders want to incorporate as many other people as possible in the accomplishment of the goal. They want to develop as wide an ownership in the vision as possible – so that when it is achieved, it is a *group victory*. The wisdom of Proverbs reminds us:

> **"For lack of guidance a nation falls, but *many advisers make victory sure."*** (Prov. 11:14).

Mature Biblical leaders are always *good partners*. To be a good partner, they must *love people* and want to include and incorporate as many others as possible in the accomplishment of their vision.

We can conclude this focus on *partnership leadership* by again reminding ourselves that *good leadership* is like *good parenting*. Wise leaders have learned what wise parents understand – that their primary job is to "work themselves out of a job." Unfortunately, many parents create *an unhealthy dependency* upon themselves. They do not adequately prepare their children to "stand on their own two feet" and "carry their own load." Because of their own "need to be needed," they create a prolonged dependency that ultimately retards and cripples the child. Ultimately the relationship becomes confining and cumbersome to both – and resented by both. Fred Smith refers to this unhealthy, prolonged dependency as "hostile dependence." He wisely points out: "Dependence can create hostility…Hostile dependence happens when a person is dependent and angry about it."[26] A parent has *only* done his or her job when they have "worked themselves out of a job." Prolonged dependency causes a relationship to become *hostile* – rather than *healthy, holy,* and *happy.*

Unfortunately, many leaders never grow to understand this principle of *parenting* and *partnership leadership*. Due to their own insecurity and immaturity, they try to create a *lifelong dependency* upon themselves. They act as though they are going to be around forever! Every good leader – just like every wise parent – will one day give up that role of leadership and headship. It will either happen by growth, individuation, or death. Maturing leaders understand the importance of *passing on leadership to others*. Let me share a few compelling quotations about the importance of *leadership legacy*, or *passing on the baton of leadership*.

- John Maxwell refers to this as the "Law of Legacy." He summarizes it this way: *"A leader's lasting value is measured by his succession."*[27]

- John Maxwell also says: *"A legacy is created only when a person puts his organization into the position to do great things without him."*[28]

- Oswald Sanders points out: *"The true test of a person's leadership is the health of the organization when the organizer is gone."*[29]

- Fred Smith notes: *"Dictators do not develop strong leaders for succession."*[30]

- Richard Phillips wisely points out: *"Unless we successfully pass the baton, and nurture successors to receive it, we will ultimately have failed as leaders...The truly worthy career does not end with its own story, but in the story of those who follow...It is important for all leaders, at all levels, to carefully oversee the appointment of a successor, if their legacy is to endure."*[31]

It has often been pointed out that there are *three phases of leadership:* First, the need to be *needed.* Second, the need to be *succeeded.* Third, the need to be *exceeded.* Not only does a wise parent want his children to grow and mature to the degree that they can *succeed* them; they want them to grow and go beyond them to the degree that they *exceed* them in life! I have often told my children that my desire for them is that they become more spiritual...more mature...more productive...more successful than I have been. I want them to "stand on my shoulders" and reach greater heights for the Kingdom of God than I have achieved by God's grace. I well know that whatever success I have experienced is because I have had the privilege of standing on the shoulders of godly parents and grandparents before me. By standing on my shoulders, I want my children – and grandchildren – to go even higher! To have your physical and spiritual children *succeed you* – and *exceed you* – is the greatest joy of parenting! It is also the greatest joy and privilege of *partnership leadership!*

"Two are better than one, because they have a good return for their work; if one falls down, his friend can help him up! But pity the man who falls and has no one to help him up! Also, if two lie down together, they will keep warm. But how can one keep warm alone? Though one may be overpowered, two can defend themselves. A cord of three strands is not quickly broken"
(Eccl. 4:9-12).

FURTHER QUOTATIONS ON
LEADERS AS PARTNERS

1. RELATIONSHIPS:

- *Relationships are essentially* transactional. *But the reality is that most of the greatest achievements and the greatest joys in life come through relationships that are* transformational. *The transactional approach grows out of the mechanical, controlling, a 'managing things' paradigm. People are essentially seen as bionic units to whom we can delegate to get more done, or as to be handled efficiently so that we can get back to our schedule...But interdependence is not* transactional; *it's* transformational. *It literally changes those who are party to it. It takes into consideration the full reality of the uniqueness and capacity of each individual and the rich, serendipitous potential of creating synergistic third alternatives that are far better than individuals could ever come up with on their own...interdependence is the richness of relationships, the adventure of discovery, the spontaneity and deep fulfillment of putting people ahead of schedules, and the joy of creating together what did not exist before...*Almost without exception, everything people identify as really important has to do with others...Our greatest joy – and our greatest pain – comes in our relationships with others.[32]

- *Genuine brotherly love, sisterly companionship, is absolutely essential for all who would pursue a path of purpose and meaning...How many people foolishly cast the living wealth of friendship into the furnace of personal ambition, sacrificing meaningful relationships for things that neither last nor satisfy the heart.[33]*

- *A good leader must value relationships. It is only as he loves and respects and serves people that they will respect and trust him.[34]*

- *It has been noted that less than 25% of an individual's success depends on skill and intelligence, while over 75% is based on their ability to build relationships. Business educator, H. Chandler Hunt surveyed business employees and found only 24% were held back by business skills. The rest were lacking in skills of human relations.[35]*

- *Leadership grows out of relationships.[36]*

- *We ought to make enemies by our position, not by our disposition. Some leaders act like they brush their teeth with gunpowder. They go around shooting off their mouth.*[37]

- *The mentor helps you answer the "dream question", "How can I make the most significant difference for God in my lifetime?"*[38]

2. PARTNERSHIPS:

- *Individuals alone, no matter how competent or charismatic, never have all the assets needed to overcome tradition and inertia except in very small organizations...Because major change is so difficult to accomplish, a powerful force is required to sustain the process.*[39]

- *Integrity grows with proper association. Our friendships not only define us, but develop and energize us.*[40]

- ...challenge those on the sidelines. *There are always many people on the sidelines...They can respond to inspired leadership, they can complain about injustice and incompetence, but left to themselves they are more than willing to* not *take a solid stand. Leaders often make the mistake...of not confronting such people. The shepherd has a bent for protecting those who are weaker, for taking all the burden on himself or herself. But in reality this is no help to t he fence-sitter; though he may survive by avoiding all confrontation, this survival comes at a fearsome cost to the soul. What is it that fence-sitters be challenged to do? To live up to the spirit of the offices they hold...Those seeking to initiate change, must challenge those on the sidelines. The calling must find expression or else it dies.*[41]

- *Be a team builder, not an empire builder...The secret to good leadership is always in getting good people. The best leader is one who has sense enough to pick good people to do what he wants done, and self-restraint enough to keep from meddling with them while they do it.*[42]

- *John D. Rockefeller said, in explaining his success: "I simply hired men who were smarter than I."*[43]

- *The true leader is concerned primarily with the welfare of others...*[44]

- *...the kind of leadership which draws together an organization is self-sacrificing leadership, forgiving leadership, and believing leadership...*[45]

- *Success is evidenced in the followers' inspiration, their growing confidence, new capabilities, and fresh achievements. Experienced leadership today does not itself produce sales or production. It produces committed and capable followers...*[46]

- *Saul could not be counted on to pursue the purposes of God, but only to serve his own. Not knowing how to follow, he could not be trusted to lead.*[47]

- *It is always a sign of trouble when an executive surrounds himself or herself with couriers unable and unwilling to offer anything but praise and adoration. Such people always seem to be available, quick to work themselves into favor through ingratiating servitude. The leader who welcomes them is avoiding, consciously or not, the truth about himself...he (Saul) settled for those insects who gravitate to the light that power radiates...he (Saul) would surround himself only with spineless creatures with slippery tongues...*[48]

- *"The most important single ingredient in the formula of success is knowing how to get along with people."* – Theodore Roosevelt, American President [49]

- *People don't care how much you know, until they know how much you care.*[50]

- You can't lead people if you need people.[51]

- *"No man will make a great leader who wants to do it all himself or get all the credit for doing it."* – Andrew Carnegie, Industrialist [52]

3. TRUST:

- *The reality is that* quality relationships *are built on principles – especially the* principle of trust. *And,* trust grows out of trustworthiness, *out of the character to make and keep commitments...It's the* personal trustworthiness that makes trust possible...*If we're duplicitous or dishonest in any role, it affects every* *role in our lives…*Trust is the glue of life. *It's the most essential ingredient in effective communication. It's the foundational principle that holds all relationships – marriages, families, and organizations of every kind – together. And* trust grows out of trustworthiness. *Both* character *and* competence *are necessary to inspire trust. The reality is that* character *and* competence *drive everything else in the organization. To nurture* character *and* competence *is the most high-leverage thing we can do to create empowerment…Again,* trust is the natural outgrowth of trustworthiness. *So the highest-leverage thing we can do to create trust is to* be trustworthy.[53]

- *Trust is the most important element in the development and maintenance of a productive work environment. Trust stimulates security and confidence, two prerequisites to innovation and creativity. On the other hand, mistrust produces frustration, insecurity, and fear – all major deterrents to creative thinking and innovative action.* [54]

- *To maintain a highly productive work environment, the leader must develop a* trust relationship *with his people, give them decision-making power that allows them to use their creativity, turn mistakes and failures into positive learning experiences, and provide proper recognition. Trust begins with the leader or manager.*[55]

4.   MANAGEMENT:

- *Great success creates a* momentum *that demands more and more* managers *to keep the growing enterprise under control while requiring little if any leadership.*[56]

- Management is about people…*All managers do the same things, whatever the purpose of their organization. All of them bring people – each possessing different knowledge – together for joint performance. All of them have to make human strengths productive in performance and human weakness irrelevant.*[57]

- *A manager, whether in a ball-bearing manufacturer or in a large church, should spend hours placing people in the job to match their strengths, helping them to define their objectives, finding the resources they need to work effectively. Management is about people, not so much about their feelings as their effectiveness. The best thing you can offer a person is the chance to contribute to a worthwhile cause... Management is ministry for helping people. It helps its employees to make a contribution to something worthwhile.*[58]

- *Management is a set of processes that can keep a complicated system of people and technology running smoothly.* The most important aspects of management include planning, budgeting, organizing, staffing, controlling, and problem-solving. *Leadership is a set of processes that creates organizations in the first place, or adapts them to significantly changing circumstances. Leadership defines what the future should look like, aligns people with that vision, and inspires them to make it happen despite the obstacles...* For every entrepreneur or business builder who is a leader, we need hundreds of managers to run their ever-growing enterprises... *The job of management is to win in the short term while making sure you're in an even stronger position to win in the future...Systematically targeting objectives and budgeting for them, creating plans to achieve those objectives, organizing for implementation and then controlling the process to keep it on track – this is the essence of management.*[59]

- *Management activity may be reduced to two basic categories: the management of* things *and* ideas. *These represent the irreducible minimums of management. Unfortunately, people often fall into the* things *category...The leader or manager interested in progress – or in an organization's existence beyond the present – must make* management of ideas his top priority. *What an organization will be tomorrow depends on how well it manages peoples' ideas today... The leader or manager is responsible for creating a* positive work environment. *People have unlimited potential to be creative and achieve greater levels of productivity.*[60]

5.   **SYNERGY:**

- *'Accomplishing tasks through people' is a different paradigm than 'building people through the accomplishment of tasks.' With one, you get things done. With the other, you get them done with far greater creativity, synergy, and effectiveness...and in the process, you build the capacity to do more in the future as well.*[61]

- *Insecure people think that all reality should be amenable to their paradigms. They have a high need to clone others, to mold them over into their own thinking. They don't realize that the very strength of the relationship is in having another point of view. Sameness is not oneness; uniformity is not unity. Unity, or oneness, is complementariness, not sameness. Sameness is uncreative...and boring. The essence of synergy is to value the differences...*[62]

6. DELEGATION & EMPOWERMENT:

- *Empower...empower...empower! It's become a politically correct mantra. The idea of helping more people to become more powerful is important. Environmental change demands organizational change.* Major internal transformation rarely happens unless many people assist. *Yet employees generally won't help, or can't help, if they feel relatively powerless. Hence the relevance of empowerment.*[63]

- *Once a leader delegates, he should show utmost confidence in the people he has entrusted...*Subordinates perform better when they feel sure of the leader's support. *This confidence comes when responsibilities have been clearly defined in writing, to eliminate any misunderstandings.*[64]

- *Administration is a necessary evil and must be done as efficiently as possible in order to minimize the time and energy devoted to it. The spiritual leader selects associates according to gifts and passion, knowing that* work delegated to people with the proper gifts and passion needs little supervision, only coordination to move the vision forward...*I have found it helpful to employ people in the area of their gifts and passions. Then you have only to coordinate them, not supervise them...Getting the right people in the right place with the right attitude is more important in a small organization than a large one...The smaller the organization, the more quality each individual must have.*[65]

- *To build a coalition that can make change happen you must:* Find the right people...create trust...develop a common goal.[66]

- *There are three important elements of delegation:* responsibility, authority, *and* accountability. Responsibility *represents the activity to be performed. When delegating responsibility, make sure the employee knows exactly what is to be done.* Authority *represents the decision-making power needed to achieve the assigned responsibility. Accountability is the obligation to perform the responsibility and exercise authority in terms of established performance standards.*[67]

7.   **LEGACY:**

- *In corporate management I was taught that the perpetuity of the healthy organization is management's first responsibility, and so leadership development at all levels is of prime importance. Successful succession is a leader's responsibility and often a test of his character.*[68]

- *Failure to make provision for the succession of leadership has spelled ruin for many missions and churches. Moses followed Jethro's advice and realized several benefits. He was able to concentrate on the biggest problems. The latent talents of many around him were discovered. Those gifted men, who could have become his critics had Moses continued alone, were now allies facing a common challenge. People-problems were solved with efficiency. And Moses laid the groundwork for effective leadership after his death.*[69]

- *Successful organizations in the twenty-first century will have to become more like incubators of leadership. Wasting talent will become increasingly costly in a world of rapid change. Developing that leadership will...demand flatter and leaner structures along with less controlling and more risk-taking cultures...People need to be encouraged to attempt to lead, at first on a small scale...to help themselves grow. In this way, through thousands of hours of trial and error, coaching, and encouragement, they will achieve their potential.*[70]

- *Our time is crying out for leaders...after God's own heart. We need the leader who is defined not by his or her own greatness, but by the greatness of the followers. Not the leader who celebrates his own abilities...but the leader who rejoices in the character and ability being cultivated in the precious human lives entrusted to him...The great military theorist and historian J.F.C. Fuller once wrote: 'What the leaders are, that, as a rule, will the men below them be.'*[71]

- *...the greatest leadership is that which creates something new in the* followers *out of the raw materials already there, and which wins not only today's battle but also gives birth to principles and values for tomorrow...*[72]

- *The late Dr. Hans Selye, in his monumental research on stress, basically says that a long, healthy, and happy life is the result of making contributions, of having meaningful projects that are personally exciting and contribute to and bless the lives of others. His ethic was "earn thy neighbor's love."*[73]

- *In the words of George Bernard Shaw,*

  "This is the true joy in life — that being used for purpose recognized by yourself as a mighty one. That being a force of nature, instead of a feverish, selfish little clod of ailments and grievances complaining that the world will not devote itself to making you happy. I am of the opinion that my life belongs to the whole community and as long as I live it is my privilege to do for it whatever I can. I want to be thoroughly used up when I die. For the harder I work the more I live. I rejoice in life for its own sake. Life is no brief candle to me. It's a sort of splendid torch which I've got to hold up for the moment and I want to make it burn as brightly as possible before handing it on to future generations..."[74]

Chapter 19

LEADERS ARE POWERFUL

*"We proclaim Him, admonishing and teaching everyone with all wisdom,
so that we may present everyone perfect in Christ.
To this end I labor, struggling with all His energy, which so
powerfully works in me"
(Col. 1:28-29).*

It has sometimes been said: *"The world is being run by tired men."* Perhaps that is one of the reasons that there is such a high "burn-out" and "drop-out" rate – resulting in a constant change in the realm of political leadership. Many public figures began with good intentions – but over time they realized that they just did not have the mental, emotional and physical energy for sustained leadership. If that is true in the world, then it is equally true that: *"Much of the church is being led by tired pastors!"*

Success in ministry or business requires *much energy.* Most *leaders that last* are "high energy people." Leadership by its very nature requires *energy* – and usually lots of it! Harvard's John Kotter wrote: "Because major change is so difficult to accomplish, *a powerful force is required to sustain the process.*"[1] Usually that "powerful force" is embodied in the life of a leader. He is that "ball of fire" that ignites others – and gets things *going, glowing,* and *growing!* Kotter further observes: "…one of the key ingredients in effective leadership is a *tremendous energy level* and a *deep desire to use that energy for supplying leadership.*"[2] It is not just *energy for energy's sake* – it is *energy for the sake of leadership.* Eugene Habecker underscores this fact and writes: "Anyone who has held, or who holds such a position of leadership, knows the need for *high energy.* A tired or exhausted leader will rarely be effective." [3]

Some studies suggest that high energy is one of the major common denominators of all leaders. Almost all leaders seem to have a disproportionate amount of energy. They are like the now-famous *Energizer Bunny* popularized in commercials: *"They just keep on going and going and going and going!"* People tend to only follow an enthusiastic leader. It is *energy that produces enthusiasm...denotes authority...projects excitement...exudes confidence...denotes purposeful activity* – and thereby *attracts a following.* It is a basic principle that *"energy attracts attention."* Therefore, *energy attracts followers.* Without it, a leader will not be able to infuse others with enthusiasm to join him in the pursuit of his vision. To lead means that you have to capture and maintain people's attention – and that requires *movement* and *motion* – which require a continuous output of *energy.*

Principle:
"Energy produces enthusiasm which results in excitement –and enthusiasm and excitement attracts followers."

It is understandable that *clams* do not have congregations! *Slugs* or *snails* don't attract much attention because they move so slowly! Their activity is almost imperceptible. I know a lot of people who move through life at a "snail's pace!" They are too slow and too "lazy to lead!" They are about as exciting as watching Jell-O melt! If those people slowed down from their normal placid pace in life – they would have to go in reverse! All they do is stand still...tread water...mark time. Their engine is always in neutral. As the old expression says, "They are going nowhere fast!" No sluggard ever became a leader! They can't even be good followers! That's why "slothful servants" are not very high on the leadership roster in the book of Proverbs (12:24, 27; 18:9; 24:30, etc)! Sluggards can't lead because they will never put forth the energy to be out front setting the pace; and they never make good followers because they cannot keep up! The core of their problem is spiritual – not physical. Oswald Sanders rightly pointed out:

> *Many who drop out of ministry are sufficiently gifted, but* have large areas of life floating free from the Holy Spirit's control. Lazy and disorganized people never rise to true leadership.[4]

By contrast, authentic leaders are people of *purposeful movement* and *positive motion.* They are able to build a *powerful momentum.* They have usually been generously endowed by both nature and God with abundant *physical energy...mental energy...emotional energy...spiritual energy.* They tend to *pulsate with energy* through their personality and presence. The moment they enter a room – the *energy level rises!* People quickly begin to be aware of their presence. Very soon they are the center of things... the focus of attention...the catalyst that sparks activity and involvement. The Apostle Paul was just that kind of energetic leader. That's why he could remind the Corinthian church:

"When I came to you, my message and my preaching were not with wise and persuasive words, but with a *demonstration of the Spirit's power"*(I Cor. 2:1-4).

Principle:
"Leaders generally have a lot of physical, mental, emotional and spiritual energy that results in their movement, motion and momentum."

As a result of their level of activity, leaders are characterized by an *energetic personality* and a *compelling drive* that causes them to "rise to the top"..."work their way up the ladder"..."be out front"...."come out on top of things." Spiritual leadership requires a high level of spiritual commitment, mental focus, and emotional energy to accomplish God given goals – often against great odds and opposition. People will not follow a leader whom they perceive to be weak, feeble, failing and inept. When a leader loses his physical strength, mental alertness and emotional energy to lead, he generally loses his followers. At that point he may move into a new role as an advisor and counselor, but he will no longer be a leader. Leadership requires energy! It's just that simple. As John Haggai said: *"A leader without energy is like a pianist without hands or a runner without feet or an orator without a voice."*[5] Therefore, *it is almost impossible to lead without energy!*

It is important to clearly understand the origin and nature of authentic *leadership energy.* It is *intrinsic* rather than *extrinsic.* It flows from *within* — instead of being imparted from without. This *power of personality* does not come about just because a person has been given a position of power, or a rank authority. True leadership ability flows from an "internal authority" rather than an "external authority." Let me illustrate.

Authentic leadership power is not like that of a policeman or soldier who has *power* because of his rank. That kind of power is demonstrated through external *signs of authority* like uniforms…badges…guns, etc. That kind of "external authority" is "put on" and "taken off" on a daily basis. That kind of *external based authority* can be given one day — and taken away the next. That kind of authority or power is totally in the hands of superiors…supervisors…higher-ups. It is not uncommon for a leader of this kind to be "stripped of his rank"…"relieved of his duties"… "demoted from his office"…"fired from his position." In those cases, his power and authority are taken away — and his leadership along with it.

Since "internal authority" cannot be imparted from man — it cannot be taken away by man. True spiritual authority is *imputed* rather than *imparted.* Jesus told His disciples to make sure they were filled with *the Holy Spirit's power* before they attempted to fulfill His Great Commission. He said: **"…stay in the city until you have been *clothed with power* from on high"** (Lk. 24:49). The KJV translates this: **"…until you be *endued with power* from on high."** We might summarize it this way: *"Endument produces energy which results in enthusiasm."*

It is our *spiritual energy* that often determines the level of our *physical energy.* That is reflected in Psalm 118:24, which says: **"The *joy of the Lord* is my *strength.*"** The greater our intimacy with the Lord, the greater our joy. The greater our spiritual joy, the greater our physical strength!

When the inner man is energized with the presence and power of the

Lord, it will infuse the outer man with strength and energy. That's why Paul prayed this prayer for the saints at Ephesus:

> "I pray that out of His glorious riches, He may *strengthen you with power through the inner being,* so that Christ may dwell in your hearts through faith. And I pray that you, being rooted and established in love, may have *power,* together with all the saints, to grasp how wide and long and high and deep is the love of Christ, and to know this love that surpasses knowledge – that you may be filled to the measure of all the fullness of God" (Eph. 4:16-19).

Authentic spiritual leaders down through the centuries have learned what Paul learned – to lay hold of God's *dunamis power (Rom. 1:16)!* They allow God's power and resources to flow in and through them. Fred Smith shared his own experiences this way:

> "I learned that with God's presence permeating the meetings, He was the source; I was only the spokesman. In other words, God was the *pump,* and I was the *pipe. The pipe never gets tired.* When I attempt to be the pump as well as the pipe, that takes more than I have. When I try to substitute my power for God's, I become powerless, dissatisfied, even frantic and defeated."[7]

"When God selects, He sends power."[8]
(Fred Smith)

We can see that all authentic spiritual power is endued from *God through His Spirit to our spirit.* This "Spirit to spirit infusion of power" produces an endument and energy in the inner man or woman that overflows to the outer man or woman. When applied to the spiritual realm, only God can *endue* or *endow* a person with true spiritual authority. Conversely, only God can strip a man of that same spiritual authority and spiritual leadership. It is an inviolate principle that *"all spiritual authority is derived."* That means: *"To have authority, one must be submitted to authority."* There are only two sources of spiritual authority in the universe: *God* and *Satan.*

Principle:
*"Since all spiritual authority is derived authority, we
must be submitted to authority to have authority."*

When the Roman centurion was in Christ's presence, he immediately
recognized an "internal spiritual authority" that was greater than his own
"eternal Roman authority." He acknowledged this by saying to Jesus: **"I
too am a man *under authority*, with soldiers under me..."** (Mt. 8:5-9).
When the centurion gave commands, his soldiers immediately obeyed.
When Jesus gave commands, demons and sickness obeyed! That's true
internal spiritual authority that is expressed with powerful external results!
That kind of *internal power* and *spiritual authority* comes only from God.
The *greater the authority we are submitted to, the greater the derived authority
we will have.* Christian leaders have the greatest Authority in the universe
authorizing their leadership!

The Bible assures us of this principle: **"God's gifts and His call are
irrevocable"** (Rom. 11:29). Even though God does not "revoke"..."take
away"..."take back" a gift of leadership that He has given to a person –
He does take away His *anointing* upon it when there has been persistent
willful disobedience. *Immature leadership* can be corrected through time
and growth. Persistent *immoral* and *iniquitous leadership* is terminal! Both
Biblical and contemporary histories are full of the tragic stories of
Christian leaders who lost their moral authorities as leaders because God
lifted His anointing upon their lives. In the process, they did not lose their
basic innate gift of leadership – but they did lose God's special blessing
upon it. Some of these "fallen leaders" continued to lead in the secular
realm since they had lost the ability to lead in the spiritual realm. But they
could no longer lead spiritually because they had forfeited their *internal
spiritual authority* that authenticated their spiritual leadership. *Internal
spiritual authority* can only be maintained through moral attributes
like *integrity...accountability...character...godliness...purity...humility.*

A good leader needs a lot of *energy* and *enthusiasm* – which must flow from
an *internal authority.* When a leader pulsates and glows with authentic
leadership authority, he will be characterized by *hard work* and *high output.*
God created work to be the most natural and immediate focal point of

man's energy. Work is not a *curse* but a *blessing!* It is this high energy level that enables effective leaders to work longer hours...stay up later...study harder...read more books...conceive more ideas...pursue more goals...make more contacts...write more letters...make more phone calls...train more people.

It is because of this principle that leaders are generally *energized by their work*. A lot of leaders are prone to over-extension and over-work. Many leaders tend to be "workaholics" because they enjoy their work so much. For most people, a vacation is an escape from work for a period of time. Most leaders find it hard to ever truly "take a vacation from their work." Wherever they may go, they carry it with them in their mind and are constantly musing about it. For many leaders a vacation is something you complete in order to get back to doing what you intensely enjoy – your work! A leader's pace often brings fatigue to others around them (my wife often reminds me of this); while it energizes the leader. It is boredom and inactivity that fatigues leaders more than their work! My wife and I often compare our personalities and temperaments like this: I relax by *doing something*, while she relaxes by *doing nothing*. One is not better than the other, it is just the difference in our temperaments. Like everyone else, leaders get physically tired and fatigued. More often than not, they are energized and nourished by their work – because it is their life. They are *refreshed, refurbished* and *refired* through the accomplishment of a meaningful goal. Only after they have completed the task...finished the job...reached the goal can they truly rest!

This principle can be seen in a situation in the life of the Lord Jesus. He had just completed an unusually busy time of ministry. By the time that He and His disciples had walked from Judea to Galilee to Samaria, they were tired and hungry. The disciples went into the town to buy food. Hot, tired and thirsty, Jesus sat down at Jacob's well. There He had the encounter with the Samaritan woman that transformed her life. Later the disciples returned with the food and said: **"Rabbi, eat something."** Jesus' response must have shocked them: **"I have food to eat that you know nothing about."** Now they were really confused! They began to ask each other: **"Could someone have bought Him food?"** Then Jesus told them: **"My food...is to do the will of Him Who sent Me and to *finish* His work"** (Jn. 4:27-34). Do you see the principle? They were physically tired because they were spiritually spent. The very act of ministering to the woman in need energized the Lord Jesus! It was doing His Father's work that was the spiritual food that fed and nourished Him.

We can see through this account that Jesus had a passion to complete the job that He had come to earth to do. Whatever the cost, He had "... to *finish* His work." And finish He did! That's why He would not be detoured from Jerusalem - and His rendezvous with the cross! As a result of that unswerving commitment, He could pray the night before His death: "**I have brought You glory on earth by *completing the work* You gave Me to do.**" (Jn. 17:4). That's the passion of every spiritual leader! That's what feeds, nourishes, replenishes and energizes him – from the *inside out!*

Fred Smith testified to the same truth in his own life as a leader:

> *Accomplishment gives me such a joy that it actually* restores my energy. *Activity for its own sake, on the other hand, is draining.*[8]

The question is this: *"Am I working for God, or is God working through me? Am I working from the outside in, or from the inside out? Am I operating in the limited energies of the flesh – or through the inexhaustible power of the Holy Spirit?*

Every authentic Biblical leader knows that the greatest aid in his life is the *Person, presence, purpose,* and *power* of God's Spirit. He alone is the source of that...

> "...*incomparably great power* for us who believe. That *power* is like the working of *His mighty strength*, which He exerted in Christ when He raised Him from the dead and seated Him at His right hand in the heavenly realms... far above all rule and authority, power and dominion... And God placed all things under His feet and appointed Him to be Head over everything for the Church, which is His body, the fullness of Him who fills everything in every way" (Eph. 1:19-23).

Christians have an incredible *leadership edge* over people of the world! They have resident within them the very same power that God used to "...**raise Jesus from the dead**" and exalt Him in heaven "...**at His right hand...far above all rule, and authority, power and dominion.**"

That's truly incredible...incomparable...incomprehensible...invincible power! That's what every humble Christian leader of integrity can lay hold of for his life and ministry! *To God be the glory!*

FURTHER QUOTATIONS ON
POWERFUL LEADERS

1. ENERGY:

- *The world belongs to the energetic. Successful leaders have energy unlimited because they are committed to what they are doing...in the end energy will prevail. My formula is: energy, plus talent, and you are a king; energy, and no talent, and you are still a prince; talent, and no energy, and you are a pauper.*[9]

2. POWER & AUTHORITY:

- *Power is necessary to get things done. It is the gasoline for the engine. Power can be used negatively to induce fear or positively as an affirming influence. There is both human power and spiritual power. Either can be used correctly or abused. Our character determines our use of power.* [10]

- *Spiritual leadership requires superior spiritual power, which can never be generated by the self. There is no such thing as a self-made spiritual leader. A true leader influences others spiritually only because the Spirit works in and through him to a greater degree than in those he leads.*[11]

- *The Spirit will not delegate authority into secular or carnal hands, even when a particular job has not direct spiritual teaching involved; all workers must be Spirit-led and filled... The prime consideration is spirituality...*[12]

- *This is what it means to be strong: to submit to a higher truth, a higher cause, a higher authority. To hold precious the legacy of the past and walk humbly before the face of the living God...*[13]

- *Followers expect the executive to exercise authority to rightly shape behavior. Especially in times of danger or uncertainty, the follower is comforted by the leader who assertively and wisely wields authority..."Your rod and your staff, they comfort me."*[14]

- *Give Decision-Making Power to People...All man-made organizations eventually become extinct. Often their demise is due to their inability to remain flexible enough to meet the needs of a changing society. In other words, the organization fails to create an ongoing work environment that continually encourages people to use their creativity and innovative ideas to meet ever-changing needs – both within the organization and among those it serves...Decision-making power can be defined as the right to determine what action will be taken. Jesus said to His disciples,* **"Go into all the world and preach the Good News to all creation"** *(Mark 16:15). Here Jesus stated the goal, but He gave the disciples decision-making power concerning how the goal was to be accomplished. As a result, they used their creativity and ingenuity to formulate plans for accomplishing the goal.* [15]

- *Gardner further notes that "holding a position of status does not make one a leader...There are government department heads, bishops, and corporate chief executive officers who could not lead a troop of Cub Scouts out of their pup tents."*[16]

- "The church is painfully in need of leaders," *lamented the English Methodist preacher William Sangster...If the world is to hear the church's voice today, leaders are needed who are authoritative, spiritual, and sacrificial. Authoritative, because people desire leaders who know where they are going and are confident of getting there. Spiritual, because without a strong relationship to God, even the most attractive and competent person cannot lead people to God. Sacrificial, because this follows the model of Jesus, who gave Himself for the whole world and who calls us to follow in His steps.*

  Churches grow in every way when they are guided by strong, spiritual leaders with the touch of the supernatural radiating in their service. The church sinks into confusion and malaise without such leadership. Today those who preach with majesty and spiritual power are few, and the booming voice of the church has become a pathetic whisper. Leaders today – those who are truly spiritual – must pass on the torch to younger people as a first-line duty...[17]

- *K. Phillips articulated an essential principle when he wrote, "The authority a person exercises is determined by the authority to which he submits."*[18]

3. PRINCIPLE-CENTERED:

- *CHARACTERISTICS OF PRINCIPLE-CENTERED PEOPLE...They're more flexible and spontaneous...They have richer, more rewarding relationships with other people... They're more synergistic...They're continually learning... they become more contribution-focused...They produce extraordinary results...They develop a healthy psychological immune system...They create their own limits...They lead more balanced lives...They become more confident and secure...They're better able to walk their talk...They focus on their Circle of Influence...They cultivate a rich inner life... They radiate positive energy...They enjoy life more...*[19]

- **A PRINCIPLE CENTER**

  By centering our lives on correct principles, we create a solid foundation for development of the four life-support factors. Our security comes from knowing that, unlike other centers based on people or things which are subject to frequent and immediate change, correct principles do not change. We can depend on them.

  Principles don't react to anything. They don't get mad and treat us differently. They won't divorce us or run away with our best friend. They aren't out to get us. They can't pave our way with shortcuts and quick fixes. They don't depend on the behavior of others, the environment, or the current fad for their validity. Principles don't die. They aren't here one day and gone the next. They can't be destroyed by fire, earthquake or theft.

  Principles are deep, fundamental truths, classic truths, generic common denominators. They are tightly interwoven threads running with exactness, consistency, beauty, and strength through the fabric of life...we can be secure in the knowledge that principles are bigger than people or circumstances, and that thousands of years of history have seen them triumph, time and time again. Even more important, we can be secure in the knowledge that we can validate them in our own lives, by our own experience...The principles don't change; our understanding of them does...The only real limitation of power is the natural consequences of the principles themselves. We are free to choose our actions, based on our knowledge of correct principles, but we are not free to choose the consequences of those actions. Remember, 'If you pick up one end of the stick, you pick up the other.'

Principles always have natural consequences attached to them. There are positive consequences when we live in harmony with the principles. There are negative consequences when we ignore them...By centering our lives on timeless, unchanging principles, we create a fundamental paradigm of effective living. It is the center that puts all other centers in perspective...[20]

- *THE HUMILITY OF PRINCIPLES: Out of the paradigm that principles exist – and that we're only effective to the degree to which we discover and live in harmony with them – comes a sense of humility. We're not in control of our lives, principles are. We cease trying to be a law unto ourselves. We cultivate attitudes of teachability, habits of continual learning. We become involved in an ongoing quest to understand and live in harmony with the Laws of Life...Our security comes from our own integrity to true north...Humility truly is the mother of all virtues. It makes us a vessel, a vehicle, an agent instead of 'the source' or the principal. It unleashes all other learning, all growth and process. With the humility that comes from being principle-centered, we're empowered to learn from the past, have hope for the future, and act with confidence in the present.*[21]

- *"Nothing can bring you peace but yourself. Nothing can bring you peace but the triumph of principles."*[22]

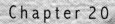

Chapter 20

LEADERS ARE PRAYERFUL

*"Do not be anxious about anything,
but in everything, by prayer and petition,
with thanksgiving, present your requests to God.
And the peace of God, which transcends all understanding
will guard your hearts and your minds in Christ Jesus"*
(Phil. 4:6-7).

I have put this matter of prayer in the life of the leader at the end of this book – not because it is of *least importance* – but because it is the *most important!* It is last only for emphasis sake. It is my desire that *last thoughts are lingering thoughts.*

Obviously, there have been many books written on this life-giving subject down through the centuries. To try and condense the matter of prayer to just one chapter is an impossibility! It is like trying to condense the oceans of the world in a teaspoon! This will not be an exhaustive "Study on Prayer" as much as it will be a brief exhortation *to pray!* Along with scores of other Christians, I too have written a longer Study Guide on the subject of prayer (It is entitled *The Dynamics of Prayer*, and can be ordered by writing our ministry – or downloaded from our Website www. jlwilliams.org). I wrote that study on prayer – not because I feel I am an authority on the subject. I wrote it to help me learn more about prayer – and become more of a *praying leader!* I am acutely and painfully aware of the *perpetual prayerlessness* of my own life and leadership! My lifelong struggle is to substitute *doing* for *being*. It is my besetting sin to spend the majority of my time in "doing things for God" – rather than just "spending time with Him." Like many other Christian leaders, I am far better at *public prayer* than I am at *private prayer*. I write this final chapter as another reminder to *me* of the vital importance of prayer for *my* life and leadership!

"I have so much business I cannot get along without spending three hours daily in prayer."[1]
(Martin Luther)

To begin, we need to remind ourselves that the supreme example of prayer in the life of a leader was the Lord Jesus. Unquestionably, He was the greatest leader of men and women the world has ever seen! No other life has had the universal, sustained, transforming impact that Christ has. He has had that impact without *doing* many of the things that we normally associate with great leadership. Could it be that His prayer life is what made the difference? The answer is obvious. If Christ's life and leadership needed to be bathed in prayer – how much more does mine need it! As Oswald Sanders pointed out, Christ's life is the perfect example of a *life totally lived in prayer*.

> *The Christian leader who seeks an example to follow does well to turn to the life of Jesus Himself. Our belief in the necessity of prayer comes from observing His life. Surely if anyone could have sustained life without prayer, it would be the very Son of God Himself. If prayer is silly or unnecessary, Jesus would not have wasted His time at it. But wait!* Prayer was the dominant feature of His life and recurring part of His teaching. *Prayer kept His moral vision sharp and clear. Prayer gave Him courage to endure the perfect but painful will of His Father. Prayer paved the way for the transfiguration. To Jesus,* prayer was not a hasty add-on, but a joyous necessity.[2]

We see this same *passion for prayer* in the life of the Apostle Paul – and in Epapharas, one of Paul's closest *prayer partners*.

> *Paul made clear that true prayer is not dreamy reverie...*

Sometimes our prayers are pale and weak compared to those of Paul or Epaphras. 'Epaphras…is always wrestling in prayer for you,' *wrote Paul in Colossians 4:12. And to the same group:* 'I want you to know how much I am struggling for you' *(Colossians 2:1). The Greek word used for 'struggle' here is the root for our words 'agony' and 'agonize.' It is used to describe a person struggling at work until utterly weary (Colossians 1:29), or competing in the arena for an athletic price (I Corinthians 9:25). It describes a soldier battling for his life (I Timothy 6:12), or a man struggling to deliver his friends from danger (John 18:36).* True prayer is a strenuous spiritual exercise that demands the utmost mental discipline and concentration.[3]

If the Lord Jesus lived in an *atmosphere of prayer,* and if the Apostle Paul constantly **"…struggled in prayer"** – how much more do I need that discipline in my life and leadership!

One of the most influential writers on prayer was E.M. Bounds. I first discovered his books when I was in Seminary. This is one of the many things he said about the role of prayer in the life of a leader:

Great praying is the sign and seal of God's great leaders. *A leader must be preeminently a man of prayer. No earnestness, no diligence, no study, no gifts will supply its lack. His heart must graduate in the school of prayer…*No learning can make up for the failure to pray.[4]

It is only through a life of personal and corporate prayer that a leader will be able to stay in touch with God and man. Without either of those relationships, authentic spiritual leadership cannot take place. John Piper observed:

I think there will be no successful spiritual leadership without extended seasons of prayer and meditation on the Scriptures. *Spiritual leaders ought to rise early in order to meet God before they meet anybody else…If you want to be a great leader of people you have to get away from people to be with God.[5]*

Dr. Wesley Duewel draws the same parallel between prayer and leadership effectiveness:

The foundation on which all ministry and leadership is built is your prayer life. Your leadership is never greater than your prayers. *Successful leadership requires much more than prayer, but no leadership can ever be ultimately successful apart from much prayer...Other things being equal, a praying leader with a praying people will be blessed of God.*[7]

As Duewel points out, leadership is *based on more than prayer* – but it is *baseless without prayer!* A *secular leader* can successfully lead without prayer. A *spiritual leader* cannot. He leads *through prayer.*

The late Andrew Murray asked the poignant question: *"What is the reason why many thousands of Christian workers in the world have not a greater influence?"* His answer:

Nothing save this – the prayerlessness of their service...It is nothing but the sin of prayerlessness which is the cause of the lack of a powerful spiritual life.[9]

**"You will never be a greater
leader than your prayers."**[8]
(Wesley Duewel)

Many studies indicate that most leaders are often *long on purpose* – but *short on prayer!* As Duewel points out: *"Every leader gives lip service to prayer. However, many have a deplorably ineffective prayer life."*[10] Over a century ago, Bishop J.C. Ryle made the same observation: *"I have come to the conclusion that the vast majority of professing Christians do not pray at all."*[11] Ouch!

Many of us as Christian leaders – myself included – do not spend nearly enough time in prayer. As a result, much of our "religious activity" lacks God's power and anointing. As Paul said: **It has the *form of godliness,* but lacks the *power"*** (II Tim. 3:5). Many of us know from painful experience that *without prayer there is no power!* We also know that purpose that is not born out of prayer is usually *polluted* with pride, self, carnality, ego, greed. Many of us as leaders go to God to ask for His blessings upon *our plans* and *our purposes* – rather than first of all going to Him through prayer to ask for His. Fred Smith points this folly out when he writes:

When we abuse prayer, we are practicing faith folly. *Too often prayer does not enter into the* setting of our goals *nearly as much as it does in the* attaining of them. *Better to seek God's will in the setting than to ask Him to bless the accomplishment. We should pour prayer over our human efforts like sauce over meat.*[12]

It is only through *prayer* that we learn to focus on Him and delight in His presence. In the crucible of that holy relationship, God will *purify our purpose* as a leader. George Mueller wrote about his own daily time with the Lord:

> *...the first great and primary business to which I ought to attend every day was to* have my soul happy in the Lord. *The first thing to be concerned about was not how much I might serve the Lord, how I might glorify the Lord; but how I might get my soul into a happy state, and how my inner man might be nourished... How different when the soul is refreshed and made happy early in the morning, from what it is when, without spiritual preparation, the service, the trials, and the temptations of the day come upon one!*[13]

Only prayer will *purify our hearts...clarify our vision...rearrange our priorities...refine our goals...cleanse our motives...sanctify our leadership.*

It is only prayer that will cause our *character* to be developed into Christlikeness. The issue of *character* brings us back to the very *heart of spiritual leadership.*

"The Christian who clings to sin closes the ear of God." [14]

(Oswald Sanders)

The English word *character* comes from *charakter*, which in turn is derived from *charasso*, meaning *"to cut into, to engrave."* The word originates from a stamp or impress, as on a coin or a seal. As a result of the "cutting" or "engraving," the features of the image correspond respectively with those of the instrument producing it. Because of this "engraving...stamping... cutting" one has the "character" or "characteristics" of the other.

It is through *seasons of prayer* through the Spirit and the Word that God increasingly engraves the *character of Christ* into our lives. Nothing other than prayer will stamp the *image of Christ* – Who alone is the *"... image of the invisible God"* (Col. 1:15) – into our lives. Only then will our leadership have the authenticating mark of the cross – signified by *selflessness. Character* is Christ-likeness *in the inner man or woman.* It is always true that our *inner character* soon manifests itself in our *outer conduct.* The more *Christ-like our character, the more Christ-like our conduct.*

Authentic Christian character is *compelling.* It causes people to be drawn to a truly spiritual leader. *Character* also *communicates* trust. It compellingly communicates trust from the leader to the followers – just as it does from a husband to a wife…a parent to a child…a politician to the people. There is just *no substitute for character in the life of a leader!*

Almost every failure of spiritual leadership is *a failure to be like Christ in character and conduct. People will not long follow a leader who has slips in character* that result in *slanderous conduct!* As we have often emphasized throughout this study, *trust* is foundational to sustained spiritual leadership. Since that is the case, *character is the cement in the foundation of trust!*

Christian leaders must have *character* that matches their *calling.* A person with a blemished character is a person who has forfeited his anointing and authority as a spiritual leader. *Spiritual character is only sustained through prayer.*

"A *prayerless leader* is a *polluted* and *powerless leader!*" It is through prayer that God leads and empowers us – so that we can in turn lead and empower others. Through prayer God shares His vision for us – so that we can share that vision with others. Through prayer God anoints us with His power, so we can in turn empower others. *Prayer propels us toward our potential,* so that we can *lead others to their potential.* Prayer must be the very life-breath of spiritual leadership!

Principle:
"Through prayer God leads and empowers the leader,
so that the leader can lead and empower others."

Let me conclude by saying that every attribute of leadership that we have looked at in this book needs to be constantly bathed and nurtured in prayer. It is only prayer that will lift these characteristics from the *human to the divine*...from the *natural to the supernatural*...from the *flesh to the spirit*...from *self to Christ!* Therefore, it is only *prayer* that will...

- Purify our *purpose*
- Make us truly *prophetic*
- Give us a *people-focus* rather than things
- Make our lives *predictable* through consistency
- Keep us *positive* and *passionate* in our pursuits
- Help us strive toward *perfection* in all we do
- Make us discerning and *perceptive* in the spirit
- Give us the wisdom to be *problem-solvers* God's way
- Impart creativity for the *promotion* of God's vision in our lives
- Motivate us to be a *pace-setter* who stays ahead through the Spirit
- Cause us to be *precipitators* who make things happen for the Kingdom
- Teach us how to be good Biblical *planners* around God's priorities
- Help us be practical and *pragmatic* in leading others
- Motivate us to be *punctual* and "on time" leaders
- Produce the needed balance of *persistence* and *patience* in our lives
- Cause us to be true *partner-leaders* who share responsibility with others
- Give us the natural and supernatural *power* we need to lead for God's glory!

Since I began this chapter with a scriptural exhortation about prayer, I want to end the same way. It is a "call to prayer" that the Apostle Paul issued to the Ephesian Christians – and is just as timely for us today. It was how he concluded his teaching to them about *spiritual warfare*, and the necessity of their daily appropriation of the **"...full armor of God"** (Eph. 6:10-17). In these verses, Paul not only exhorted them to saturate every area of their lives in prayer, he also asked that they regularly pray for him and his ministry. I would request those of you reading this book to do the same for me.

> **"And *pray in the Spirit on all occasions* with all kinds of prayers and requests. With this in mind, *be alert* and *always keep on praying for all the saints.***

Pray also for me, that whenever I open my mouth, words may be given me so that I will fearlessly make known the mystery of the Gospel for which I am an ambassador in chains. *Pray that I may declare it fearlessly, as I should"* (Eph. 6:18-20).

Principle:

"No cross, no leadership" [15]

FURTHER LESSONS ON
LEADERSHIP AND PRAYER

1. PRAYER:

- *Prayer is the most ancient, most universal, and most intensive expression of the religious instinct. It includes the simplest speech of infant lips and the sublime entreaties of older age. All reach the Majesty on high.* Prayer is indeed the Christian's vital breath and native air...[16]

- ...*'When I go to prayer,'* confessed an eminent Christian, *'I find my heart so loath to go to God, and when it is with Him, so loath to stay.'* Then self-discipline has a role. *'When you feel most indisposed to pray, yield not to it,'* he counseled, *'but strive and endeavor to pray, even when you think you cannot.'* [17]

- We cannot learn about prayer except by praying. *No philosophy has ever taught a soul to pray. The intellectual problems associated with prayer are met in the joy of answered prayer and closer fellowship with God.*[18]

- *Paul made clear that true prayer is not dreamy reverie. 'All vital praying makes a drain on a man's vitality. True intercession is a sacrifice, a bleeding sacrifice,' wrote J.H. Jowett. Jesus performed miracles without a sign of outward strain, but 'He offered up prayers and petitions with loud cries and tears' (Heb. 5:7). Sometimes our prayers are pale and weak compared to those of Paul or Epapharas. 'Epaphras...is always wrestling in prayer for you,' wrote Paul in Colossians 4:12. And to the same group: 'I want you to know how much I am struggling for you' (Colossians 2:1). The Greek word used for 'struggle' here is the root for our words 'agony' and 'agonize.' It is used to describe a person struggling at work until utterly weary (Colossians 1:29), or competing in the arena for an athletic price (I Corinthians 9:25). It describes a soldier battling for his life (I Timothy 6:12), or a man struggling to deliver his friends from danger (John 18:36)* True prayer is a strenuous spiritual exercise that demands the utmost mental discipline and concentration.[19]

- *God will not cooperate with prayers of mere self-interest, or prayers that come from impure motives. The Christian who clings to sin closes the ear of God. Least of all will God tolerate unbelief, the chief of sins. 'Anyone who comes to Him must believe...' (Hebrews 11:6). In our prayers the paramount motive is the glory of God.*[20]

- *We naively think that the more we grow as Christians, the easier it will be to discern the will of God. But the opposite is often the case. God treats the mature leader as a mature adult, leaving more and more to his or her spiritual discernment and giving fewer bits of tangible guidance than in earlier years. The resulting perplexity adds inevitably to a leader's pressure.*[21]

- *The Desert Fathers spoke of 'busyness as moral laziness.' He writes that 'busyness acts to repress our inner fears and personal anxieties, as we scramble to achieve an enviable image to display to others. We become 'outward people' obsessed with how we appear, rather than 'inward people,' reflecting on the meaning of our lives...We define ourselves by what we do, rather than by any quality of what we are inside...Since prayer belongs to the relational side of human life to 'who I am' rather than to 'what I do', it is inevitable that prayer will have a very low priority, at the very best, for people who live busy lives.* None of us is too busy for the things that we regard as priorities.[22]

- *The Spirit's help in prayer is mentioned in the Bible more frequently than any other help He gives us. All true praying comes from the Spirit's activity in our souls. Both Paul and Jude teach that effective prayer is* 'praying in the Spirit.' *That phrase means that we pray along the same lines, about the same things, in the same name, as the Holy Spirit. True prayer rises in the spirit of the Christian from the Spirit who indwells us.*[23]

2. CHARACTER:

- *If we are to do God's work God's way, we must start with character...*[24]

- *In my sixty years in business, nobody has said, "I have a flawed character." It is much easier to admit a lack of skill than to admit to a character weakness. Yet from 75 to 80 percent of the failures I've seen have been character failures. The church must be involved in character building, helping men and women to grow into the maturity of Christ. Leaders are responsible for modeling and encouraging character and integrity.* [25]

- *B. F. Wescott once remarked, "Great occasions do not make heroes or cowards; they simply unveil them to the eyes of men. Silently and imperceptibly, as we wake or sleep, we grow strong or we grow weak, and at last some crisis shows us what we have become."* [26]

- *...what makes a champion. Not strength of arms, not wizardry at spreadsheets, not a charismatic speaking style, but strength of heart, conviction, and passionate faith...* [27]

- *... "The within is ceaselessly becoming the without," said James Allen, author of the classic* As a Man Thinketh. *"From the state of a man's heart proceed the conditions of his life; his thoughts blossom into deeds, and his deeds bear the fruitage of character and destiny."* [28]

- *Building character strength is like building physical strength. When the test comes, if you don't have it, no cosmetics can disguise the fact that it just isn't there. You can't fake it.* [29]

- *Educating the heart is the critical complement to educating the mind. In the words of American educator John Sloan Dickey:*

  "The end of education is to see men made whole, both in competence and in conscience. For to create the power of. As John Haggai said: *"A leader without energy is like a pianist without hands or a runner without feet or an orator without corresponding direction to guide the use of that power is bad education. Furthermore, competence will finally disintegrate apart from conscience."* [30]

- *"That which we persist in doing becomes easier to do," said Emerson, "not that the nature of the thing has changed, but that our ability to do has increased." As we learn to ask with intent, listen without excuse, and act with courage, we build our ability to live a principle-centered life...Over time, listening to and living by conscience becomes the fundamental habit of the heart.*[31]

- *The soul can't be fed with ambition, accomplishment, and acquisition. The soul is fed by the Spirit and the words that proceed from God...*[32]

- *Wong Ming-Dao, the great Chinese Christian also known as a "Man of Iron," passed the potent verdict, "A person with a blemished character is a person unworthy to work for God."*[33]

POSTSCRIPT

In closing this study on leadership, I want to point out several things that I hope will help keep this study in balance.

1. First, as I stated at the beginning, *no single leader has ALL of these characteristics* – any more than any Christian has ALL of the gifts of the Holy Spirit. If any of us had all of these spiritual and natural attributes, we would not need anyone! We would be complete and sufficient in ourselves. But only Jesus Christ is history's one Perfect Man. He alone was perfect and complete in Himself. However, He chose to incorporate people just like you and me into His Holy calling of building His Kingdom. In fact, it was for that purpose alone that He came. If Jesus Christ, as the world's only perfect leader, called others into fellowship and partnership with Himself – how can we not do the same?

2. Second, all of these characteristics of leadership that I have discussed in this chapter can be either *good* or *bad*. Each one is a *double-edged sword*. All of these characteristics can be used in the *flesh* or in the *Spirit*. These characteristics represent both a leader's potential *strength* - and possible *weakness!*

3. Third, almost all of these qualities of leadership are the same characteristics of both *secular* and *spiritual* leaders. Non-Christian leaders can exemplify many of these characteristics by virtue of their natural endowment. Many people are leaders by *nurture* more than by *nature*. As we saw at the beginning of this study, these people are *built leaders* more than they are *born leaders*. They have studied and learned many of the principles and "techniques of leadership" from the mentoring of other leaders. We should not be surprised to see many very capable leaders in the secular world. But *we should be surprised and concerned when we do not see more excellent leaders in the church!* Jesus Christ ordained that

His church would be the *greatest trainer of leaders in the world!* The church should be the most *leadership intensive organization in society!* Jesus entrusted the leadership of His church to His redeemed people. The church should be raising up the best leaders of all. Christian leaders have everything the secular leader has through natural endowment – but they also have the supernatural endowment that only comes through God's Spirit!

4. Fourth, since all leadership gifts come from God – whether they are *natural or supernatural* - they must be *broken* and *sanctified* to be fully used by Him! Until our gifts of leadership are broken, sanctified and purified, they will be *polluted with self* through and through. Like all valid spiritual experiences, this sanctification of our leadership gifts is both a *crisis* and *process*. It must consciously begin at some point – but it will continue throughout time, and even continue into eternity. No leader becomes completely freed from the many *self-sins* against which we all struggle. That is a leadership battle that will be a lifelong struggle of *daily surrenders!*

As we close this section, may our prayers as leaders be what King David prayed about his life and leadership...

> **"You know my folly, O God; my guilt is not hidden from You.** *May those who hope in You not be disgraced because of me, O Lord...may those who seek You not be put to shame because of me..."* (Ps. 69:5-6).

REFERENCES

Introduction

1. Paul Powell, *Getting the Lead Out of Leadership*, published by the author, Tyler, Texas, 1997, p. 12.

2. Richard D. Phillips, *The Heart of an Executive: Lessons on Leadership from the Life of King David*, Doubleday, New York, 1999, pp. 37-38.

3. Phyllis Thompson, *D. E. Hoste*, China Inland Mission, London, n.d., p. 122. This was referenced in Oswald Sanders' *Spiritual Leadership*, Moody Press, Chicago, 1994, p. 28.

4. John Piper, "The Marks of a Spiritual Leader," *http://www.desiringgod.org*, July 2000. (Desiring God Ministries, Minneapolis, MN)

5. Ibid.

6. Oswald Sanders, *Spiritual Leadership*, Moody Press, Chicago, 1994, p. 18.

7. John Edmund Haggai, *Lead On*, BAC Printers, Singapore, 1986, p. 4.

8. Bobb Biehl, *Mentoring*, Broadman & Holman Publishers, Nashville, TN, 1996, p. 145.

9. Paul Powell, *Getting the Lead Out of Leadership*, published by the author, Tyler, Texas, 1997, p. 15.

10. Ibid., p. 55.

11. Herman Cain, *Leadership is Common Sense,* Van Nostrand Reinhold, New York, 1997, p. xiv.

12. Ibid., p. xiv.

13. John C. Maxwell, *The 21 Irrefutable Laws of Leadership,* Thomas Nelson, inc., Nashville, 1998, p. 138.

14. Gunter Krallmann, *Mentoring for Mission: A Handbook on Leadership Principles Exemplified by Jesus Christ,* Jensco Limited, Hong Kong, 1994, p. 124.

15. Paul Powell, *Getting the Lead Out of Leadership,* published by the author, Tyler, Texas, 1997, p. 94.

Chapter One

1. Oswald Sanders, *Spiritual Leadership,* Moody Press, Chicago, 1994, p. 5.

2. Paul Powell, *Getting the Lead Out of Leadership,* published by the author, Tyler, Texas, 1997, p. 30.

3. Ibid., pp. 24-26.

4. Ibid., p. 24.

5. Richard Nixon, *Leaders,* Warner Books, Inc., New York, 1982, p. 5.

6. Paul Powell, *Getting the Lead Out of Leadership,* published by the author, Tyler Texas, 1997, pp. 19, 24.

7. Bobb Biehl, *Mentoring: Confidence in Finding a Mentor and Becoming One,* Broadman & Holman Publishers, Nashville, 1996, p. 49.

8. Paul Powell, *Getting the Lead Out of Leadership,* published by the author, Tyler Texas, 1997, p. 24.

9. Ibid., p. 56.

10. Franklin Graham, *Living Beyond the Limits*, Thomas Nelson, Inc., Nashville, 1998, p. 203.

11. Paul Powell, *Getting the Lead Out of Leadership*, published by the author, Tyler Texas, 1997, pp. 56-57.

12. Ibid., p. 71.

13. John Piper, "The Marks of a Spiritual Leader," *http://www.desiringgod.org*, July 2000. (Desiring God Ministries, Minneapolis, MN)

14. John C. Maxwell, *The 21 Indispensable Qualities of a Leader*, Thomas Nelson, Inc., Nashville, 1999, p. 150.

15. Fred Smith, *Leading with Integrity*, Bethany House Publishers, Minneapolis, 1999, p. 76.

16. Stephen R. Covey, *The 7 Habits of Highly Effective People: Powerful Lessons in Personal Change*, Simon & Schuster, New York, 1989, p. 99.

17. Paul Powell, *Getting the Lead Out of Leadership*, published by the author, Tyler Texas, 1997, p. 53.

18. John P. Kotter, *Leading Change*, Harvard Business School Press, Boston, 1996, pp. 7, 71.

19. Ibid., p. 81.

20. Ibid., p. 51.

21. John Edmund Haggai, *Lead On*, BAC Printers, Singapore, 1986, pp. 18-19).

22. Ibid., pp. 18-19.

23. Paul Powell, *Getting the Lead Out of Leadership*, published by the author, Tyler, Texas, 1997, p. 117.

24. Richard D. Phillips, *The Heart of an Executive: Lessons on Leadership from the Life of King David*, Doubleday, New York, 1999, p. 10).

25. Ibid., p. 268.

26. Ibid., p. 31.

27. Paul Powell, *Getting the Lead Out of Leadership*, published by the author, Tyler, Texas, 1997, p. 116.

28. John C. Maxwell, *The 21 Irrefutable Laws of Leadership*, Thomas Nelson, Inc., Nashville, 1998, p. 190.

29. Fred Smith, *Leading With Integrity*, Bethany House Publishers, Minneapolis, p. 169.

30. Paul Powell, *Getting the Lead Out of Leadership*, published by the author, Tyler, Texas, 1997, p. 103.

31. Fred Smith, *Leading with Integrity*, Bethany House Publishers, Minneapolis, 1999, p. 65.

32. A. W. Tozer, in *The Reaper*, February 1962, 459. This was referenced in Oswald Sanders' *Spiritual Leadership*, Moody Press, Chicago, 1994, pp. 29-30.

33. John C. Maxwell, *The 21 Indispensable Qualities of a Leader*, Thomas Nelson, Inc., Nashville, 1999, p. 151.

34 Fred Smith, *Leading With Integrity*, Bethany House Publishers, Minneapolis, p. 42.

35. Herman Cain, *Leadership is Common Sense*, Van Nostrand Reinhold, New York, 1997, p. 16.

36. John C. Maxwell, *The 21 Indispensable Qualities of a Leader*, Thomas Nelson, Inc., Nashville, 1999, p. 34.

37. Ibid., p. 36.

38. Stephen R. Covey, *The 7 Habits of Highly Effective People: Powerful Lessons in Personal Change*, Simon & Schuster, New York, 1989, p. 148.

39. Ibid., p. 146.

40. John C. Maxwell, *The 21 Irrefutable Laws of Leadership*, Thomas Nelson, Inc., Nashville, 1998, p. 128.

41. Stephen R. Covey, *The 7 Habits of Highly Effective People: Powerful Lessons in Personal Change*, Simon & Schuster, New York, 1989, p. 161.

42. Ibid., p. 98.

43. Paul Powell, *Getting the Lead Out of Leadership*, published by the author, Tyler, Texas, 1997, p. 25.

44. Fred Smith, *Leading with Integrity*, Bethany House Publishers, Minneapolis, 1999, p. 172.

45. Stephen R. Covey, *First Things First*, Simon & Schuster, New York, 1994, p. 116.

46. Ibid., pp. 103-104.

47. Victor E. Frankl, *Man's Search for Meaning*, Pocket Books, New York, 1959, p. 172.

48. John P. Kotter, *Leading Change*, Harvard Business School Press, Boston, 1996, p. 93.

49. Ibid., p. 85.

50. Paul Powell, *Getting the Lead Out of Leadership*, published by the author, Tyler, Texas, 1997, pp. 115-116.

51. Ibid., p. 21.

52. Stephen R. Covey, *First Things First*, Simon & Schuster, New York, 1994, p. 140.

53. Stephen R. Covey, *The 7 Habits of Highly Effective People: Powerful Lessons in Personal Change*, Simon & Schuster, New York, 1989, pp. 99, 103.

54. Ibid., p. 134.

55. Herman Cain, *Leadership is Common Sense*, Van Nostrand Reinhold, New York, 1997, p. 4.

56. Ibid., p. 171.

57. Ibid., p. 172.

58. Paul Powell, *Getting the Lead Out of Leadership*, published by the author, Tyler, Texas, 1997, p. 115.

59. Richard D. Phillips, *The Heart of an Executive: Lessons on Leadership from the Life of King David*, Doubleday, New York, 1999, p. 122.

60. Fred Smith, *Leading with Integrity*, Bethany House Publishers, Minneapolis, 1999, pp. 95-98.

61. Ibid., pp. 99-100.

62. Stephen R. Covey, *The 7 Habits of Highly Effective People: Powerful Lessons in Personal Change*, Simon & Schuster, New York, 1989, pp. 156-157.

63. Herman Cain, *Leadership is Common Sense*, Van Nostrand Reinhold, New York, 1997, p. 12.

64. Tim Stafford, *The Business of the Kingdom*, Christianity Today, November 15, 1999, p. 46.

65. Fred Smith, *Leading with Integrity*, Bethany House Publishers, Minneapolis, 1999, p. 42.

66. Tim Stafford, *The Business of the Kingdom*, Christianity Today, November 15, 1999, p. 44.

67. Oswald Sanders, *Spiritual Leadership*, Moody Press, Chicago, 1994, p. 95.

68. Stephen R. Covey, *First Things First*, Simon & Schuster, New York, 1994, p. 44.

69. Ibid., p. 87.

70. Ibid., p. 206.

71. Stephen R. Covey, *The 7 Habits of Highly Effective People: Powerful Lessons in Personal Change*, Simon & Schuster, New York, 1989, p. 98.

72. Ibid., p. 98.

73. Ibid., p. 161.

74. Oswald Sanders, *Spiritual Leadership*, Moody Press, Chicago, 1994, p. 97.

75. Fred Smith, *Leading with Integrity*, Bethany House Publishers, Minneapolis, 1999, p. 173.

76. Ibid., p. 156.

Chapter Two

1. Paul Powell, *Getting the Lead Out of Leadership*, published by the author, Tyler, Texas, 1997, p. 52.

2. Lettie Cowman, *Charles E. Cowman*, Oriental Missionary Society, Los Angeles, 1928, p. 258. This was referenced in Oswald Sanders' *Spiritual Leadership*, Moody Press, Chicago, 1994, p. 121.

3. John P. Kotter, *Leading Change*, Harvard Business School Press, Boston, 1996, pp. 68-70.

4. Ibid., p. 97.

5. Richard Nixon, *Leaders*, Warner Books, Inc., New York, 1982, p. 5.

6. Eugene B. Habecker, *The Other Side of Leadership*, SP Publications, Wheaton, IL, 1987, p. 51.

7. Oswald Sanders, *Spiritual Leadership*, Moody Press, Chicago, 1994, p. 18.

8. Ibid., p. 115.

9. Ibid., p. 116.

10. A. W. Tozer, in The Reaper, February 1962, p. 459. This is referenced in J. Oswald Sanders' *Spiritual Leadership*, Moody Press, Chicago, 1994, pp. 29-30.

11. Richard D. Phillips, *The Heart of an Executive: Lessons on Leadership from the Life of King David*, Doubleday, New York, 1999, p. 244.

12. Paul Powell, *Getting the Lead Out of Leadership*, published by the author, Tyler Texas, 1997, p. 52.

13. Oswald Sanders, *Spiritual Leadership*, Moody Press, Chicago, 1994, p. 118.

14. Ibid., p. 118.

15. Ibid., p. 118.

Chapter Three

1. John C. Maxwell, *The 21 Irrefutable Laws of Leadership*, Thomas Nelson, Inc., Nashville, 1998, p. 74.

2. Herman Cain, *Leadership is Common Sense*, Van Nostrand Reinhold, New York, 1997, pp. xiii-xiv.

3. Stephen R. Covey, *The 7 Habits of Highly Effective People: Powerful Lessons in Personal Change*, Simon & Schuster, New York, 1989, pp. 161, 169.

4. Richard D. Phillips, *The Heart of an Executive: Lessons on Leadership from the Life of King David*, Doubleday, New York, 1999, p. 154.

5. John C. Maxwell, *The 21 Indispensable Qualities of a Leader*, Thomas Nelson, Inc., Nashville, 1999, p. 40.

6. Ibid., p. 140.

7. Oswald Sanders, *Spiritual Leadership*, Moody Press, Chicago, 1994, p. 15.

8. Richard D. Phillips, *The Heart of an Executive: Lessons on Leadership from the Life of King David*, Doubleday, New York, 1999, pp. 3-4.

9. Ibid., p. 6.

10. Ibid., p. 7.

11. Ibid., p. 12.

12. Stephen R. Covey, *First Things First*, Simon & Schuster, New York, 1994, p. 262.

13. Ibid., p. 26.

14. Paul Powell, *Getting the Lead Out of Leadership*, published by the author, Tyler, Texas, 1997, p. 87.

15. Ibid., p. 87.

16. Fred Smith, *Leading with Integrity*, Bethany House Publishers, 1999, p. 171.

17. Oswald Sanders, *Spiritual Leadership*, Moody Press, Chicago, 1994, p. 15.

18. Ibid., p. 125.

19. Stephen R. Covey, *The 7 Habits of Highly Effective People: Powerful Lessons in Personal Change*, Simon & Schuster, New York, 1989, p. 299.

20. Bryant S. Hinckley, *Not by Bread Alone*, Bookcraft, Salt Lake City, 1955, p. 25. This is referenced in Stephen R. Covey's *First Things First*, Simon & Schuster, New York, 1994, p. 306.

21. Paul Powell, *Getting the Lead Out of Leadership*, published by the author, Tyler, Texas, 1997, p. 91.

22. Quotes from C. S. Lewis' *Mere Christianity*, Macmillan, New York, 1952, pp. 109-110. Stephen R. Covey, *First Things First*, Simon & Schuster, New York, 1994, pp. 289.291.

23. Oswald Sanders, *Spiritual Leadership*, Moody Press, Chicago, 1994, p. 61.

24. Stephen R. Covey, *First Things First*, Simon & Schuster, New York, 1994, p. 251.

Chapter Four

1. Stephen R. Covey, *The 7 Habits of Highly Effective People: Powerful Lessons in Personal Change*, Simon & Schuster, New York, 1989, p. 62.

2. Oswald Sanders, *Spiritual Leadership*, Moody Press, Chicago, 1994, p. 115.

3. Herman Cain, *Leadership is Common Sense*, Van Nostrand Reinhold, New York, 1997, p. 5.

4. Oswald Sanders, *Spiritual Leadership*, Moody Press, Chicago, 1994, p. 82.

5. Ibid., p. 82.

6. Stephen R. Covey, *The 7 Habits of Highly Effective People: Powerful Lessons in Personal Change*, Simon & Schuster, New York, 1989, p. 305.

7. Richard D. Phillips, *The Heart of an Executive: Lessons on Leadership from the Life of King David*, Doubleday, New York, 1999, p. 125.

8. Fred Smith, *Leading with Integrity,* Bethany House Publishers, Minneapolis, 1999, p. 170.

9. Ibid., p. 26.

10. John C. Maxwell, *The 21 Irrefutable Laws of Leadership,* Thomas Nelson, Inc., Nashville, 1998, p. 168.

11. Richard D. Phillips, The Heart of an Executive: Lessons on Leadership from the Life of King David, Doubleday, New York, 1999, p. 71.

12. Stephen R. Covey, *The 7 Habits of Highly Effective People: Powerful Lessons in Personal Change,* Simon & Schuster, New York, 1989, p. 46.

13. Ibid., p. 93.

14. Ibid., pp. 148-149.

15. John P. Kotter, *Leading Change,* Harvard Business School Press, Boston, 1996, p. 183.

16. Oswald Sanders, *Spiritual Leadership,* Moody Press, Chicago, 1994, p. 53.

17. Richard D. Phillips, *The Heart of an Executive: Lessons on Leadership from the Life of King David,* Doubleday, New York, 1999., p. 49.

Chapter Five

1. Richard D. Phillips, *The Heart of an Executive: Lessons on Leadership from the Life of King David,* Doubleday, New York, 1999, p. 60.

2. Oswald Sanders, *Spiritual Leadership,* Moody Press, Chicago, 1994, p. 165.

3. John Piper, "The Marks of a Spiritual Leader," *http://www.desiringgod, org,* July 2000. (Desiring God Ministries, Minneapolis, MN).

4. Stephen R. Covey, Stephen R. *The 7 Habits of Highly Effective People: Powerful Lessons in Personal Change*, Simon & Schuster, New York, 1989, pp. 219-220.

5. Ibid., pp. 219-220.

6. Ibid., pp. 219-220.

7. Ibid., pp. 219-220.

8. Fred Smith, *Leading with Integrity*, Bethany House Publishers, Minneapolis, 1999, p. 175.

9. Stephen R. Covey, *The 7 Habits of Highly Effective People: Powerful Lessons in Personal Change*, Simon & Schuster, New York, 1989, p. 93.

10. Paul Powell, *Getting the Lead Out of Leadership*, published by the author, Tyler, Texas, 1997, p. 51.

11. Ibid., p. 57.

12. Ibid., p. 79.

13. Ibid., p. 95.

14. Ibid., p. 108.

15. Ibid., p. 108-109.

16. John C. Maxwell, *The 21 Indispensable Qualities of a Leader*, Thomas Nelson, Inc., Nashville, 1999, p. 92.

17. Ibid., p. 121.

18. Ibid., p. 121.

19. Herman Cain, *Leadership is Common Sense*, Van Nostrand Reinhold, New York, 1997, p. 29.

20. Fred Smith, *Leading with Integrity*, Bethany House Publishers, Minneapolis, 1999, p. 146.

21. Victor E. Frankl, *Man's Search for Meaning* (New York: Pocket Books, 1959), p. 104. This is referenced in Stephen R. Covey's *First Things First*, Simon & Schuster, New York, 1994, p. 169.

22. Stephen R. Covey, *First Things First*, Simon & Schuster, New York, 1994, p. 289.

23. Myron Rush, *Management: A Biblical Approach*, Victor Books, Wheaton, IL, 1987, p. 173.

24. Oswald Sanders, *Spiritual Leadership*, Moody Press, Chicago, 1994, pp. 25, 37.

25. Fred Smith, *Leading with Integrity*, Bethany House Publishers, Minneapolis, 1999, p. 85.

26. John C. Maxwell, *The 21 Indispensable Qualities of a Leader*, Thomas Nelson, Inc., Nashville, 1999, p. 91.

27. Ibid., p. 88.

28. Fred Smith, *Leading with Integrity*, Bethany House Publishers, Minneapolis, 1999, p. 175.

29. Bobb Biehl, *Mentoring: Confidence in Finding a Mentor and Becoming One*, Broadman & Holman Publishers, Nashville, 1996, p. 37.

30. Fred Smith, *Leading with Integrity*, Bethany House Publishers, Minneapolis, 1999, p. 173.

31. Ibid., p. 175.

32. Dr. James J. Seymour, *"The Value of a Good Attitude"*.

33. Richard D. Phillips, *The Heart of an Executive: Lessons on Leadership from the Life of King David*, Doubleday, New York, 1999, p. 264.

34. Ibid., p. 109.

35. Myron Rush, *Management: A Biblical Approach*, Victor Books, Wheaton, IL, 1987, p. 178.

36. Franklin Graham, *Living Beyond the Limits*, Thomas Nelson, Inc., Nashville, 1998, p. 199.

37. Myron Rush, *Management: A Biblical Approach*, Victor Books, Wheaton, IL, 1987, p. 93.

38. Stephen R. Covey, *The 7 Habits of Highly Effective People: Powerful Lessons in Personal Change*, Simon & Schuster, New York, 1989, pp. 219-220.

Chapter Six

1. John C. Maxwell, *The 21 Indispensable Qualities of a Leader*, Thomas Nelson, Inc., Nashville, 1999, p. 41.

2. Ibid., p. 85.

3. John C. Maxwell, *The 21 Irrefutable Laws of Leadership*, Thomas Nelson, Inc., Nashville, 1998, p. 83.

4. Ibid., p. 27.

5. John C. Maxwell, *The 21 Indispensable Qualities of a Leader*, Thomas Nelson, Inc., Nashville, 1999, p. 84.

6. Bob Biehl, *Mentoring: Confidence in Finding a Mentor and Becoming One*, Broadman & Holman Publishers, Nashville, 1996, p. xiv.

7. Richard D. Phillips, *The Heart of an Executive: Lessons on Leadership from the Life of King David*, Doubleday, New York, 1999, p. 67.

8. Ibid., pp. 244, 268.

9. Ibid., p. 141.

10. Ibid., p. 191.

11. Fred Smith, *Leading With Integrity*, Bethany House Publishers, Minneapolis, p. 33.

12. Ibid., p. 31.

13. Ibid., p. 31.

14. Ibid., p. 31.

15. Ibid., p. 32.

16. Ibid., p. 31.

17. John C. Maxwell, *The 21 Indispensable Qualities of a Leader*, Thomas Nelson, Inc., Nashville, 1999, p. 86.

18. Fred Smith, *Leading With Integrity*, Bethany House Publishers, Minneapolis, pp. 32-33.

19. John C. Maxwell, *The 21 Indispensable Qualities of a Leader*, Thomas Nelson, Inc., Nashville, 1999, p. 148.

20. Fred Smith, *Leading With Integrity*, Bethany House Publishers, Minneapolis, p. 77.

21. John C. Maxwell, *The 21 Indispensable Qualities of a Leader*, Thomas Nelson, Inc., Nashville, 1999, p. 83.

22. John P. Kotter, *Leading Change*, Harvard Business School Press, Boston, 1996, p. 82.

23. Fred Smith, *Leading With Integrity*, Bethany House Publishers, Minneapolis, p. 112.

24. John C. Maxwell, *The 21 Irrefutable Laws of Leadership*, Thomas Nelson, Inc., Nashville, 1998, p. 108.

25. Herman Cain, *Leadership is Common Sense*, Van Nostrand Reinhold, New York, 1997, p. 9.

26. Richard D. Phillips, *The Heart of an Executive: Lessons on Leadership from the Life of King David*, Doubleday, New York, 1999, p. 271.

27. John C. Maxwell, *The 21 Indispensable Qualities of a Leader*, Thomas Nelson, Inc., Nashville, 1999, p. 34.

28. Ibid., p. 114.

29. John Gardner, *Excellence*, Harper & Brothers, New York, 1961, p. 86. This is referenced in Eugene B. Habecker's *The Other Side of Leadership*, SP Publications, Wheaton, IL, 1987, p. 132.

30. Jon Johnston, *Christian Excellence*, Baker Book House, Grand Rapids, Mich., 1985, p. 30. This is referenced in Eugene B. Habecker's *The Other Side of Leadership*, SP Publications, Wheaton, IL 1987, p. 134.

31. Fred Smith, *Leading With Integrity*, Bethany House Publishers, Minneapolis, p. 170.

32. John C. Maxwell, *The 21 Irrefutable Laws of Leadership*, Thomas Nelson, Inc., Nashville, 1998, p. 83.

33. Ibid., p. 85.

34. Fred Smith, *Leading With Integrity*, Bethany House Publishers, Minneapolis, pp. 26-27.

35. Paul Powell, *Getting the Lead Out of Leadership*, published by the author, Tyler, Texas, 1997, p. 56.

36. Ibid., p. 64.

37. Ibid., p. 111.

38. Sherwood E. Wirt, *Jesus: Man of Joy*, Harvest House Publishers, Eugene, Oregon, 1999, p. 21.

39. Ibid., p. 22.

40. Ibid., pp. 45-46.

41. Ibid., p. 49.

42. Ibid., p. 53.

43. Paul Powell, *Getting the Lead Out of Leadership*, published by the author, Tyler, Texas, 1997, p. 107.

44. Ibid., pp. 107-110.

45. Richard D. Phillips, *The Heart of an Executive: Lessons on Leadership from the Life of King David*, Doubleday, New York, 1999, p. 72.

46. Ibid., p. 149.

47. Ibid., p. 158.

48. Ibid., p. 256.

49. Ibid., p. 269.

50. Ibid., p. 269.

51. Ibid., p. 269.

52. Stephen R. Covey, *First Things First*, Simon & Schuster, New York, 1994, p. 175.

53. Ibid., pp. 142-144.

54. Oswald Sander, *Spiritual Leadership*, Moody Press, Chicago, 1994, p. 69.

55. Ibid., p. 72.

56. Ibid., p. 111.

57. John P. Kotter, *Leading Change*, Harvard Business School Press, Boston, 1996, p. 82.

58. Stephen R. Covey, *The 7 Habits of Highly Effective People: Powerful Lessons in Personal Change*, Simon & Schuster, New York, 1989, p. 299.

59. Fred Smith, *Leading With Integrity*, Bethany House Publishers, Minneapolis, p. 31.

60. Ibid., p. 125.

61. Eknath Easwaran, *Gandhi, the Man, 2nd Edition,* Nilgin Press, 1978, p. 145. This is referenced in Stephen R. Covey's *First Things First,* Simon & Schuster, New York, 1994, p. 121.

62. Stephen R. Covey, *First Things First,* Simon & Schuster, New York, 1994, p. 167.

63. Stephen R. Covey, *The 7 Habits of Highly Effective People: Powerful Lessons in Personal Change,* Simon & Schuster, New York, 1989, pp. 70, 310.

64. John P. Kotter, *Leading Change,* Harvard Business School Press, Boston, 1996, p. 65.

65. John C. Maxwell, *The 21 Indispensable Qualities of a Leader,* Thomas Nelson, Inc., Nashville, 1999, p. 34.

Chapter Seven

1. Paul Powell, *Getting the Lead Out of Leadership,* published by the author, Tyler, Texas, 1997, p. 109.

2. Ibid., p. 104.

3. Ibid., p. 104.

4. Ibid., p. 105.

5. Ibid., p. 105.

6. Ibid., p. 106.

7. Stephen R. Covey, *First Things First,* Simon & Schuster, New York, 1994, p. 246.

8. Stephen R. Covey, *The 7 Habits of Highly Effective People: Powerful Lessons in Personal Change,* Simon & Schuster, New York, 1989, p. 49.

9. Ibid., p. 61.

10. Fred Smith, *Leading with Integrity*, Bethany House Publishers, Minneapolis, 1999, p. 128.

11. C. S. Lewis, *The Quotable Lewis*, edited by Wayne Martindale and Jerry Root, Tynedale House of Publishers, Wheaton, IL, 1989, p. 232. This is referenced in Stephen R. Covey's First Things First, Simon & Schuster, New York, 1994, p. 68.

12. Stephen R. Covey, *The 7 Habits of Highly Effective People: Powerful Lessons in Personal Change*, Simon & Schuster, New York, 1989, p. 305.

13. Richard D. Phillips, *The Heart of an Executive: Lessons on Leadership from the Life of King David*, Doubleday, New York, 1999, p. 37.

14. Ibid., p. 38.

15. Ibid., p. 232.

Chapter Eight

1. Richard D. Phillips, *The Heart of an Executive: Lessons on Leadership from the Life of King David*, Doubleday, New York, 1999, p. 40.

2. John P. Kotter, *Leading Change*, Harvard Business School Press, Boston, 1996, p. 39.

3. John C. Maxwell, *The 21 Indispensable Qualities of a Leader*, Thomas Nelson, Inc., Nashville, 1999, p. 20.

4. John C. Maxwell, *The 21 Irrefutable Laws of Leadership*, Thomas Nelson, Inc., Nashville, 1998, p. 99.

5. Franklin Graham, *Living Beyond the Limits*, Thomas Nelson, Inc., Nashville, 1998, pp. 63, 65.

6. Ibid., p. 172.

7. Stephen R. Covey, *First Things First*, Simon & Schuster, New York, 1994, p. 175.

8. *The Chronicle of Higher Education*, May 28, 1986, p. 20. This is referenced in Eugene B. Habecker's *The Other Side of Leadership*, SP Publications, Wheaton, IL, 1987, p. 17.

9. Fred Smith, *Leading with Integrity*, Bethany House Publishers, Minneapolis, p. 112.

10. Franklin Graham, *Living Beyond the Limits*, Thomas Nelson, Inc., Nashville, 1998, p. 16.

Chapter Nine

1. Stephen R. Covey, *The 7 Habits of Highly Effective People: Powerful Lessons in Personal Change*, Simon & Schuster, New York, 1989, p. 154.

2. John C. Maxwell, *The 21 Indispensable Qualities of a Leader*, Thomas Nelson, Inc., Nashville, 1999, p. 95.

3. Fred Smith, *Leading with Integrity*, Bethany House Publishers, Minneapolis, 1999, p. 172.

4. John C. Maxwell, *The 21 Indispensable Qualities of a Leader*, Thomas Nelson, Inc., Nashville, 1999, p. 100.

5. Eugene B. Habecker, *The Other Side of Leadership*, SP Publications, Wheaton, IL, 1987, p. 102.

6. Oswald Sanders, *Spiritual Leadership*, Moody Press, Chicago, 1994, p. 132.

7. Ibid., p. 132.

8. John C. Maxwell, *The 21 Indispensable Qualities of a Leader*, Thomas Nelson, Inc., Nashville, 1999, p. 95.

9. Fred Smith, *Leading with Integrity*, Bethany House Publishers, Minneapolis, 1999, p. 78.

10. John C. Maxwell, *The 21 Indispensable Qualities of a Leader*, Thomas Nelson, Inc., Nashville, 1999, p. 48.

11. Herman Cain, *Leadership is Common Sense*, Van Nostrand Reinhold, New York, 1997, p. 24.

12. Ibid., p. 25.

13. John P. Kotter, *Leading Change*, Harvard Business School Press, Boston, 1996, p. 122.

14. Stephen R. Covey, *The 7 Habits of Highly Effective People: Powerful Lessons in Personal Change*, Simon & Schuster, New York, 1989, p. 89.

15. Ibid., p. 85.

16. Ibid., p. 232.

17. Herman Cain, *Leadership is Common Sense*, Van Nostrand Reinhold, New York, 1997, p. 18.

18. Attributed to *Spirella*, referenced in Herman Cain's *Leadership is Common Sense*, Van Nostrand Reinhold, New York, 1997, p. 64.

19. John C. Maxwell, *The 21 Indispensable Qualities of a Leader*, Thomas Nelson, Inc., Nashville, 1999, p. 111.

20. Stephen R. Covey, *The 7 Habits of Highly Effective People: Powerful Lessons in Personal Change*, Simon & Schuster, New York, 1989, p. 71.

21. Richard D. Phillips, *The Heart of an Executive: essons on Leadership from the Life of King David*, Doubleday, New York, 1999, p. 20.

22. Stephen R. Covey, *First Things First*, Simon & Schuster, New York, 1994, p. 238.

23. *Myron Rush, Management: A Biblical Approach, Victor Books, Wheaton, IL, 1987, p. 112.*

24. *Ibid., p. 201.*

25. *Ibid., p. 205.*

26. *Ibid., p. 212*

27. *Ibid., p. 216.*

28. John P. Kotter, *Leading Change*, Harvard Business School Press, Boston, 1996, p. 61.

29. Richard D. Phillips, *The Heart of an Executive: Lessons on Leadership from the Life of King David*, Doubleday, New York, 1999, p. 96.

30. Oswald Sanders, *Spiritual Leadership*, Moody Press, Chicago, 1994, p. 75.

31. Ibid., p. 126.

32. Fred Smith, *Leading with Integrity*, Bethany House Publishers, Minneapolis, 1999, p. 171.

33. Stephen R. Covey, *The 7 Habits of Highly Effective People: Powerful Lessons in Personal Change*, Simon & Schuster, New York, 1989, p. 91.

34. John P. Kotter, *Leading Change*, Harvard Business School, Boston, 1996, p. 122.

35. Eugene B. Habecker, *Leading with a Follower's Heart*, SP Publications, Wheaton, 1990. p. 119.

36. Ibid., p. 120.

Chapter Ten

1. John C. Maxwell, *The 21 Indispensable Qualities of a Leader*, Thomas Nelson, Inc., Nashville, 1999, p. 27.

2. Fred Smith, *Leading with Integrity*, Bethany House Publishers, Minneapolis, 1999, p. 164.

3. John C. Maxwell, *The 21 Indispensable Qualities of a Leader*, Thomas Nelson, Inc., Nashville, 1999, p. 23.

4. John Edmund Haggai, *Lead On*, BAC Printers, Singapore, 1986, pp. 107.

5. Ibid., pp. 107-111.

6. Ibid., pp. 107-109.

7. Ibid., p. 111.

8. Herman Cain, *Leadership is Common Sense*, Van Nostrand Reinhold, New York, 1997, p. 88.

9. John C. Maxwell, *The 21 Indispensable Qualities of a Leader*, Thomas Nelson, Inc., Nashville, 1999, p. 23.

10. John P. Kotter, *Leading Change*, Harvard Business School Press, Boston, 1996, pp. 89-90.

11. Ibid., pp. 76-77.

12. Ibid., pp. 94-95.

13. Myron Rush, *Management: A Biblical Approach*, Victor Books, Wheaton, IL, 1987, pp. 114-115.

14. Ibid., p. 129.

15. Stephen R. Covey, *The 7 Habits of Highly Effective People: Powerful Lessons in Personal Change*, Simon & Schuster, New York, 1989, p. 238.

16. Ibid., p. 255.

17. Paul Powell, *Getting the Lead Out of Leadership*, published by the author, Tyler, Texas, 1997, p. 55.

18. Stephen R. Covey, *First Things First*, Simon & Schuster, New York, 1994, p. 112.

19. Herman Cain, *Leadership is Common Sense*, Van Nostrand Reinhold, New York, 1997, p. 10.

20. John C. Maxwell, *The 21 Indispensable Qualities of a Leader*, Thomas Nelson, Inc., Nashville, 1999, p. 8.

21. Stephen R. Covey, *The 7 Habits of Highly Effective People: Powerful Lessons in Personal Change*, Simon & Schuster, New York, 1989, p. 143.

22. John C. Maxwell, *The 21 Indispensable Qualities of a Leader*, Thomas Nelson, Inc., Nashville, 1999, p. 58.

23. Ibid., p. 58.

24. Ibid., p. 63.

Chapter Eleven

1. John Piper, "The Marks of a Spiritual Leader," *http://www.desiringgod.org*, July 2000. (Desiring God Ministries, Minneapolis, MN)

2. John R. W. Stott, *Involvement: Social and Sexual Relationships in the Modern World*, Vol. II, Fleming H. Revell Company, 1984, 1985, Old Tappan, NJ, 1984, 1985, p. 249. This is referenced in Eugene B. Habecker's *The Other Side of Leadership*, SP Publications, Wheaton, IL, 1987, p. 61.

3. Lawrence Miller, *American Spirit: Visions of a New Corporate Culture*, William Morrow and Company, Inc., New York, 1984, p. 15. This is referenced in Eugene B. Habecker's *The Other Side of Leadership*, SP Publications, Wheaton, IL, 1987, p. 61.

4. Fred Smith, *Leading with Integrity*, Bethany House Publishers, Minneapolis, 1999, p. 170.

5. Oswald Sanders, *Spiritual Leadership*, Moody Press, Chicago, 1994, p. 113.

6. Ibid., p. 113.

7. Ibid., p. 28.

8. Herman Cain, *Leadership is Common Sense*, Van Nostrand Reinhold, New York, 1997, p. 83.

9. Oswald Sanders, *Spiritual Leadership*, Moody Press, Chicago, 1994, p. 117.

10. Ibid., p. 117.

11. John C. Maxwell, *The 21 Irrefutable Laws of Leadership*, Thomas Nelson, Inc., Nashville, 1998, p. 141.

12. Paul Powell, *Getting the Lead Out of Leadership*, published by the author, Tyler, Texas, 1997, p. 72.

13. Ibid., p. 90.

14. Ibid., p. 111.

15. Franklin Graham, *Living Beyond the Limits*, Thomas Nelson, Inc, Nashville, 1998, p. 67.

Chapter Twelve

1. Oswald Sanders, *Spiritual Leadership*, Moody Press, Chicago, 1994, p. 58.

2. Richard D. Phillips, *The Heart of an Executive: Lessons on Leadership from the Life of King David*, Doubleday, New York, 1999, p. 95.

3. Ibid., p. 96.

4. Ibid., p. 268.

5. Ibid., p. 168.

6. Stephen R. Covey, *The 7 Habits of Highly Effective People: Powerful Lessons in Personal Change*, Simon & Schuster, New York, 1989, p. 72.

7. John P. Kotter, *Leading Change*, Harvard Business School Press, Boston, 1996, pp. 11, 42, 119.

8. Ibid., pp. 4–5, 36, 43.

9. John C. Maxwell, *The 21 Indispensable Qualities of a Leader*, Thomas Nelson, Inc., Nashville, 1999, p. 40.

10. Herman Cain, *Leadership is Common Sense*, Van Nostrand Reinhold, New York, 1997, p. 13, 166.

11. Franklin Graham, *Living Beyond the Limits*, Thomas Nelson, Inc., Nashville, 1998, p. 16.

12. Oswald Sanders, *Spiritual Leadership*, Moody Press, Chicago, 1994, p. 127.

13. John C. Maxwell, *The 21 Indispensable Qualities of a Leader*, Thomas Nelson, Inc., Nashville, 1999, p. 145.

14. Oswald Sanders, *Spiritual Leadership*, Moody Press, Chicago, 1994, p. 127.

15. Marcus Loane, *Archbishop Mowll*, Hodder & Stoughton, London, 1960, p. 249. This was referenced in Oswald Sanders' *Spiritual Leadership*, Moody Press, Chicago, 1994, p. 128.

16. Fred Smith, *Leading with Integrity*, Bethany House Publishers, Minneapolis, 1999, p. 171.

17. Eugene B. Habecker, *The Other Side of Leadership*, SP Publications, Wheaton, IL, 1987, p. 27.

18. Oswald Sanders, *Spiritual Leadership*, Moody Press, Chicago, 1994, p. 127.

19. Ibid., p. 127.

20. John P. Kotter, *Leading Change*, Harvard Business School Press, Boston, 1996, p. 30.

21. Ibid., p. 45.

22. Eugene B. Habecker, *The Other Side of Leadership*, SP Publications, Wheaton, IL, 1987, pp. 24-25.

23. Richard D. Phillips, *The Heart of an Executive: Lessons on Leadership from the Life of King David*, Doubleday, New York, 1999, pp. ix, 95-100.

24. (Marilyn Ferguson) Stephen R. Covey, *The 7 Habits of Highly Effective People: Powerful Lessons in Personal Change*, Simon & Schuster, New York, 1989, pp. 60-61.

25. Ibid., p. 108.

26. John C. Maxwell, *The 21 Indispensable Qualities of a Leader*, Thomas Nelson, Inc., Nashville, 1999, p. 144.

27. Paul Powell, *Getting the Lead Out of Leadership*, published by the author, Tyler, Texas, 1997, pp. 111-112.

28. Ibid., p. 112.

29. Ibid., p. 112.

30. Ibid., p. 114.

31. John P. Kotter, *Leading Change*, Harvard Business School Press, Boston, 1996, p. 95.

32. Stephen R. Covey, *The 7 Habits of Highly Effective People: Powerful Lessons in Personal Change*, Simon & Schuster, New York, 1989, pp. 29, 31, 125.

33. Paul Powell, *Getting the Lead Out of Leadership*, published by the author, Tyler, Texas, 1997, p. 10.

34. Ibid., p. 48.

35. Ibid., p. 49.

36. Ibid., p. 50.

37. Ibid., pp. 51-52.

38. Ibid., p. 53.

39. Ibid., p. 69.

40. Ibid., p. 71.

41. Ibid., p. 71.

42. Ibid., p. 72.

43. Ibid., p. 111.

44. *Myron Rush, Management: A Biblical Approach, Victor Books, Wheaton, IL, 1987, p. 107.*

Chapter Thirteen

1. Oswald Sanders, *Spiritual Leadership*, Moody Press, Chicago, 1994, p. 74.

2. Stephen R. Covey, *First Things First*, Simon & Schuster, New York, 1994, p. 72.

3. Fred Smith, *Leading with Integrity*, Bethany House Publishers, Minneapolis, 1999, p. 171.

4. Ibid., pp. 143, 171.

5. John Edmund Haggai, *Lead On*, BAC Printers, Singapore, 1986, p. 32.

6. Paul Powell, *Getting the Lead Out of Leadership*, published by the author, Tyler, Texas, 1997, p. 37.

7. Ibid., p. 38.

8. Ibid., p. 40.

9. Ibid., p. 45.

10. Myron Rush, *Management: A Biblical Approach*, Victor Books, Wheaton, IL, 1987, p. 80.

11. Stephen R. Covey, *First Things First*, Simon & Schuster, New York, 1994, p. 77.

12. Paul Powell, *Getting the Lead Out of Leadership*, published by the author, Tyler, Texas, 1997, p. 30.

13. Ibid., p. 32.

14. Ibid., p. 33.

15. Ibid., p. 35.

16. Ibid., p. 56.
17. Ibid., p. 82.

18. Oswald Sanders, *Spiritual Leadership*, Moody Press, Chicago, 1994, p. 32.

19. Stephen R. Covey, *First Things First*, Simon & Schuster, New York, 1994, p. 136.

20. Myron Rush, *Management: A Biblical Approach*, Victor Books, Wheaton, IL, 1987, p. 175-178.

Chapter Fourteen

1. Fred Smith, *Leading with Integrity*, Bethany House Publishers, Minneapolis, 1999, p. 66.

2. Ibid., p. 158.

3. Paul Powell, *Getting the Lead Out of Leadership*, published by the author, Tyler, Texas, 1997, p. 47.

4. Franklin Graham, *Living Beyond the Limits*, Thomas Nelson, Inc., Nashville, 1998, p. 53.

5. John P. Kotter, *Leading Change*, Harvard Business School Press, Boston, 1996, p. 171.

Chapter Fifteen

1. Maxwell, John C. *The 21 Indispensable Qualities of a Leader*, Thomas Nelson, Inc., Nashville, 1999, p. 71.

2. Smith, Fred *Leading With Integrity*, Bethany House Publishers, Minneapolis, 1999, p. 160.

3. Richard D. Phillips, *The Heart of an Executive: Lessons on Leadership from the Life of King David*, Doubleday, New York, 1999, p. 121.

4. Oswald Sanders, *Spiritual Leadership*, Moody Press, Chicago, 1994, p. 94.

5. Ibid., pp. 93-94.

6. Ibid., p. 98.

7. Ibid., p. 98.

8. Ibid., p. 94.

9. Herman Cain, *Leadership is Common Sense*, Van Nostrand Reinhold, New York, 1997, p. 175.

10. Oswald Sanders, *Spiritual Leadership*, Moody Press, Chicago, 1994, p. 95.

11. Fred Smith, *Leading with Integrity*, Bethany House Publishers, Minneapolis, 1999, p. 161.

12. John C. Maxwell, *The 21 Indispensable Qualities of a Leader*, Thomas Nelson, Inc., Nashville, 1999, p. 128.

13. Fred Smith, *Leading with Integrity*, Bethany House Publishers, Minneapolis, 1999, p. 172.

14. Oswald Sanders, *Spiritual Leadership*, Moody Press, Chicago, 1994, p. 93.

15. W. Y. Fullerton, *F. B. Meyer*, Marshall, Morgan & Scott, London, n.d., p. 70. This is referenced in Oswald Sanders' *Spiritual Leadership*, Moody Press, Chicago, 1994, p. 97.

16. Oswald Sanders, *Spiritual Leadership*, Moody Press, Chicago, 1994, p. 94.

17. Stephen R. Covey, *First Things First*, Simon & Schuster, New York, 1994, pp. 105-106.

18. Franklin Graham, *Living Beyond the Limits*, Thomas Nelson, Inc., Nashville, 1998, p. 66.

Chapter Sixteen

1. Oswald Sanders, *Spiritual Leadership*, Moody Press, Chicago, 1994, p. 119.

2. Fred Smith, *Leading with Integrity*, Bethany House Publishers, Minneapolis, 1999, pp. 58, 172, 174.

3. Richard D. Phillips, *The Heart of an Executive: Lessons on Leadership from the Life of King David*, Doubleday, New York, 1999, p. 151.

4. John C. Maxwell, *The 21 Indispensable Qualities of a Leader*, Thomas Nelson, Inc., Nashville, 1999, p. 89.

5. John P. Kotter, *Leading Change*, Harvard Business School Press, Boston, 1996, p. 132.

6. Ibid., pp. 132-133.

7. John C. Maxwell, *The 21 Irrefutable Laws of Leadership*, Thomas Nelson, Inc., Nashville, 1998, p. 165.

8. Paul Powell, *Getting the Lead Out of Leadership*, published by the author, Tyler, Texas, 1997, p. 52.

9. Ibid., p. 75.

10. Ibid., p. 76.

11. Ibid., p. 76.

12. Ibid., p. 79.

13. Ibid., pp. 105-106.

14. Ibid., p. 117.

15. Ibid., p. 117.

16. Richard D. Phillips, *The Heart of an Executive: Lessons on Leadership from the Life of King David*, Doubleday, New York, 1999, p. 187.

17. Paul Powell, *Getting the Lead Out of Leadership*, published by the author, Tyler, Texas, 1997, p. 52.

18. Ibid., pp. 77, 94-95.

19. Ibid., p. 79.

20. John C. Maxwell, *The 21 Indispensable Qualities of a Leader*, Thomas Nelson, Inc., Nashville, 1999, p. 129.

21. Stephen R. Covey, *First Things First*, Simon & Schuster, New York, 1994, p. 264.

22. Myron Rush, *Management: A Biblical Approach*, Victor Books, Wheaton, IL, 1987, p. 43.

23. Oswald Sanders, *Spiritual Leadership*, Moody Press, Chicago, 1994, p. 15.

24. Ibid., p. 154.

25. John C. Maxwell, *The 21 Irrefutable Laws of Leadership*, Thomas Nelson, Inc., Nashville, 1998, p. 171-174.

26. John P. Kotter, *Leading Change*, Harvard Business School Press, Boston, 1996, p. 36.

27. Ibid., p. 59.

28. Ibid., p. 133.

29. Herman Cain, *Leadership is Common Sense*, Van Nostrand Reinhold, New York, 1997, p. xv.

30. Ibid., p. 10.

31. Ibid., p. 155.

32. Ibid., p. 166.

33. Stephen R. Covey, *First Things First*, Simon & Schuster, New York, 1994, p. 170.

34. Richard D. Phillips, *The Heart of an Executive: Lessons on Leadership from the Life of King David*, Doubleday, New York, 1999, p. 124.

35. Ibid., pp. 119-200.

36. Herman Cain, *Leadership is Common Sense*, Van Nostrand Reinhold, New York, 1997, p. 29.

37. Ibid., p. 35.

38. Ibid., 61.

39. Ibid., p. 106.

40. Ibid., p. 106.

Chapter Seventeen

1. Oswald Sanders, *Spiritual Leadership*, Moody Press, Chicago, 1994, p. 70.

2. Franklin Graham, *Living Beyond the Limits*, Thomas Nelson, Inc., Nashville, 1998, p. 83.

3. John C. Maxwell, *The 21 Irrefutable Laws of Leadership*, Thomas Nelson, Inc., Nashville, 1998, p. 27.

4. Stephen R. Covey, *The 7 Habits of Highly Effective People: Powerful Lessons in Personal Change*, Simon & Schuster, New York, 1989, p. 62.

5. Oswald Sanders, *Spiritual Leadership*, Moody Press, Chicago, 1994, p. 70.

6. Ibid., p. 70.

7. John Edmund Haggai, *Lead On*, BAC Printers, Singapore, 1986, p. 76.

8. Oswald Sanders, *Spiritual Leadership*, Moody Press, Chicago, 1994, p. 44.

9. Fred Smith, *Leading with Integrity*, Bethany House Publishers, Minneapolis, 1999, p. 38.

10. Oswald Sanders, *Spiritual Leadership*, Moody Press, Chicago, 1994, p. 143.

Chapter Eighteen

1. Myron Rush, *Management: A Biblical Approach*, Victor Books, Wheaton, IL, 1987, p. 48.

2. Bobb Biehl, *Mentoring: Confidence in Finding a Mentor and Becoming One*, Broadman & Holman Publishers, Nashville, 1996, p. 32.

3. Richard D. Phillips, *The Heart of an Executive: Lessons on Leadership from the Life of King David*, Doubleday, New York, 1999, p. 117.

4. Myron Rush, *Management: A Biblical Approach*, Victor Books, Wheaton, IL, 1987, p. 67.

5. Ibid., p. 67.

6. Oswald Sanders, *Spiritual Leadership*, Moody Press, Chicago, 1994, p. 137.

7. John C. Maxwell, *The 21 Indispensable Qualities of a Leader*, Thomas Nelson, Inc., Nashville, 1999, p. 118.

8. Myron Rush, *Management: A Biblical Approach*, Victor Books, Wheaton, IL, 1987, p. 132.

9. Eugene B. Habecker, *The Other Side of Leadership*, SP Publications, Wheaton, IL, 1987, p. 30.

10. Daniel Katz and Robert L. Kahn, *The Social Psychology of Organizations*, 2nd ed., John Wiley & Sons, New York, 1978, p. 571. This was referenced in Eugene B. Habecker's *The Other Side of Leadership*, SP Publications, Wheaton, IL, 1987, p. 30.

11. Myron Rush, *Management: A Biblical Approach*, Victor Books, Wheaton, IL, 1987, p. 57.

12. Oswald Sanders, *Spiritual Leadership*, Moody Press, Chicago, 1994, p. 138.

13. Stephen R. Covey, *The 7 Habits of Highly Effective People: Powerful Lessons in Personal Change*, Simon & Schuster, New York, 1989, p. 171.

14. Fred Smith, *Leading with Integrity*, Bethany House Publishers, Minneapolis, 1999, p. 83.

15. Oswald Sanders, *Spiritual Leadership*, Moody Press, Chicago, 1994, p. 137.

16. Stephen R. Covey, *The 7 Habits of Highly Effective People: Powerful Lessons in Personal Change*, Simon & Schuster, New York, 1989, pp. 262-283.

17. Herman Cain, *Leadership is Common Sense*, Van Nostrand Reinhold, New York, 1997, p. 23.

18. John P. Kotter, *Leading Change*, Harvard Business School Press, Boston, 1996, p. 51.

19. Stephen R. Covey, *First Things First*, Simon & Schuster, New York, 1994, p. 28.

20. Ibid., pp. 48, 245.

21. Quoting Peter Drucker, Stephen R. Covey, *The 7 Habits of Highly Effective People: Powerful Lessons in Personal Change*, Simon & Schuster, New York, 1989, p. 101.

22. Eugene B. Habecker, *The Other Side of Leadership*, SP Publications, Wheaton, IL, 1987, p. 20.

23. Stephen R. Covey, *The 7 Habits of Highly Effective People: Powerful Lessons in Personal Change*, Simon & Schuster, New York, 1989, p. 148.

24. Ibid., pp. 101-102.

25. Brian Friel, *Drucker on Management*, March 23, 1998, p. 2.

26. Fred Smith, *Leading with Integrity*, Bethany House Publishers, Minneapolis, 1999, p. 111.

27. John C. Maxwell, *The 21 Irrefutable Laws of Leadership*, Thomas Nelson, Inc., Nashville, 1998, p. 215.

28. Ibid., p. 221.

29. Oswald Sanders, *Spiritual Leadership*, Moody Press, Chicago, 1994, p. 143.

30. Fred Smith, *Leading with Integrity*, Bethany House Publishers, Minneapolis, 1999, p. 55.

31. Richard D. Phillips, *The Heart of an Executive: Lessons on Leadership from the Life of King David*, Doubleday, New York, 1999, pp. 224-255.

32. Stephen R. Covey, *First Things First*, Simon & Schuster, New York, 1994, pp. 27, 195-197.

33. Richard D. Phillips, *The Heart of an Executive: Lessons on Leadership from the Life of King David*, Doubleday, New York, 1999, pp. 79, 81.

34. Paul Powell, *Getting the Lead Out of Leadership*, published by the author, Tyler, Texas, 1997, pp. 83-84.

35. Ibid., p. 84.

36. Ibid., p. 85.

37. Ibid., p. 90.

38. Bobb Biehl, *Mentoring: Confidence in Finding a Mentor and Becoming One*, Broadman & Holman Publishers, Nashville, 1996, p. 102.

39. John P. Kotter, *Leading Change*, Harvard Business School Press, Boston, 1996, pp. 6, 51.

40. Fred Smith, *Leading with Integrity*, Bethany House Publishers, Minneapolis, 1999, p. 34.

41. Richard D. Phillips, *The Heart of an Executive: Lessons on Leadership from the Life of King David*, Doubleday, New York, 1999, pp. 117-119.

42. Paul Powell, *Getting the Lead Out of Leadership*, published by the author, Tyler, Texas, 1997, p. 93.

43. Ibid., p. 93.

44. Oswald Sanders, *Spiritual Leadership*, Moody Press, Chicago, 1994, p. 125.

45. Richard D. Phillips, *The Heart of an Executive: Lessons on Leadership from the Life of King David*, Doubleday, New York, 1999, p. 175.

46. Ibid., p. 8.

47. Ibid., p. 35.

48. Ibid., p. 50.

49. John C. Maxwell, *The 21 Indispensable Qualities of a Leader,* Thomas Nelson, Inc., Nashville, 1999, p. 103.

50. Ibid., p. 103.

51. Ibid., p. 118.

52. Ibid., p. 118.

53. Stephen R. Covey, *First Things First,* Simon & Schuster, New York, 1994, pp. 57, 199, 203, 241-243.

54. Myron Rush, *Management: A Biblical Approach,* Victor Books, Wheaton, IL, 1987, p. 34.

55. Ibid., p. 46.

56. John P. Kotter, *Leading Change,* Harvard Business School Press, Boston, 1996, p. 59.

57. Quoting Peter Drucker, Tim Stafford, *The Business of the Kingdom,* Christianity Today, November 15, 1999, p. 46.

58. Tim Stafford, *The Business of the Kingdom,* Christianity Today, November 15, 1999, p. 46.

59. John P. Kotter, *Leading Change,* Harvard Business School Press, Boston, 1996, pp. 25-27, 125, 128.

60. Myron Rush, *Management: A Biblical Approach,* Victor Books, Wheaton, IL, 1987, pp. 20, 46.

61. Stephen R. Covey, *First Things First,* Simon & Schuster, New York, 1994, p. 256.

62. Stephen R. Covey, *The 7 Habits of Highly Effective People: Powerful Lessons in Personal Change*, Simon & Schuster, New York, 1989, p. 274.

63. John P. Kotter, *Leading Change*, Harvard Business School Press, Boston, 1996, pp. 101-102.

64. Oswald Sanders, *Spiritual Leadership*, Moody Press, Chicago, 1994, p. 138.

65. Fred Smith, *Leading with Integrity*, Bethany House Publishers, Minneapolis, 1999, pp. 66, 113-114.

66. John P. Kotter, *Leading Change*, Harvard Business School Press, Boston, 1996, p. 66.

67. Myron Rush, *Management: A Biblical Approach*, Victor Books, Wheaton, IL, 1987, p. 144.

68. Fred Smith, *Leading with Integrity*, Bethany House Publishers, Minneapolis, 1999, p. 56.

69. Oswald Sanders, *Spiritual Leadership*, Moody Press, Chicago, 1994, p. 139.

70. John P. Kotter, *Leading Change*, Harvard Business School Press, Boston, 1996, p. 166.

71. Richard D. Phillips, *The Heart of an Executive: Lessons on Leadership from the Life of King David*, Doubleday, New York, 1999, pp. 40, 49.

72. Ibid., p. 134.

73. Stephen R. Covey, *The 7 Habits of Highly Effective People: Powerful Lessons in Personal Change*, Simon & Schuster, New York, 1989, p. 299.

74. Ibid., p. 299.

Chapter Nineteen

1. John P. Kotter, *Leading Change*, Harvard Business School Press, Boston, 1996, p. 51.

2. John P. Kotter, *The Leadership Factor*, The Free Press, New York, 1988, p. 28. This is referenced in Eugene B. Habecker's *Leading with a Follower's Heart*, SP Publications, Wheaton, IL, 1990, p. 109.

3. *Eugene B. Habecker, Leading with a Follower's Heart, SP Publications, Wheaton, IL, 1990, p. 109.*

4. Oswald Sanders, *Spiritual Leadership*, Moody Press, Chicago, 1994, p. 52.

5. John Edmund Haggai, *Lead On*, BAC Printers, Singapore, 1986, p. 136.

6. Fred Smith, *Leading with Integrity*, Bethany House Publishers, Minneapolis, 1999, p. 25.

7. Ibid., p. 24.

8. Ibid., p. 83.

9. Paul Powell, *Getting the Lead Out of Leadership*, published by the author, Tyler, Texas, 1997, p. 106.

10. Fred Smith, *Leading with Integrity*, Bethany House Publishers, Minneapolis, 1999, p. 173.

11. Oswald Sanders, *Spiritual Leadership*, Moody Press, Chicago, 1994, p. 28.

12. Ibid., pp. 79-80.

13. Richard D. Phillips, *The Heart of an Executive; Lessons on Leadership from the Life of King David*, Doubleday, New York, 1999, p. 257.

14. Ibid., p. 9.

15. Myron Rush, *Management: A Biblical Approach*, Victor Books, Wheaton, IL, 1987, p. 38.

16. John W. Gardner, *The Nature of Leadership*, Independent Sector, Washington, D.C., 1986. This is referenced in Eugene B. Habecker's *The Other Side of Leadership*, SP Publications, Wheaton, IL, 1987, p. 20.

17. Oswald Sanders, *Spiritual Leadership*, Moody Press, Chicago, 1994, p. 18.

18. Gunter Krallmann, *Mentoring for Mission: A Handbook on Leadership Principles Exemplified by Jesus Christ*, Jensco Limited, Hong Kong, 1994, p. 137.

19. Stephen R. Covey, *First Things First*, Simon & Schuster, New York, 1994, pp. 291-294.

20. Stephen R. Covey, *The 7 Habits of Highly Effective People: Powerful Lessons in Personal Change*, Simon & Schuster, New York, 1989, pp. 122-123.

21. Stephen R. Covey, *First Things First*, Simon & Schuster, New York, 1994, pp. 72-73.

22. Ralph Waldo Emerson, *"Self Reliance"* in *Essays: First and Second Series*, in *The Complete Works*, Volume 1, Houghton Mifflin, Boson, 1921, p. 90. This is referenced in Stephen R. Covey's *First Things First*, Simon & Schuster, New York, 1994, p. 303.

Chapter Twenty

1. Richard J. Foster, *Celebration of Discipline*, Harper & Row, San Francisco, 1978, p. 31. This was referenced in Eugene B. Habecker's *Leading with a Follower's Heart*, SP Publications, Wheaton, IL, 1990, p. 90.

2. Oswald Sanders, *Spiritual Leadership*, Moody Press, Chicago, 1994, pp. 86-87.

3. Ibid., p. 87.

4. Wesley L. Duewel, *Ablaze for God*, (Grand Rapids: Francis Asbury Press, 1989), pp. 211, 213. This was referenced in Eugene B. Habecker's *Leading with a Follower's Heart*, SP Publications, Wheaton, IL, 1990, p. 89.

5. John Piper, "The Marks of a Spiritual Leader," *http://www.desiringgod.org*, July 2000. (Desiring God Ministries, Minneapolis, MN)

6. Wesley L. Duewel, *Ablaze for God*, (Grand Rapids: Francis Asbury Press, 1989), pp. 211, 213. This was referenced in Eugene B. Habecker's *Leading with a Follower's Heart*, SP Publications, Wheaton, IL, 1990, p. 89.

7. Ibid., pp. 89-90.

8. Ibid., p. 106.

9. Ibid., p. 89.

10. Ibid., p. 90.

11. Ibid., p. 91.

12. Fred Smith, *Leading with Integrity*, Bethany House Publishers, Minneapolis, 1999, p. 155.

13. John Piper, "The Marks of a Spiritual Leader," *http://www.desiringgod.org*, July 2000. (Desiring God Ministries, Minneapolis, MN)

14. Oswald Sanders, *Spiritual Leadership*, Moody Press, Chicago, 1994, p. 92.

15. Ibid., p. 116.

16. Ibid., p. 11.

17. Ibid., p. 86.

18. Ibid., p. 86.

19. Ibid., p. 87.

20. Ibid., p. 92.

21. Ibid., p. 121.

22. *Eugene B. Habecker, Leading with a Follower's Heart, SP Publications, Wheaton, IL, 1990, p. 93.*

23. Oswald Sanders, *Spiritual Leadership*, Moody Press, Chicago, 1994, p. 88.

24. Fred Smith, *Leading with Integrity*, Bethany House Publishers, Minneapolis, 1999, p. 14.

25. Ibid., pp. 14–15.

26. Cyril J. Barber, *The Books of Samuel*, vol. 1, Loizeaux, Neptune, N.J., 1994, p. 151. This is referenced in Richard D. Phillips' *The Heart of an Executive: Lessons on Leadership from the Life of King David*, Doubleday, New York, 1999, p. 45.

27. Richard D. Phillips, *The Heart of an Executive: Lessons on Leadership from the Life of King David*, Doubleday, New York, 1999, p. 64.

28. James Allen, *As a Man Thinketh*, Vol. 2, MindArt, Bountiful, Utah, 1988, p. 83. This is referenced in Stephen R. Covey's *First Things First*, Simon & Schuster, New York, 1994, p. 28.

29. Stephen R. Covey, *First Things First*, Simon & Schuster, New York, 1994, p. 138.

30. John Sloan Dickey, U.S. educator, quoted in a private university's plans and goals report. This is referenced in Stephen R. Covey's *First Things First*, Simon & Schuster, New York, 1994, p. 180.

31. Often quoted and originally attributed to Ralph Waldo Emerson. This is referenced in Stephen R. Covey's *First Things First*, Simon & Schuster, New York, 1994, p. 179.

32. Fred Smith, *Leading with Integrity*, Bethany House Publishers, Minneapolis, 1999, p. 83.

33. Gunter Krallmann, *Mentoring for Mission: A Handbook on Leadership Principles Exemplified by Jesus Christ*, Jensco Limited, Hong Kong, 1994, p. 124.

BIBLIOGRAPHY

Biehl, Bobb, *Mentoring: Confidence in Finding a Mentor and Becoming One*, Broadman & Holman Publishers, Nashville, TN, 1996.

Cain, Herman, *Leadership is Common Sense*, Van Nostrand Reinhold, New York, 1997.

Covey, Stephen R., *First Things First*, Simon & Schuster, New York, 1994.

Covey, Stephen R., *The 7 Habits of Highly Effective People: Powerful Lessons in Personal Change*, Simon & Schuster, New York, 1989.

Frankl, Victor E., *Man's Search for Meaning*, Pocket Books, New York, 1959.

Friel, Brian, *Drucker on Management*, March 23, 1998.

Graham, Franklin, *Living Beyond the Limits*, Thomas Nelson, Inc., Nashville, 1998.

Habecker, Eugene B., *Leading with a Follower's Heart*, SP Publications, Wheaton, IL 1990.

Habecker, Eugene B., *The Other Side of Leadership*, SP Publications, Wheaton, IL, 1987.

Haggai, John Edmund, *Lead On*, BAC Printers, Singapore, 1986.

Kotter, John P., *Leading Change*, Harvard Business School Press, Boston, 1996.

Krallmann, Gunter, *Mentoring for Mission: A Handbook on Leadership Principles Exemplified by Jesus Christ*, Jensco Limited, Hong Kong, 1994.

Maxwell, John C., *The 21 Indispensable Qualities of a Leader*, Thomas Nelson, Inc., Nashville, 1999.

Maxwell, John C., *The 21 Irrefutable Laws of Leadership*, Thomas Nelson, Inc., Nashville, 1998.

Nixon, Richard, *Leaders*, Warner Books, Inc., New York, 1982.

Phillips, Richard D., *The Heart of an Executive: Lessons on Leadership from the Life of King David*, Doubleday, New York, 1999.

Piper, John, "The Marks of a Spiritual Leader," *http://www.desiringgod. org*, July 2000. (Desiring God Ministries, Minneapolis, MN)

Powell, Paul, *Getting the Lead Out of Leadership*, published by the author, Tyler, Texas, 1997.

Rush, Myron, *Management: A Biblical Approach*, Victor Books, Wheaton, IL, 1987.

Sanders, Oswald, *Spiritual Leadership*, Moody Press, Chicago, 1994.

Seymour, Dr. James J., *The Value of a Good Attitude"*.

Smith, Fred, *Leading with Integrity*, Bethany House Publishers, Minneapolis, 1999.

Stafford, Tim, *The Business of the Kingdom*, Christianity Today, November 15, 1999.

Wirt, Sherwood E., *Jesus: Man of Joy*, Harvest House Publishers, Eugene, Oregon, 1999.